THE CHICKEN TRAIL

THE CHICKEN TRAIL

Following Workers, Migrants, and Corporations across the Americas

KATHLEEN C. SCHWARTZMAN

ILR PRESS

AN IMPRINT OF

CORNELL UNIVERSITY PRESS

ITHACA AND LONDON

First published 2013 by Cornell University Press
First printing, Cornell Paperbacks, 2013
Printed in the United States of America

Library of Congress Cataloging-in-Publication Data

Schwartzman, Kathleen Crowley, 1948–
   The chicken trail : following workers, migrants, and corporations
across the Americas / Kathleen C. Schwartzman.
      p. cm.
   Includes bibliographical references and index.
   ISBN 978-0-8014-5116-4 (cloth : alk. paper)
   ISBN 978-0-8014-7809-3 (pbk. : alk. paper)
   1. Chicken industry—United States.   2. Chicken industry—Mexico.
3. Foreign workers, Mexican—United States.   4. Unemployment—
United States.   5. Unemployment—Mexico.   6. United States—
Emigration and immigration.   7. Mexico—Emigration and immigration.
8. United States—Commerce—Mexico.   9. Mexico—Commerce—
United States.   I. Title.
   HD9437.U62S49   2013
   338.1'76500973—dc23   2012027611

Cornell University Press strives to use environmentally responsible
suppliers and materials to the fullest extent possible in the publishing of
its books. Such materials include vegetable-based, low-VOC inks and
acid-free papers that are recycled, totally chlorine-free, or partly composed
of nonwood fibers. For further information, visit our website at
www.cornellpress.cornell.edu.

Cloth printing   10 9 8 7 6 5 4 3 2 1
Paperback printing   10 9 8 7 6 5 4 3 2 1

The Chicken Trail, where the externalities of economic theory become the social problems of nations and the tragedies of individuals.

CONTENTS

PREFACE

The relationship between immigration and unemployment has become a particularly controversial topic in the United States. This book is about immigration and unemployment, but it is also about bi-national business restructuring and bi-national labor reorganization. *The Chicken Trail* ties them together. I have two goals in writing this book: first, to outline and analyze the causes and consequences of immigration; and second, to dispel some of the common beliefs about immigration by replacing them with a more historically nuanced sociological analysis. While I do not directly engage the current debate, I offer an alternative framework for understanding the perplexing realities of immigration. This I take to be the sociological mandate: to offer an analysis of how society works and to reflect on policy options. My hope is that those concerned with policy as well as students will find it useful.

I use metaphor of the chicken trail to investigate highly important patterns and transitions that affect America and the entire world. My framework folds the immigration story into the ongoing processes of U.S. and

Mexico labor reorganization and displacement, which it then connects to global transformations. The labor displacement and immigration stories become part of a twenty-first-century "Global Dilemma" and "American Dilemma." The Global Dilemma is that in developing nations, as rural survival continues to be undermined by international trade, people attempt to alleviate their poverty by abandoning first the countryside and then their country. The American Dilemma is that economic transformations have left the United States with jobs that "nobody wants," jobs that are shipped overseas, and jobs for which American workers are unqualified.

This book materialized out of several experiential and intellectual encounters. During visits to Alabama, U.S.A., and Sonora, Mexico, I was struck by the presence of unemployed young black men on the streets of Alabama and of ghost villages in Sonora. While America appears to have accepted growing populations of unemployed and imprisoned African Americans, it seems to be at war with, or at least ambivalent about, immigrants. The ambivalence I experienced in Arizona, currently a major thoroughfare for immigrant traffic and engulfed in a firestorm of contentious debate.

The Sonoran-Arizona desert is a space where the reality of immigration and climate interact. It is considered one of the most dangerous frontiers in the world. It is burning hot and inhabited by venomous species. It is also a place where immigrants are assaulted or abandoned by their coyotes (smugglers). Humanitarian groups, alarmed by the deaths of immigrants without documents trying to enter illegally through the Arizona desert, have launched ameliorative actions. Some set up water tanks and first aid stations (Arcs of Covenant); others offer Good Samaritan assistance on the immigrant trails. To publicize the hardships that immigrants endure trying to enter illegally without documentation, groups have organized marches tracing immigrant paths from the Mexican border towns to Tucson, Arizona. Immigrant-rights groups stress the number of Mexicans who die while trying to cross the desert from Mexico into Arizona (estimates of crossings begin at 2,000 per day and go up from there) or the tragedy of family separation when undocumented mothers are deported leaving behind "birthright citizen" children.

On the other side of the Arizona debate are groups advocating immigration restrictions. They are frequently characterized as mean-spirited, unfair, "driven by hate," or racists—some are even linked to national white-supremacy groups. Those who oppose immigration (with or without guest labor status) express concern over cultural conflicts as well as economic costs. Here one finds advocates of denying public goods (such as drivers' licenses, free hospitalization, "in-state" university tuition, or birthright citizenship) to illegal immigrants. Some vigilante groups have attempted to stop illegal immigrant flows with border watches. The heated debate continues with bills such as Arizona Senate Bill 1070. Signed into law in April 2010, SB 1070 gave Arizona law enforcement the authority to stop people whom officers have "reasonable suspicion" of being in the country illegally, detain these individuals while verifying immigration status, and arrest undocumented immigrants for transfer to the custody of U.S. Immigration and Custom Enforcement (ICE). SB 1070 was followed by Arizona Senate and House bills passed in January and February 2011 to deny birthright citizenship to babies of undocumented parents born on U.S. soil.

I am frustrated by the immigration debate, which feeds into public policies that offer inadequate long-term solutions. Why? First, the debate is polarized between what some pejoratively call "racists" and "bleeding-heart liberals." Battle lines are drawn in legislation, on the border, and also in the language of the debate. A perusal of immigrant-rights commentaries, for example, will reveal the attribution of "racism" to opponents. In 2007, Mexican President Felipe Calderón began a media campaign aimed at influencing American public opinion. The sentiment of many immigrant-rights groups is reflected in the quote of a Mexico City accountant who said, "They don't treat the Russians or English or other white Europeans like that, and so for me they are a bunch of racists" (Schwartz 2007).

Labels are social constructs that emerge from political debates and carry an emotional charge, whether laudatory or pejorative. Some commentators have suggested, for example, that the very use of the term *anchor-baby* is hate speech. Polarization can also be found in the terms used to describe immigrants. Since U.S. government documents use a variety of labels, I adhere to the labels employed by the respective sources.1 Apart from these, I interchange them to avoid alignment with any one political position.

Second, the debate is impaired by tunnel vision. The set of stakeholders is reduced to two: immigrants with supporters and those who would restrict immigration. This oversimplified model must be expanded to include stakeholders such as businesses, governments, native workers, unions, and African Americans.

Third, each side "demonizes" the other. Certainly, there is no analytical value in denigrating immigrants, businesses, or those advocating limited immigration. Because this debate has become so contentious, it is important to differentiate analysis from slander. Facts should not be considered libelous. From an analytical perspective, it is more pragmatic to assume that each group of stakeholders (U.S. business owners, displaced workers, native citizens, and immigrants) lives within its respective institutional framework of incentives. In response to those incentives, they behave as rational actors and pursue their perceived best interests. Slander and sanctification are poor substitutes for analysis. The sociological contribution is to describe the complex intersection of multiple incentive frameworks. In short, this book is not intended to incriminate, "villainize," or sanctify industries, individuals, or ethnic groups.

Set in the dichotomous frame of "humanitarians" versus "racists," the debate cannot be resolved. Only by examining immigration in a wider context of labor and global changes do we have any chance of breaking through the heated, uncivil, divisive, and sometimes violent discussions. Chicken may seem like a weak analytical weapon, but the study of its production and distribution is well suited to depict the nexus of immigration, labor displacement, and globalization and to provide the foundation for a more grounded approach to immigration.

Why another book on immigration, on Mexico, on globalization, on poultry, on unions, on the plight of African Americans? Each has been the focus of considerable research, together totaling thousands of pages. Some of the work is single-issue research and some combines several topics. The challenge is to build on and extend that research. Excellent publications have detailed Mexico-U.S. migration: its origin, its destination, and the conditions that affect its flow, ranging from poverty in Mexico to U.S. border policies. Several large scale research programs (e.g., Marcelli and Cornelius 2001; Martinez 2007; Massey et al. 1994) have yielded multiple insights into migratory flows. Ethnic succession—one ethnic group stepping into the jobs or neighborhoods of another—in the southeastern United States has received substantial ethnographic and journalistic attention. Such work documents the arrival of Hispanic migrants in a region that had not been a traditional migrant destination. Reports address the tensions of integration, competition with residents for jobs and services, and the actions of community and church members to bring Hispanics and blacks together (Swarns 2006a, 2006b).

The political and economic consequences of Mexico's ongoing global integration have been, and continue to be, the subject of extensive and multifaceted research. Authors document how global integration undermined PRI's political monopoly in Mexico (Castells and Laserna 1989); how corn and hog imports undercut Mexican producers (Oxfam 2003; Wise 2003); and how various agents of globalization (including the Mexican business community) encouraged the Mexican government to liberalize many of the previously controlled aspects of the economy (Gates 2009). Likewise, the U.S. poultry industry has been the unwilling target of many exposes by journalists, consumer advocates, and anthropologists. Salmonella in my soup describes how factory farms are fertile breeding grounds for microorganisms, especially salmonella (Bruce 1990), listeria infestations, and avian influenza. Inside the processing plants, the chilling tanks get special attention because they become so filthy that they are referred to as producing fecal soup. Undercover journalists and anthropologists highlight the gruesome work conditions, the injuries, and the low pay. Animal advocates describe the plight of the birds with subheadings such as "treatment of unwanted male chick" and "pain and suffering in birds," and environmentalists worry about the discharge of animal waste into the waters.

For several decades, scholars have investigated the immigrant-native job tradeoff. One common focus is the immigrant impact on the occupational dislocation and employment chances of less skilled and less educated native workers, particularly African Americans. There is no agreement. Some argue that immigrants are not in competition with teenagers, women, or minorities. Neither the garment industry nor agriculture, they argue, could fill its labor needs with teenagers. Such conclusions are based on the observation that immigrants often enter different labor market streams for reasons having to do with the human capital (education, language, and legal status) and an acceptance of low-wage or seasonal/temporary labor. Thus, any observed increase in impoverishment or income inequality cannot be attributed to immigrants.

The other perspective maintains that immigrants are responsible for labor substitution and the decrease in the earnings of native workers.

Borjas (2001) and Briggs (2001) both describe the negative effect of immigration on low-skilled native workers and highlight a more detrimental effect for African Americans. Borjas assesses the claim that immigrants offer a net benefit to the nation. His book, based on a plethora of empirical analyses, including his own, concludes that the correct way to evaluate the immigrant impact is in terms of income redistribution. Because the bulk of contemporary immigrants are low-skilled workers, it is the less-skilled native workers who suffer the most from the economic integration of immigrants. Briggs also uses multiple empirical studies along with his own historical analysis. He demonstrates how, historically, immigration has had the same negative redistributive effect for less-skilled native workers. In addition, Briggs highlights a crucial intervening mechanism, namely the negative impact of immigration on union density. Another important and often overlooked question is how immigrants come to occupy certain jobs in the first place. Waldinger's (1997) conclusions, based on the cross-sectional surveys, suggest what should be included in an analysis. He outlines a process that ends with African Americans being "excluded" (not displaced) from the labor market.

    I share subject matter and theoretical principles with scholars in the fields of globalization, immigration, race relations, and labor studies. The title of this book was inspired by Tom Miller's *The Panama Hat Trail* (1986).2 He traced the journey of the straw hat from the *Carludovica palmata* green stalks in the coastal lowlands of Ecuador, to weavers and preliminary processors in Ecuador, to finishers in St. Louis and New York, and finally to buyers in retail outlets such as Western Hat Works in San Diego. In a somewhat similar fashion, Deborah Barndt's Tomasita project explored the shifting role of women in the tomato's journey from a Mexican field to a Canadian fast food restaurant (1999). Miller's "actual commodity" journey and Barndt's "same-commodity at different points" journey are single-commodity versions of the global commodity chains described in *Commodity Chains and Global Capitalism* (Gereffi and Korzeniewicz 1994). They define a global commodity chain (GCC) as "the production of a single commodity [that] often spans many countries, with each nation performing tasks in which it has a cost advantage. The components of the Ford Escort, for example, were made and assembled in fifteen countries across three continents" (1994, 1). Authors in that volume followed disaggregated stages of production and consumption as commodities (organized as interconnected firms or enterprises) crossed national boundaries. The GCC framework defined by Hopkins and Wallerstein (1986, 159) demonstrates how production and consumption connect households, enterprises, and nations.

This work has informed my analysis; however, *The Chicken Trail* is a metaphorical commodity chain. I do not follow an actual product from beginning to end, nor do I follow a single commodity assembled from multiple decentralized networks of labor and production. I do share the GCC perspective of searching for the macro-micro links at the global, national, and local levels as a way to understand contemporary changes. I use the metaphor of a "trail" to link unconnected "poultry sites" in an analytical way. I begin with a trail of migrants to poultry factories in the southeastern United States and then follow a trail of exported poultry and investment to Mexico. I end with a trail of migrants to the United States. As in the GCC essays, my analysis switches back and forth between a developed nation and an "emerging" economy, binding households, industries, and nations to one another within the world system. The value-added contribution of this book is its conceptual linking of global and bi-national economic transformations with bi-national local labor market reorganization and migration. Tracing the intersection of the poultry and emigrant streams exposes the bi-national connections among commodity, capital, and labor flows—the very essence of globalization.

I draw from multiple theoretical perspectives, including world-systems (Wallerstein 1974), split-labor markets (Bonacich 1972), and labor regimes (Przeworski 1985). A wide range of material is cited in the text and in the reference list. Because I have included as many theoretical and empirical contributions as possible, along with contemporary work on immigration and neoliberalism, the bibliography is lengthy. Despite that, I hope that in my survey of these vast literatures, I have not unintentionally overlooked any authors.

My research strategy has been eclectic: following the principle that good narratives need quantitative data and good data need ethnographic narratives. Neither side stands alone; each fortifies and lends credibility to the other. I use as much quantitative data as possible. I have done extensive analysis of the data collections published by branches of the Mexican and U.S. governments. I have used government, corporate, and union press releases. I also used corporate reports, media reports and commentaries, scholarly monographs, published interviews, and my own ethnography and informal interviews. Most of my conversations in Mexico were conducted in Spanish, and many of the research monographs are written in Spanish. While some books benefit from a single methodological approach, this book weaves together multiple methodologies to construct the trail. At times the path between two trail markers is navigated by data presentation and analysis, other times by ethnographic studies; and still others by deduction.

There were research highs and lows along the way. The two most "exciting" were being evicted from a poultry plant parking lot in Alabama and chasing a rooster in Sonora trying to record its crow for a PowerPoint presentation. Conversations with Americans who migrated from Mexico more than a decade ago and remember purchasing "illegal" American chickens smuggled into Mexico; with undocumented Mexicans who arrived more recently in the United States; with Mexican residents in Sonora; and with former Mexican poultry executives were extremely informative. My conversations with unemployed African Americans and labor leaders in the Southeast provided a human face to the story of ethnic succession. On the other hand, the unsuccessful attempts to acquire more recent data from certain branches of both governments were frustrating. Equally frustrating is the internet: it giveth and it taketh. It is not only blogs that disappear; academic papers, organization reports, newspaper articles, and official government publications and data sets vanish as well.

The book is organized as follows. Chapter 1 introduces the conceptual and empirical elements of this multifaceted framework, and begins the trail with ethnic succession in the United States. Chapters 2–5 describe major historical transformations in the U.S. poultry industry and economy, which contributed to that "ethnic succession." Chapters 6–8 follow the "chicken trail" of exports to Mexico and examine the effects of trade. Imports rarely enter a country without disturbing the equilibrium. Here the narrative focuses on the impact and the reactions that open commodity and capital markets had on Mexican industry and on Mexican rural subsistence. The concluding chapter reflects on the connections between globalization and local labor displacement in the two countries.

The mechanisms that bind globalization and bi-national labor displacements are neither straightforward nor singular. While industry transformation in the United States rearranged the labor force, it also contributed to a rearrangement of the labor force in Mexico. NAFTA did much more than facilitate trade flows. As a recent face of neoliberalism, it rearranged relationships among concerned stakeholders: the Mexican government, Mexican commercial producers, Mexican farmers, Mexico's trade partners, foreign investors, and American labor. By analyzing jointly the separate spheres of public policies—immigration reform, NAFTA, and domestic economic development—we derive a more complete and complex understanding of the societal causes and consequences of immigration.

As a sociologist, I hope I have shed light on the deeper process of immigration and moved us beyond what appears as an impassioned conflict between vilified "racist Americans" and denigrated "illegal immigrants." We must be hopeful for the future of both the American unemployed and displaced as well as others displaced from work and country. While Adam Smith theorized that the outcome of individual rational action was a collective good, the outcome for many of the stakeholders described in this book is a collective tragedy.

The author would like to thank Claude Rubinson, Sondra Barringer, Lisa Thiebaud, and Eleanor Simpson for assistance; Ruth Milkman and anonymous reviewers for their suggestions; Fran Bensen for her guidance in manuscript preparation; Michael Burawoy for helpful comments all along the way ;and Alfonso Parks and Fernando G. Tapia for sharing their insights about and lived experiences in Alabama and Sonora. The work was funded in part by a grant from the Rogers Program in Law and Society, Rogers College of Law, University of Arizona.

ABBREVIATIONS

AFL-CIO	American Federation of Labor and Congress of Industrial Organizations
BIP	border industrial program
CONASUPO	National Company of Popular Subsidies (Mexico)
CPS	Current Population Survey, U.S. Census
FAO	Food and Agriculture Organization (United Nations)
GAO	Government Accounting Office (U.S.)
GATT	General Agreement on Trade and Tariffs
LIUNA	Laborers' International Union of North America
NAFTA	North American Free Trade Agreement
NAICS	North American Industry Classification System (formerly SIC)
NLRB	National Labor Relations Board
OSHA	Occupational Health and Safety Administration
RC	NLRB election for Certification of Representative
RD	NLRB election for Decertification of Representation

RWDSU	Retail, Wholesale, Department Store Union; affiliate of AFL-CIO
SAGARPA	Secretary of Agriculture, Livestock, Rural Development, Fish, and Nutrition (Mexico)
SAP	Structural Adjustment Programs (International Monetary Fund)
SIC	Standard Industrial Classification
SSA	Social Security Administration
SSM	special safeguard mechanisms (World Trade Organization)
TRQ	tariff rate quotas
UFCW	United Food and Commercial Workers
ULP	Unfair Labor Practice (NLRB)
UNA	Union Nacional de Avicultures (National Union of Poultry Producers)

THE CHICKEN TRAIL

1

Why Follow Chickens?

Displaced labor has many expressions, three of which are depicted in this book: unemployed African Americans, ghost villages in Sonora, and Mexican immigrants to the United States. In following the "chicken trail," I connect the U.S. labor shortage and the Mexican labor surplus. While transformations in the U.S. poultry industry and its labor-management regime created new demands for cheap labor, changes in the Mexican economy, including poultry production, contributed to labor displacement. Many of the displaced entered the migrant stream to the United States. By the 1990s, that stream was flowing past traditional gateway locations (such as California) into southeastern states. Here migrants happened upon an ongoing labor displacement of African Americans.

One theme in the current immigration debate is the link between Mexican immigration and U.S. labor displacement. In this book, I expand upon that theme to include Mexican labor displacement and dynamics of globalization. In so doing, the immigration story becomes part of a new "American Dilemma"—we are a nation that generates some jobs that "nobody wants," jobs that people want that are shipped overseas, and other jobs that people want but for which they are unqualified. By broadening the analysis to include globalization, the "American Dilemma" becomes part of a new "Global Dilemma"—in nations where subsistence survival has been undermined by international trade, citizens have attempted to remedy their poverty by abandoning their country.

Ethnic Succession and Immigration

In the brief two-hundred-plus years since its founding, the United States has wrestled with the immigration question many times. While older nations periodically endeavored to prevent their citizens from leaving (Portugal in 1720, Britain in the eighteenth century, and Italy in 1902), the United States periodically has erected barriers to prevent migrants from entering.

Today, some immigration advocates emphasize that immigrants (particularly the undocumented) fill occupational slots that have been rejected by native workers. In a national Gallup poll conducted in 2008, 79 percent of the respondents agreed that "illegal immigrants mostly take low-paying jobs that Americans don't want"—up from 74 percent in 2006 (Gallup Organization 2008). The debate highlights the work that immigrants do in the agricultural sector. In fact, the lettuce picker became the iconic "hard-working immigrant" doing the job that native workers will not do. On May 13, 2005, President Vicente Fox of Mexico praised Mexican immigrants in the United States for their dignity, great contributions, willingness and ability to work in jobs that "not even blacks were willing to do" (Orlandi 2005).

A closer examination of specific industries, however, reveals that some jobs currently occupied by immigrants were previously filled by native labor. Milkman (2006) describes the ethnic succession in occupations such as building services and truck driving in Los Angeles. The labor force in some southern industries has also undergone an ethnic succession in the last two decades. In poultry processing, Hispanics have become a substantial proportion of a workforce that was previously dominated by African American females. Did these recently arrived immigrants take jobs "disdained" by native workers, thereby filling a labor-market vacuum? Did they supplement the existing native labor force? Did they displace native workers? These questions motivated my research.

The unemployment rate for African Americans is catastrophically high. For several decades, the black unemployment rate has towered above the white rate by roughly a factor of two. In 2005, the national unemployment rate was 5.1 percent. In contrast, the unemployment rate for blacks was 12.4 percent in Mississippi and 9.7 in Arkansas (DOL 2005). U.S. Census data present a grave situation—a permanent recession for blacks. Some traditional explanations still have relevance: the geographic mismatch between suburban jobs and urban residents and the rejection of personal networks in job searches. Other explanations point to more recent economic shifts such as globalization. Outsourcing, offshoring, just-in-time production, and technological substitution have all contributed to widespread industry reorganization and labor displacement. Displacement has been more detrimental for all those at the bottom of the occupational hierarchy. However, in Michigan, which experienced greater deindustrialization and has a larger African American population than the national average, the 2005 unemployment rate for blacks was more than twice that of whites (12.6% and 5.7%, respectively).

Another constant in the CPS data is the persistent plight of young black men without a high school diploma. Like many workers, they were affected by transformations that gave rise to new labor regimes, such as temporary and part-time work. In addition, they may have been especially vulnerable to the ethnic succession that was occurring in certain labor markets. Since the CPS only defines the unemployed as those non-institutionalized persons actively searching for a job, these numbers underestimate the plight of African Americans, as they do for all "discouraged workers." They also underestimate unemployment due to the high rates of incarceration for African Americans. In midyear 2005, the Alabama prison and jail incarnation rate per 100,000 was 542 for whites and 1,916 for blacks. In Arkansas, it was 478 for whites and 1,846 for blacks; in Georgia, 623 and 2,068; in Mississippi, 503 and 1,742; and in North Carolina, 320 and 1,727 (Mauer and King 2007). In this book I explore the factors connecting ethnic secession and immigration.

Trade and Immigration

Trade is one important component of the totality of global exchanges. Mexico and the United States historically have had a close economic relationship. In contemporary times, vast quantities of people, commodities, capital, and credit cross the border daily. In 1980, 63.2 percent of Mexico's exports went to the United States, and 65.6 percent of its imports came from the United States. By 1999, those figures had risen to 88.3 and 74.1 percent, respectively (UCLA 2002, 770). The 1990s was a time of exceptional trade growth: U.S. agricultural exports to Mexico grew 12 percent annually from 1990 to 1993. Although the 1995 Mexican peso crisis and ensuing recession triggered a 23 percent downturn in U.S. exports, they recovered by 1997, and the growth rate rebounded to almost 11 percent per year. By 1998, Mexico was the third-largest market for *all* U.S. agricultural exports, exceeded only by Japan and Canada (United States-Mexico Chamber of Commerce 1999b). However, there is an appreciable asymmetry between Mexico and the United States. In 1998, Mexico received 12 percent of all U.S. agricultural exports, while the United States received 60 percent of all Mexico's agricultural exports. Agriculture represented only 2 percent of the U.S. gross domestic product (GDP) and 2.7 percent of the labor force, whereas it contributed 8 percent to the Mexican GDP and occupied 22 percent of its labor force (United States-Mexico Chamber of Commerce 1999b).

During the same period, the migratory flow from Mexico was on the rise and seemed unstoppable. Scholars note that the Mexican-born population living in the United States has been augmented by rising legal and illegal flows. The accelerated migrant flow that started in the mid-1990s continued until the end of the decade followed by a decline from 2001 to 2004 (Passel and Suro 2005).

This increase in migration was not predicted. The explicit assumption associated with globalization in general, and the North American Free Trade Agreement (NAFTA) in particular, is that free trade based on the respective comparative advantages of the trading partners would benefit all. According to a letter addressed to President Bill Clinton and signed by a phalanx of professional economists, the bottom line should be "a net positive for the United States, both in terms of employment creation and overall economic growth . . . moreover, beyond employment gains, an open trade relationship." In 1993, U.S. secretary of agriculture Mike Espy said, "American Agriculture will be a winner under the NAFTA"—by increasing exports of capital-intensive grains and meats.

At the same time, according to Rupert, "mainstream economists have argued that NAFTA is likely to have modest positive effects on the U.S. economy and somewhat larger positive effects upon the Mexican [economy]"

(1995, 666). Both Mexico and the United States had comparative advantages. Mexico would increase production of crops that were labor-intensive and better suited to its climate. NAFTA advocates predicted that the treaty would ameliorate Mexican unemployment and poverty, thereby reducing the incentive to emigrate. Mexico's president at the time, Carlos Salinas, envisioned a trade deal that would allow Mexico to export "tomatoes, not tomato pickers." Although a new equilibrium would be established, and some workers might be displaced as "specialization according to comparative advantage unfolds through the operation of market forces" (Rupert 1995, 666), such dislocations theoretically would be offset by the gains that trade would produce. Cornelius and Martin (1993) forecast that rural workers displaced from agricultural sectors such as corn would gain opportunities in new rural sectors.

Mexico's leaders promised its citizens that the agreement would help modernize the Mexican countryside by converting low-yield peasant plots into productive commercial farms growing fruits, vegetables, and noncompetitive crops such as coffee and tropical fruits for the U.S. market (Wise 2003). The 1992 constitutional amendment transformed land tenure laws: it gave small landholders new opportunities to own their own land, acquire new land, and engage in more effective and cost-efficient farming. In addition, increased foreign direct investment would create additional employment in Mexico. The promises by Mexico's leaders and the capital openings and ease of export that would help Mexicans shift to cash crops—which would in turn provide employment—provided the grounds for optimism. Some analysts recognized that the restructuring could bring about a "migration hump"— pressures leading to increased migration in the short term. But this initial period of higher migration would be followed by one of decreased migration once faster economic and job growth arrived (Martin 1998–1999, 424).

Real (1997) describes how one adjustment unfolded in San Rafael, a village in the state of Guanajuato. Farmers had worked on a part-time basis for a Mexican firm (founded in 1986) that harvested, froze, and labeled broccoli and cauliflower for export to Birds Eye Vegetables in the United States. Laborers had adapted to the presence of this agribusiness and had no need to abandon their traditional production of corn and beans. When the firm decided to shift its land use to fodder for livestock, they would have been displaced. Just then, Pilgrim's Pride, a multinational subsidiary in Mexico, opened up an incubator and "growing-out" farms in the area, offering alternative employment. The less fortunate, however, did face dislocation and emigration.

Neoliberalism and Labor

Since 1980, neoliberalism has been the face of globalization. The globalization effect varies by a country's location in the world-system paradigm. In the United States, globalization and neoliberalism are characterized by the breakdown of the traditional labor market, which had been divided into primary and secondary sectors. That segmentation was associated with the nature of the firms and the qualifications of job seekers. In contrast to the primary sector, which hired skilled workers, the secondary sector drew its labor force from the unskilled (Edwards 1973). Changes in industrial societies, including rapid developments in technology, growing international and price competition, and corporate financial restructuring in capital markets, eroded those employment arrangements (Kallenberg 2003, 154). Firms now pursue flexibility in their production processes and employment systems through nonstandard work arrangements: shifting the workforce to part-time and temporary employees or removing employees from the payroll by using outside agencies. To this list of "flexible" hiring strategies used by employers to tackle price competition and profit losses, I argue that we must add employers' use of undocumented immigrant labor.

In emerging markets (previously designated as third-world or semiperipheral countries) promoters of neoliberalism have encouraged governments to reduce regulations on foreign investments, capital flows, and labor systems. Following this advice, Mexico and other countries privatized state-owned enterprises, eliminated price controls, and reduced government subsidies and safety nets for workers. Like it or not, no nation has entirely escaped neoliberalism and its transformative effects. Neoliberalism has been praised by some as the panacea for world poverty and political instability—and denounced by others for aggravating poverty and displacing workers.

Neoliberalism and Its Challengers

In July 2008, the Doha Round of the World Trade Organization (WTO), begun in Doha, Qatar, in 2001, was declared a failure. The final breakdown was the product of a fundamental disagreement between developed and developing countries on the issue of special safeguard mechanisms (SSMs) for agriculture. Nations of the EU and the United States sought to expand the WTO, thereby giving their own (and subsidized) agribusinesses lower-tariff access to the markets of developing countries. In opposition, India and other developing nations sought the right to protect their at- or near-subsistence farming sectors. For them, global trade between highly developed and underdeveloped countries had destructive consequences, consequences that Marx predicted in the 1840s:

> The bourgeoisie, by the rapid improvement of all instruments of production, by the immensely facilitated means of communication, draws all, even the most barbarian nations into civilisation. The cheap prices of its commodities are the heavy artillery with which it batters down all Chinese walls, with which it forces the barbarians' intensely obstinate hatred of foreigners to capitulate. It compels all nations, on pain of extinction, to adopt the bourgeois mode of production, it compels them to introduce what it calls civilisation into their midst, i.e. to become bourgeois themselves. In one word, it creates a world after its own image. ([1848] 1964)

The debate regarding the winners and losers of NAFTA echoes that surrounding the WTO. As in the Doha Round, NAFTA advocates promised that the expansion of trade of goods and services would raise rural living standards and real income. But like the failures of WTO agreements, critics argue, NAFTA has produced some negative realities.

NAFTA brought advantages and disadvantages to Mexican commercial poultry producers. The principle advantages were Mexico's access to global technological developments in the pharmaceutical industry and cheaper producers' goods. Authors who identify disadvantages of free trade for Mexico, the least developed of the three NAFTA signatories, highlight the injurious effects that imports has had on domestic producers. Analysts predicted that the drop in import tax, duty-free quotas with a sliding tariff above the quota, and the streamlined import-permit application process would produce a "poultry crisis," in other words a "debacle" (Hernandez et al. 1996).

Hirschman's 1970 book *Exit, Voice, and Loyalty: Responses to Decline in Firms, Organizations, and States* offers a cogent way to describe Mexican responses to global integration. Emigration (exit) and protest (voice) represent the two ends of his exit-voice continuum. While small barnyard producers chose emigration, the larger commercial poultry producers protested.

Do trade agreements promoting the free flow of commodities also lead to the flow of migrants? Both occur in fully integrated common markets where labor and commodities are freed from border regulations, but what about nations at unequal levels of development bound by multilateral treaties such as NAFTA in which commodities are freely traded but labor flows are restricted by national legislation? Subsistence farmers around the world have adopted different strategies to deal with the liabilities of trade. One Indian farmer, unable to repay his loans, used his final loan to buy enough pesticide to kill himself (Sengupta 2006). Indian politicians point out that in 2003, "free" trade in cotton provoked 17,107 farmer suicides. Mexican farmers have responded by selling their livestock or borrowing money from relatives in order to pay a coyote to be smuggled into the United States.

Can illegal immigration be understood as a consequence of market adjustments and the competitive "disadvantages" with which Mexico entered NAFTA? There is an astonishing parallel in the rise of U.S. poultry exports to Mexico and undocumented Mexican migration to the United States (fig. 1.1). The vertiginous increase of U.S. exports to Mexico after 1990 was expected; the increase of Mexican migration to the United States was not. While this association between U.S. poultry exports and Mexican

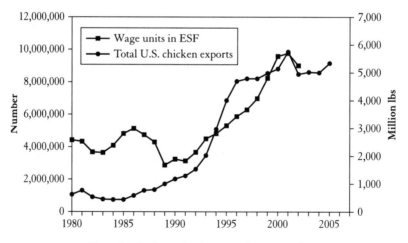

Figure 1.1. Poultry and undocumented immigrant flows

Source: Author's compilation based on data from USDA (2009) and SSA (2002) updated by the SSA as of October 2004 (personal email from Carolyn Puckett, SSA).

emigration might appear to be a statistical absurdity, it is not spurious. My goal is to elucidate the connections. I use the poultry sector and the metaphor of the chicken trail to examine the effects of the NAFTA-mandated trade and investment liberalization on the development of Mexico, the sustainability of Mexican agriculture, Mexican emigration, and ongoing production and labor transformations in the United States. Tracing the interface of the poultry-emigrant streams exposes the bi-national connections among commodity, capital, and labor flows—the very essence of globalization.

Theoretical and Methodological Challenges to the "Globalization" Explanation

Studies of globalization have been part of the fabric of sociology since Wallerstein launched the world-systems paradigm in 1974. At the 2009 American Sociological Association meetings, of the 475 sessions, 34 titles included the words *neoliberal* or *globalization* (including variations but excluding *international*) and only 10 with the word *national* (and variations). Perhaps for social scientists of today, the concept of globalization is what industrialization was for those writing at the beginning of the twentieth century. On the positive side, both industrialization and globalization are conceptual, methodological, and value-added ways to understand social reality. Just as the industrialization paradigm offered scholars a conceptual way to link the micro to the macro (such as linking alienation with urbanization), the globalization paradigm links the regional and national to the international. However, globalization also may be the sociological parallel to the astronomers' spinning black hole that engages in cosmic feeding frenzies that devour all matter. We must guard against globalization (or neoliberalism) becoming that theoretical eating machine from which no social phenomena can escape.

In other words, NAFTA cannot be solely responsible for all of Mexico's economic difficulties. Poultry exports to Mexico and rural-migrant flows to the United States are small streams within the cross-border torrents of commodities and migrants. In addition, the totality of transformations in Mexican poultry cannot be attributed solely to U.S. imports. The challenge is to persuade readers of a causal connection while not overdetermining the outcome. That risk certainly exists. NAFTA critics have been accused of popularizing a "demonizing myth" in which trade is blamed for all the country's ills and of promoting "emporiophobia," an irrational fear of trade (Rupert 1995, 683). As De Janvry warns, "Because the potential economic, income distribution, and environmental effects of NAFTA are serious and contentious issues, many of the negative occurrences in the three North American countries since 1994 have been blamed on NAFTA" (1996, 4).

A related challenge is to convince readers that the empirical covariations are not spurious, that there is a causal relationship. Przeworski argues that "the motor of history is endogeneity" and that the difficulty is "to distinguish the effects of causes from the effects of conditions under which they operate." From the perspective of social science, "there are good reasons to think that institutions, policies, and events are endogenous" (Przeworski 2007, 168). Stated in terms of my investigation, *both* emigration and the adoption of neoliberal policies, such as structural adjustment programs (SAPs) or WTO-encouraged trade liberalization, are more likely in developing countries. The challenge is to see if emigration exists because of neoliberal programs or because neoliberal programs also occur under conditions that give rise to emigration. With this in mind, I focus on the growth of emigration in the mid-1990s, a moment when there was a shift in neoliberal policy implementation.

Note on Data and Methodology

Research linking globalization to local/national transformations or an "immigrant impact" typically is based on case studies or on aggregate quantitative studies. Case studies provide the opportunity to study a single firm or place over time, chronicling the local repercussions of a global shift. Aggregate studies offer the advantage of comparisons over years or among countries. While case studies are more vulnerable to overestimating the causal effect, aggregate data studies are more vulnerable to spurious correlations and are more opaque in terms of historical variations and potential causal paths. Since a single approach seemed inadequate, my research strategy has been eclectic, combining ethnographic narratives with my analysis of quantitative data.

I did extensive analysis on data available from U.S. government branches such as the Social Security Administration, the Census Bureau, the Departments of Agriculture and of Labor, and the National Labor Relations Board as well as the publicly available Mexican Migration Project data set. I have also analyzed data available from various Mexican government sources such as the Secretary of Commerce, the Secretary of Agriculture, and the Bank of Mexico. I treat U.S. Supreme Court decisions, media reports, and press releases from government agencies, corporations, and unions as data. These two streams of evidence are often corroborated by the research monographs of specialists on whose work I also rely. As indicated in the preface, I had conversations with Mexicans (in Mexico and in Tucson) who were associated with commercial poultry production. I had informal discussions with residents in several small villages in Sonora and with Mexican-American residents in Tucson who had migrated in the 1990s or before. I do not treat those informal interviews or my own ethnography as evidence but rather as "the human face" of what has transpired. This data fusion may appear awkward because of the customary divide between case studies and quantitative-statistical analyses, but it offers a fuller understanding of the unfolding struggles and shifting composition of labor markets.

What constitutes proof that the interpretations that I have drawn from the data are valid, an improved interpretation of history? I follow a strategy of linking two variables at a time. At each point along the explanatory chain (the chicken trail), I introduce competing hypotheses and counterfactuals drawn from the relevant schools of thought on immigration and globalization. In short, I pay attention to the methodological hazards but believe that examining the interface of the poultry-emigrant streams helps to delineate the mechanisms connecting global integration and global migration. This "chicken trail" is metaphorical, but it is also empirical.

Sampling

I sample from four domains: the industrial sector (poultry), global exchanges (U.S.-Mexico trade, investment, and migration), time (the 1980s and 1990s), and U.S. location (five southeastern states). This is intentional:

the commodity matters, the international exchanges matter, the place matters, and the timing matters. The intersection of one commodity, traded between two particular countries, at a specific historical conjuncture, and from one U.S. region illuminates the impact of global and national economic transformations on local labor markets.

I use the case of poultry to examine global-local connections. Poultry exports to emerging markets have been on the rise. The Food and Agriculture Organization of the United Nations (FAO) has studied the damaging impact of poultry imports on local poultry industries and domestic production (declines in retail prices and losses of rural jobs). FAO researchers echoed those who interpreted the 2008 collapse of the Doha Round as a reaction by developing nations to rising imports. Mexico underwent import surges similar to those that FAO regards as part of globalization. Imports made up 13.3 percent of Mexican poultry consumption by 2003, up from 5 percent in 1990 (UNA 2005). Even with such modest percentages, examining the interface of the poultry-emigrant streams helps to identify the mechanisms connecting global integration and global migration and exposes the unintended and unexpected consequence of NAFTA, or what I would call the "real" NAFTA blowback.

I focus on U.S.-Mexico exchanges: in particular, poultry going south and migrants coming north. The U.S.-Mexico border has the unique trait of being the longest contiguous border of any two countries with distinctly different levels of development. Poultry exports to Mexico and rural-migrant flows to the United States are part of the commodity and migrant streams. Although the bulk of my analysis describes the NAFTA effect, limiting globalization to NAFTA commodity flows misspecifies the model—it overestimates the NAFTA-trade effect and underestimates the "real" globalization effect. NAFTA was only one milestone in the Mexico's ongoing global integration. Mexico's integration was intensified by its 1982 debt renegotiations and its 1986 adherence to the General Agreement on Tariffs and Trade (GATT). In addition to these, I describe certain policies reactions to earlier stages of global integration; some might classify these policies as strictly domestic. It was not simply the "invisible hand" of the market that transported globalization into Mexico's countryside but exogenous pressures from the United States, the IMF, the World Bank, and Wall Street that led to restructuring state-civil-society relations.

I focus on the decade of the 1990s. It was a transitional period, a critical juncture. Something qualitatively different began then, and the legacies persist in Mexico and the United States to this day. On the Mexican side, although NAFTA was implemented in 1994, it was not until January 1, 2008, that the last remaining quotas and import taxes on U.S. poultry legs and quarters were eliminated. In 2008, President Calderón extended through 2012 PROCAMPO, a program of monetary transfers to rural producers initiated by the Mexican government at the end of 1993 that had been scheduled to phase out. PROCAMPO was said to reach about 40 percent of rural producers in agriculture and livestock. On the U.S. side, higher fertility rates and family reunification caused the migrant population to grow. From 2006 through 2010, State Department figures show that Mexicans who have become American citizens legally brought in 64 percent more immediate relatives compared to the previous five years (Cave 2011). Tracing one industry from 1980 to 2000 captures the unique conjuncture of a new world economic order, conflicts within U.S. labor, radical changes in the Mexican economy, and the rise of Hispanic immigrant inflows to nontraditional destinations.

I chose five states (Alabama, Arkansas, Georgia, Mississippi, and North Carolina) that have a significant concentration in poultry processing *and* saw·significant increases in Hispanic inflows between 1990 and 2000. They

TABLE 1.1. Poultry production by state

	Number of firms 1997*	Number of paid employees 1997*	Value of U.S. shipments 1997**	Value of U.S. broiler production 1997**
Alabama	30	19,944	7.34%	11.679%
Arkansas	43	33,409	15.58%	14.121%
Georgia	41	29,587	12.02%	16.088%
Mississippi	25	15,952	5.25%	8.662%
N. Carolina	29	18,166	8.95%	9.296%
5-state subtotal	168 (35.59%)	117,058 (52.19%)	49.14%	59.846%
United States	472 (100%)	224,309 (100%)	100%	$14,152,519

* Author's calculations based on U.S. Census (1997) for the poultry processing sector, North American Industry Classification System (NAICS) code 311615.
** Author's calculations from USDA (1999), Table 8-48.

are a strategic site for analyzing the relationship between global economic restructuring and global labor replacement. In 1997 there were 472 poultry processing plants in the United States (U.S. Census 1997). These five states contained 35 percent of the enterprises, 52.3 percent of the paid employees, and 49.1 percent of the value of U.S. shipments were located in (table 1.1). In FY 2006, these five states accounted for 45.4 percent of U.S. exports of poultry and poultry products. Chicken has become to Arkansas what microchips were to Silicon Valley and autos to Detroit. Arkansas produced a billion broilers a year during this period and was by far the state's dominant employer, supporting one out of every twelve citizens (Behar 1992). Most of the excluded states had only a few plants; important exceptions included Minnesota and Pennsylvania (19 plants each), California (29), and Missouri (24 plants; 12,215 paid employees). Although Missouri captured 6.2 percent of national sales in 1997 in contrast to Mississippi's 5.2 percent, Mississippi had one more plant, a larger payroll, and 3,737 more employees.

These same five states became new hosts to Hispanics. Of all U.S. states, these five both had a higher percent of poultry processing workers and the greatest increase in their Hispanic population. This statistical overlap between poultry workers and the rise in Hispanic population held to some extent at the country level.[1] Hall County, Georgia, for example, had the highest number of plants (10) and recorded a high 19.6 percent Hispanic, with 20 percent of the population speaking a language other than English in the home. By spotlighting one industry in the limited geographic area of the South, this analysis speaks to the high unemployment rate of one group that has been identified by researchers as more vulnerable to an immigrant effect, namely, unskilled African Americans.

My own thoughts on methodology, sampling, and data are captured elegantly by Gledhill: "I look through the lens of the small fragments of social reality that I can observe . . . at some of the cracks in the world order of late capitalist civilization. I explore the increasingly problematic nature of sociality within local rural communities swept up in the restructuring of the Mexican economy. . . . I emphasize the way these changes are resonances of a larger conjuncture of crisis in the New World Order" (1995, 13).

2

ETHNIC SUCCESSION IN THE SOUTH

The South has changed. It was Al Parks who showed me around Birmingham. Al is a 60-year-old African American man who had spent the first eighteen years of his life in that city. We visited several places where he and his friends had worked as young men. One such place was a large municipal (wholesale and retail) fruit and vegetable market. According to Al[1] and other locals, African Americans did much of the loading, stocking, and selling through the 1980s. By 2004, the absence of African Americans had become obvious, as had the presence of Hispanic workers. I spoke with Marisala,[2] an undocumented Mexican worker who worked as a clerk in a retail stand in the market. She, her children, her husband, and her mother, all originally from Michoacán, had spent some years in California before arriving in Alabama in 2002.

What accounts for this apparent ethnic succession? One familiar explanation is employer preferences based on stereotypical notions of work readiness. In the retail section of the market, I had a casual conversation with a young white man, a high school senior who was helping with the family's vegetable business. His opinion seemed to be that Mexican workers were the fastest-growing group in wholesale work, although he also saw many in construction. He thought that they were good workers, can put up a house in three days, and work for lower pay (pers. com. 2004). In contrast to these words of praise, an African American resident of Hobson City, the oldest black town in Alabama, told journalist Jason Zengerle that his community was plagued by drug problems and voluntary idleness. The town's main engines of growth were bingo and crack (2003, 13).

Such stereotypical portraits, however, misrepresent those who *would* work those loading jobs, were they to become available. In another part of Birmingham, I was introduced to Nathan[3] a 40-year-old African American man known to Al. He had dropped out of school after the fifth grade. From 1978 until 1997, he worked in that same market stacking tomatoes, but then the employer let him go. Since then, he has worked as a day laborer in Birmingham and Selma. In 2004, he was back in Birmingham, unemployed, unable to find work, and on the street. Clearly the story is more complex than employer choice among applicants in a given labor pool.

The social science notions of immigrant "assimilation" and ethnic succession embrace cultural, residential, political, and occupational dimensions. The early sociological work of Park (1936) posited that as cities evolve, residential distributions will shift along a city's concentric zones. Each new wave of immigrants encounters and adapts to the preexisting urban ecology, resulting in residential segregation for the new group and spatial mobility with eventual assimilation for the previous waves. Similar ethnic and racial succession occurs in labor markets—this is even true for organized crime. As earlier waves move up the ladder to higher-status jobs, vacancies are created that can be filled by new immigrant groups. These theorized successions are benign representations of a succession processes generated by the market's "invisible hand" that pushes migrants from their country of origin and pulls them into available residential or labor niches.

The ethnic succession detailed in this chapter is one of the three that transpired in the meat and poultry plants during the twentieth and beginning of the twenty-first century. For meat, the first succession transpired as factories moved from the industrial Midwest farther south. Earlier workers were mostly white—many immigrants from Eastern and Southern Europe—along with African American men. Numerous scholars have documented the ethnic transition that accompanied the relocation (Brueggemann and Brown 2003; Fink 2003; Halpern and Horowitz 1996; Horowitz 1997; Stull and Broadway 2004).

In poultry, the workforce shifted from African American women to Hispanics. As a plant manager told one researcher, "When I came to Gainesville, I couldn't see a Mexican on the street. But now when you go, all you see are Mexicans . . . at the beginning, we had only white folks. Then blacks. Then Vietnamese people. They are mostly gone . . . now we have Hispanics" (Guthey 2001, 61). This succession started during the 1990s.

In poultry, a third succession, involving a growing Somali population (and in some cases political refugees from Burma, Laos, or Sudan), began around 2000. This transition is described by reporters, often as they chronicled ICE (Immigration and Customs Enforcement) activities. In Cactus, Texas, a December 2006 ICE raid of a Swift & Co. beef processing plant led to the arrest of 297 Mexican and Central American workers on immigration violations. It triggered a population exodus of an estimated 600 who feared additional raids. Swift filled its labor gap with refugees from Burma and Somalia (McLemore 2008). The case of a Mexican American worker alludes to the second succession (which included his own arrival) and describes the third. Raul, who had been living and working in Nebraska since 1994, "watched with some discomfort as hundreds of Somali immigrants have moved into town in the past couple of years, many of them to fill jobs once held by Latino workers taken away by immigration raids" (Semple 2008). Conflict over the Somali's request for fifteen-minute prayer breaks and the management decision to cut both the work day and pay by fifteen minutes to afford time for prayer led to several days of strikes and disruption by more than a thousand Latino workers. In that instance, management abandoned the plan. In contrast, Tyson signed an agreement with the union (RWSDU) representing the Tennessee workers to allow prayer breaks for Muslim workers.

ICE raids in other parts of the country have prompted similar ethnic turnover. Three-hundred and twenty-five Karens (an ethnic minority displaced by Myanmar's military junta) were given refugee status and located in Denver. Nearby agribusiness hoped that they would solve a labor shortage aggravated by the 2007 immigration raids (Draper 2008). Because my research focus is the second succession in poultry (from mostly African American women to Hispanics), I concentrate on the 1980 to 2000 period.[4]

Speaking Spanish in the South

Hispanics are relatively recent arrivals in some southern states. In the 1980 U.S. Census, over 75 percent of the nearly 15 million foreign-born Hispanics were concentrated in four states: California, New York, Texas, and Florida (Portes and Truelove 1987, 360). By 1998, 30 percent of legal immigrant flows were avoiding these destinations (Massey et al. 2002, 127). The South had not been a typical destination for Hispanic migrants (with the exceptions of Texas, Florida, Louisiana, and Tennessee). For some, moving to the South was a "secondary migration," a "settling out" for those who first migrated into agriculture and then, with the acquisition of some human capital (particularly English), moved into other economic sectors and places. The clerk with whom I spoke in Birmingham said that after migrating from Michoacán, they left California because the wages were too low and Alabama offered better employment. Secondary migration of the foreign-born away from high-saturation gateway states, particularly California and New Jersey, comes from the need for better pay and benefits—health care, housing, and education for children (Perry and Schachter 2003). This becomes more critical as the initial settlers are joined by family members. Massey et al. offer several reasons for this diaspora. First, the 1986 IRCA legislation liberated 55 percent of those in California from the servitude of illegal status and gave them the confidence and freedom to strike out in search of better opportunities. Second, the appearance of labor shortages in the Northeast, the Midwest, and the Southeast in industries such as meatpacking, poultry processing, seafood canning, construction, and agribusiness encouraged movement. And third, conditions in California—increased militarization of the border, an unusually deep recession, and anti-immigrant mobilization—contributed to the shift away from traditional receivers (2002, 127).

Why Choose the South?

The immigrant movement to the Southeast represented a new era in locational choice. The Refugee Act of 1980 and the Refugee Resettlement Program identified the South as a place to settle refugees from Southeast Asia, the former Soviet Union, Eastern Europe, and Africa who were not being sponsored in other parts of the country (Duchon and Murphy 2001, 1).

During this period there was an influx of groups such as the Hmong, who had been airlifted into Minnesota and then resettled in Morganton, Burke County, North Carolina (a quiet industrial center of 16,000 people), with help from churches and federal monies (Fink 2003, 10). Between 1990 and 2000, there was an 88 percent increase in number of "foreign-born" living in the South, and Hispanics had joined the flow. The foreign-born made up 8.6 percent of the population of the South in 2000 (an 87.9 percent change from 1990). And 31.6 percent of all "foreign-born" in the South were from Mexico. Using the 2000 U.S. Census county data, I calculated the overlap between "foreign-born" and Latino for the 483 counties in my five-state sample (Alabama, Arkansas, Georgia, Mississippi, and North Carolina). The overlap is quite high (correlation: .897).

Hispanics worked in various industries. Dalton, Georgia, for example, has experienced industry and population growth since the 1980s. Dalton produces more than half of the carpets in the United States, and executives credit Mexican immigrants with helping the industry survive and grow. The carpet industry underwent a change with the new tufted-carpet technology. This led to rise of specialized firms offering machinery, dyeing and finishing services, and wholesale services, and it created a labor shortage. The first industry response was to increase wages. Overall, the 1987 manufacturing wage in Whitfield County, where Dalton is located, was 83.5 percent of the national average, and unemployment was below Georgia's rates (Engstrom 2001, 46–47). According to Engstrom, because the area offered the advantages of a specialized industrial district, the carpet industry didn't move offshore as so many others have. Moving offshore would have compromised production. Simultaneously an immigrant-labor option became available. The poultry processing industry in northern Georgia was attracting Mexican workers, and this flow offered a solution for the carpet industry. Management also offered a "worker preference" explanation for the shift to an immigrant population. The industry executives praised the work ethic and the "industriousness and tirelessness" of Mexican immigrants. Responding to the "job displacement" criticism, management claimed that it was labor shortage; immigrants were not taking jobs away from anyone but instead were taking jobs that would otherwise have remained unfilled (Engstrom 2001, 50–52). Numerous southern industries turned to Hispanic labor. Dale et al. report that in the summer 1997, a shipbuilding firm in Morgan City, North Carolina, hired two hundred immigrant workers who were housed in fifteen trailers on commercial property owned by the firm (2001, 110). The Hispanic population increase noted in the U.S. Census data is reflected in these hiring stories.

Once established, an immigration flow is self-perpetuating; chain migration makes labor recruitment unnecessary. Zavodny finds that the "most important determinant of immigrants' locational choices within the United States is the presence of earlier immigrants" (1999, 1015). She also finds that, for new recipients of legal permanent resident status between 1989 and 1994, economic conditions matter, and for refugees, the level of welfare benefits is a significant determinant (1999, 1028). Massey portrays migration as a process that unfolds according to its own internal logic, with its own momentum (1986, 670). A crucial aspect of this logic is the social capital accumulated by successive waves of immigrants. Increased emigration from a location makes subsequent emigration more likely by reducing the risk and cost for later migrants who can benefit from the knowledge, assistance, and organizations of those who went before them (Massey et al. 1994, 1493).

When and How Many?

In a few southern locations—not counting Texas and Florida—some analysts noticed a shift to Mexican labor before 1990. In their study of the peach and pecan industries, Studstill and Nieto-Studstill quoted one grower who dated the labor force changeover from African Americans to Hispanics in the 1970s. He attributed this to the African American exodus from seasonal farm work to nearby industries with better pay money and benefits (2001, 79). Some Hispanics moved into poultry processing plants in Georgia in the 1980s as the Texas construction boom slowed and the economy declined (Engstrom 2001, 48). Louisiana sweet potato farmers began to employ Hispanics as early as 1986. Generally, however, employers of poultry farms, along with ornamental plant nurseries, construction firms, canning factories, forestry, and manufacturing, first increased their hiring in the 1990s. Louisiana's Allen Canning Company, for example, which makes cans for sweet potatoes, sought a Hispanic labor force in late 1990s "due to the difficulty of retaining local workers" (Manger 1999).

Multiple data sources point to the 1990s as the decisive decade for the transformation of the volume and nature of the migration flow. Even

Mexican asylum claims jumped during FYs 1995–97. Mexicans submitted 18,820 asylum applications in FY 1997 (up from 122 in FY 1990), the most of any country during that fiscal year (DHS 2001).[5] U.S. Census data show a sizable rise in the Hispanic population after 1990. On the timing of the secondary migration to the South, the U.S. Census reported virtually no Hispanic population in 1970 and 1980 in Alabama, Arkansas, Georgia, Mississippi, and North Carolina.[6] Albeit small in absolute size, the Hispanic increases in those states from 1990 to 2000 are 100 percent or greater, outpacing total state growth (table 2.1). In the U.S. Census county ranking of Hispanic or Latino population growth between 1990 and 2000, Webster County, Georgia, ranked second with a 6,500 percent increase. Seven counties in Georgia and two in Alabama ranked in the top twenty-five nationwide.[7] These indicate relative change although, as already mentioned, the absolute size of the Hispanic population in 2000 was still modest (Alabama, 1.7%; Arkansas, 3.2%; Georgia, 5.3%; Mississippi, 1.4%; and North Carolina, 4.7%).

Accumulated anecdotal information (increases in the number of Hispanic grocery stores, English classes, public school enrollment, and Hispanics with bogus driver's licenses, fake identification, or no vehicle insurance stopped for traffic violations) corroborates the U.S. Census data on the magnitude and timing of this growth. For example, in 1998, two of the six Dalton County elementary schools reached a Hispanic student population

TABLE 2.1. Population increases by state, 1990–2000

	Percent increase in total population*	Percent increase in Hispanic population**	Percent increase in unauthorized immigrant population***
U.S.	13.2%	57.9%	138%
South	17.3%	71.2%	
Alabama	10.1%	207.9%	400%
Arkansas	13.7%	337.0%	500%
Georgia	26.4%	299.6%	614%
Mississippi	10.5%	148.4%	100%
North Carolina	21.4%	394.0%	740%

* Data from Perry and Mackun (2001).
** Data from Brewer and Suchman (2001); Malone et al. (2003).
*** Author's calculations based on data from Passel and Cohn (2009, 23).

of 70 percent, and the overall Hispanic attendance in the school district rose from 4 percent in 1989 to 42 percent in 1998 (Engstrom 2001, 49). The public school population in Atkinson County, Georgia, grew from 7 percent Hispanic in 1995 to nearly 30 percent in 2006, and state spending for teaching English to speakers of other languages (including indigenous languages) soared from $18,296 to $102,002.[8] On the timing, a nonrandom survey of Dalton County Hispanics found that 35 percent had arrived in the decade of the 1990s, almost equal to the 40 percent that arrived before the 1986 passage of IRCA (Zuniga and Hernandez-Leon 2001, 129). Regarding timing, Hernandez-Leon, in his household survey of Monterrey, Mexico, found that of those who were migrating to the United States, half had done so since 1987 and 33 percent since 1994 (2004, 436).

The growing population was matched by the growth in Mexican-oriented services, ranging from tortilla sales to Mexican consulates. In 1995, Mission Foods, originally of Monterrey, opened a tortilla plant in Jefferson, Georgia. In 1997 the Atlanta metropolitan area had three Hispanic newspapers; by 1999 there were eleven (Rees 2001, 39). And, the actions of the Mexican government coincided with this timing. In 1992, the Atlanta, Georgia, consulate became a consulate-general; in 2009 it sponsored twenty-seven mobile consulates in Alabama, Georgia, and Tennessee. In November 2000, the Mexican government opened a new consulate-general in Raleigh, North Carolina, to attend to the estimated five hundred thousand Mexicans living in the Carolinas.

Most commentators agree: the actual population increases were larger still. Precisely because many are illegal, the U.S. Census may not reflect the full magnitude of migration. It is extremely difficult to estimate the size of a hidden population because, fearing deportation, many avoid the U.S. Census canvass. The INS estimate of the unauthorized population identified California, Texas, Illinois, Arizona, Georgia, and North Carolina as the states with the largest increases in the 1990s. The Census estimated that in 2000, Mexican immigrants made up about 70 percent of the undocumented population, followed by El Salvador, Guatemala, Colombia, Honduras, China, and Ecuador (INS 2003).

Firms in the southeastern United States were represented among the major employers of the undocumented. A 1993 Social Security Administration survey identified the top hundred companies that submitted "no match" items (SSA 1999).[9] Seven companies from four of the five states (not Mississippi) made the list, contributing 7.07 percent of the wage items. In follow-ups, the SSA determined that those same seven firms contributed 7.27 percent in 1996 and 7.29 percent in 2000.[10] One firm in North Carolina (ranking 90th in 1993) had a 476 percent increase in the number of suspended W-2 forms between Tax Years (TY) 1993 and 1996. In TY 2002, North Carolina and Georgia ranked among the top ten states in suspended wage items. Using this metric, the five states all had spikes in estimated unauthorized population between 1990 and 2000 that surpassed the national rate. With a 740 percent increase, Georgia ranked first.[11]

Speaking Spanish on the Chicken Line

"If there weren't Hispanic workers, nobody in America would be eating chicken," said one plant manager (Guthey 2001, 61). Because meatpacking requires little training or English-language skills, it attracts immigrants. By 2000, a high percentage of poultry workers in certain parts of the United States were Hispanic and immigrant. Evidence of the Hispanic immigrant presence comes from official U.S. government data as well as ethnographic and media reports. The U.S. Government Accounting Office (GAO) reports on all meat and poultry plants in the nation in 2003 lists workers as: 32 percent white, 20 percent African American, and 46 percent Hispanic (with 26 percent of the latter being foreign-born) (2005b). The Hispanic figure is up from 25 percent in 1994. In addition, as the GAO points out, some of the largest meat and poultry processors subcontract independent cleaning and sanitation companies. The three independent subcontracted companies interviewed by the GAO employed over five thousand non-union workers and operated 140 different plants across the country. All three companies employed workers who tended to be young and Hispanic (GAO 2005b). When the sanitation workers are added, the number of foreign-born noncitizens in the meat and poultry industry rises to 38 percent. The United Food and Commercial Workers (UFCW) cites another report that estimated that at least half of the 250,000 laborers in 174 major U.S. chicken factories were Latino (2005).

The GAO report notes that foreign-born noncitizens are more highly represented in the meat and poultry workforce than in manufacturing as a whole (26 percent and 10 percent, respectively).[12] Other government sources support this observation. In reference to a lawsuit against Tyson for back wages, Secretary of Labor Elaine L. Chao was quoted in a Department of Labor news release saying "Most poultry workers are immigrants who earn less than $7.00 an hour" (DOL 2002).

What about plants in the Southeast? As summarized above, U.S. Census data document the substantial rise in the Hispanic population for the five states between 1990 and 2000. I merged the U.S. Census county data with the U.S. Economic Census data. Counties with poultry processing enterprises are also counties with increases in the Hispanic population. Hall County, Georgia, for example, which includes Gainesville, the self-proclaimed "poultry capital of the world," listed ten poultry processing establishments in 1997, and the Hispanic population rose from 4.2 percent of the county total in 1990 to 19.6 percent in 2000.

In 1990, the county-level correlation between Hispanic percentage (1990)[13] and the number of poultry plants (1987) was .163; a decade later it had risen to .385 (Latinos in 2000 and plants in 1997, respectively).[14] While statistically significant, this evidence has several shortcomings: first, the correlations measure Hispanic presence at the county level, not the firm level, and workers sometimes cross county lines to work. Second, the U.S. Census undercounts illegal immigrants by an estimated 10 percent.[15] Nevertheless, merging these two data sets situates Hispanics in the vicinity of the poultry plants, shows a strengthening spatial overlap from 1990 to 2000, and corroborates findings from the GAO study and media reports.

Industry, union, media reports, academic studies, and court records affirm that Hispanics are likely to make up a majority of the workforce in some plants and a substantial portion in others. In the late 1990s, "according to a court testimony, 600 to 700 Hispanics made up nearly 75 percent of the [Tyson-Shelbyville] plant's workers" (Rosenbloom 2003). Another source reports that by the late 1990s the overall Tyson workforce was very heavily Hispanic—40 percent according to Tyson and 60 percent according to union officials (Stein 2002). The significance of the immigrant workforce was clear to one employer who provided regular bus service between Gainesville, Georgia ("the world poultry capital"), and Mexico. Plants even changed their vacation policy, permitting a week of unpaid leave after a year so that workers could return to Mexico for two weeks and still keep their jobs (Guthey 2001, 60). In reporting on union organizing at the Koch Foods poultry plant in Tennessee, Greenhouse commented that of the "700 poultry workers here, most of them [are] Mex-icans" (2005).

Katz used the employee roster on a Hudson Foods Inc. factory wall in Noel, Missouri, to illustrate the change. Not a single Latino surname was listed among the workers hired between 1959 and 1990. In 1994, Hudson expanded bird processing from 850,000 to 1.3 million a week and expanded its workforce from 750 to 1,200. The new employees all had Latino names (1996). According to *Rural Migration News* (1998), a 1997 *St. Louis Post-Dispatch* news story guessed that Noel—a town with just 1,300 total in-habitants a few years earlier—had 2,000 Hispanics. In 1993–94, McDonald County schools had no Hispanics; by 1997–98, one third of the children in Noel Elementary School were Hispanic. Hudson Foods helped to start the multicultural center and donated land for a soccer field. An even greater jump was recorded in Morganton, North Carolina, where a Case Farms poultry plant is located. There were 344 Hispanics in the 1990 Census; by 1997, the Hispanic population was estimated at 10,000 (*Rural Migration News* 1998). Ethnographic reports echo this. Striffler, who did ethno-graphic work inside a plant in Springdale, Arkansas in 2001, made two observations about the demographic profile of workers: (1) about three-quarters were Latin American, with Southeast Asians and Marshallese ac-counting for most of the remaining workers; and (2) two-thirds were men (2002, 307). In commenting on the demography of the twenty-odd workers on the line where poultry are cut up, Striffler noted that he was one of the few white employees (2005, 114).

The evidence supports the claim that not only documented immigrants worked in the meat and poultry businesses. In FY 1997, the INS appre-hended unauthorized foreigners in Iowa and Nebraska. The INS Omaha office estimates that 25 percent of the meatpacking workers are unauthor-ized (*Rural Migration News* 1998). One Mexican worker interviewed in an INS detention center said, "After four years of living as an illegal immi-grant in Maryland, working a succession of menial jobs with forged work permits and sending money home each month to his parents in Veracruz, [his] luck had run out." He sat in the detention center, still wearing the black rubber boots that normally protected him from chicken blood in the Showell, Maryland, processing plant. The twenty-seven illegal immigrants caught in the raid were from Mexico and Central America. In the previ-ous five years (1990–95), the reporter notes, Showell Farms and another poultry plant had been fined $2,800 and $90,000, respectively, after illegal immigrants were discovered on their payrolls (Constable 1995).

Although my analysis focuses on undocumented Mexican immigrants who work in the poultry industry, documented Guatemalans sometimes appear in the story. Some refugees with papers had an employment advantage over other Latinos: some were legalized under IRCA (1986), and Guatemalans with seven years of residence in the United States hoped for papers under the Nicaragua Adjustment and Central American Relief Act (1997). The late 1980s through the mid-1990s were golden years of employment opportunity for the U.S.-bound Guatemalan emigrant (Fink 2003, 20). They were also golden years for employers in search of a new labor pool. Data from these diverse sources imply that undocumented Mexican immigrants represented a substantial part of the workforce. Overall, multiple data sources (U.S. Census, media, and ethnographies) point to the mid-1990s as the time of a major shift in the ethnic composition of the labor force.

These two trends, the poultry industry use of Mexican immigrants and of undocumented workers, continued into the twenty-first century. In describing the July 5, 2005, immigration raid of the Petit Jean Poultry plant in Arkadelphia, Arkansas, the media reported that 115 of the 119 workers arrested by federal officials were Mexican. A former worker admitted to the unlawful sale of Social Security cards and other documents (*New York Times* 2005).

Before 2005, enforcement was relaxed; only 445 unauthorized workers were arrested in FY 2004 (GAO 2005a). In 2005, ICE made about 1,300 worksite arrests of undocumented immigrants, 4,400 in 2006, and nearly 5,000 in 2007. ICE targeted several industries, but meat processing drew disproportionate attention. In December, 2006, ICE launched "Operation Wagon Train," the largest worksite operation in history, which netted about 1,300 people at six Swift & Co. meat processing plants located around the country.[16] In 2007, ICE targeted meat and poultry processing factories. Pilgrim's Pride, the nation's biggest chicken supplier, lost more than 3 percent of its nationwide production staff when federal immigration agents raided poultry plants in Chattanooga and four other cities (Flessner 2008). Workers arrested in the roundup were from Mexico and Central America. In April 2008, ICE conducted a widely publicized raid at a meat processing plant in Postville, Iowa. Over 300 of the roughly 850 workers at the plant were arrested. In conclusion, the reports on the raids show the extent to which poultry, Mexican workers, and the undocumented were intertwined.

When Poultry Workers Were African American

In 2005, President Vicente Fox, speaking to the Texas-Mexico Frozen Food Council in Puerto Vallarta, praised Mexican immigrants for a willingness to do jobs that American blacks would not do (Orlandi 2005). President Fox triggered an avalanche of criticism. His remarks were called shameful and racist. The Rev. Jesse Jackson and the Rev. Al Sharpton both scheduled trips to Mexico in pursuit of an apology for the African American community. Fox, of course, was only repeating a phrase commonly heard in the contemporary debate on U.S. immigration—"they take the jobs that nobody wants." He went one step further, emphasizing that even African Americans view these jobs with disdain. Foreign Relations Secretary Luis Derbez told a reporter in the Mexican state of Jalisco, "The president didn't make a declaration in the racist sense"; Fox was making the point that "Mexican migrants are making great contributions in the United States." His comment followed Mexico's announcement that it would protest the proposed U.S. immigration reforms of 2005, including the decisions to extend walls along the border and to curb illegal immigration (Associated Press 2005).

The assumption that immigrant labor fills an otherwise empty labor market ignores the earlier history. In southern plants, the workforce was predominantly black, female, and non-Hispanic white. Long after King Cotton had fallen from its southern throne, poultry, textiles, and furniture were the "royal" contenders, and in the pre-1990 period, the labor force was African American. As Horwitz (1994) put it, the onetime Cotton Belt now belongs to a "broiler belt," stretching from Delaware to East Texas and studded with what are, in effect, company towns. Similarly, one shop steward said, "This is the Old South. They freed the slaves, and then they just put them to work in the chicken plants" (Applebome 1989). Dangerous, dirty, and underpaid as it was, there was a workforce before Hispanics arrived. Two data sources support the claim of an African American and non-Hispanic white labor force. The first are the above-cited U.S. Census data that documents the virtual absence of a Latino population in these states in 1980. Industries located there had to be operating with a non-Hispanic labor force. The second data source comes from media, academic, government, company, and union reports about the industry during the 1980s and early 1990s.

The predominance of an African American workforce in media reports is unmistakable. "Mostly black women" is a phrase that appears often in news reports. In 1979, for example, when workers received no response to their complaints about the working conditions at the Sanderson chicken processing plant in Laurel, Mississippi, some 200 workers—"mostly black women"—decided to strike (McCarthy 1980). Many years later, Mike Cockrell, the chief financial officer of Mississippi's largest poultry company, Sanderson Farms, reported that in the Laurel plant: "Jobs in chicken processing have been traditionally filled by black women. Many of these women are single mothers without much education" (Cobb 2004, 5). Commenting on the low wages and bad working conditions in the "New South," the poultry workforce in North Carolina was described as poor black women without a high school diploma (Diebel 1993).

In September 1991, a fire broke out in a chicken processing plant in Hamlet, North Carolina. Workers were prevented from escaping because of locked exits. Ella Mae Blackstock, a survivor, said that the company kept doors locked so workers could not steal their chicken. Twenty-five women died, consumed by flames and smoke. Jesse Jackson accused government officials of gross negligence and compared the fire to famous civil rights conflagrations (Hoodfires 1992). News accounts identify the race of the workers as "mostly black and more than three-quarters women, the workforce of more than 200 people gathered each day to cut, bag, weigh, and fry chicken pieces for use in fast-food restaurants" (Tabor 1991). Published interviews with the fifty-six injured survivors and relatives of the deceased leave little doubt that the workforce was predominantly African American female. The lists of deceased and survivors contain no Latino names, and the biographies of the Hamlet fire victims reflect a typical work history of rural African Americans. Survivor Mattie Fairley had picked cotton peaches, and tobacco before going to work in the plant. Loretta Goodwin told the reporter that her father was a railroad worker and as a teen she had picked cotton, tobacco, and peaches (Tabor 1991).

Describing the 1990 strike by workers at Mississippi's Delta Pride catfish plant, the reported noted that the confrontation involved "impoverished black catfish workers, many of whom once worked in the cotton fields and still are waiting for their day to come. . . . This is a struggle of people who've been held down for 300 years" (Dine 1990a). In 2007, ICE raided the Crider plant in Stillman, Georgia. ICE suspected seven hundred workers of having false work documents. About 70 percent of the workers were African American in 1996, but by the time of the raid, 75 percent of its 900-member workforce was Hispanic and 14 percent African American (Perez and Dade 2007). Yes, there had been a workforce, and it was overwhelmingly African American.

Conclusion

This survey of five southern states establishes that (1) there was a rise of Hispanic population in the 1990s; (2) a significant portion of the workforce was undocumented; and (3) Hispanics, some undocumented, were now found in occupations that had been the domain of African Americans. In the 1980s, there were few Hispanics in those southeastern states that subsequently led in poultry production. Even though employees, Occupational Health and Safety Administration (OSHA) analysts, union organizers, and academic and journalistic muckrakers all describe the work as distasteful, stressful, and dangerous, African Americans had worked those jobs. What explains this apparent ethnic occupational succession? The two explanations offered most often are that African American workers were upwardly mobile leaving job vacancies, or that industry expansion created labor shortages that were filled by Hispanic workers.

3

WHERE HAVE ALL THE WORKERS GONE?

Many southern industries experienced a labor-force turnover after 1990. In poultry, Hispanics became a substantial proportion of a workforce that was previously dominated by African American females. What accounts for this ethnic succession? I present the strongest case for the two conventional explanations: that Hispanics filled vacancies, and that Hispanics supplemented the existing workforce. Then I offer arguments and data that challenge them. My interpretation of the data is that this was labor displacement, an industry solution to labor-management conflict.

The first explanation—recent immigrants took the jobs that nobody wanted—asserts that labor market vacancies existed because native labor turned away from undesirable, dangerous, and poorly compensated jobs.[1] These vacancies were filled by available Hispanic workers. A second explanation—immigrants supplemented the existing labor force—directs the investigation toward new labor shortages and asserts that as industry expanded, so too did the need for labor. In other words, Hispanics were hired to supplement the existing labor force.

Vacancies: No U.S. Worker Wants These Jobs

The contemporary debate often emphasizes that immigrants (particularly illegal immigrants) fill occupational slots that have been rejected by native workers. Immigration advocates cite the sectors of agricultural, landscaping, and construction where they say that native workers have rejected jobs. Representatives of agribusiness echo the same theme. In 2005, Senators Larry E. Craig (R-Idaho) and Edward M. Kennedy (D-Mass.) promoted an immigration bill that offered permanent residency to certain immigrant workers (*Washington Post* 2005). Senator Craig justified the bill by saying that 72 to 78 percent of the agricultural force in Idaho was illegal and that agroindustry would collapse without these workers; if immigrants were denied these jobs, no native workers would fill them.

Intentional or not, immigrant advocates presume that the U.S. labor force is *still* divided into primary and secondary sectors, the latter comprised of jobs that nobody wants and are occupied by immigrants. Primary sector jobs (with higher wages, better working conditions, stable employment, and substantial returns to human capital) are assumed to be unavailable to immigrant labor.[2] Since many immigrants have less skill or education than natives (Bean and Stevens 2003, 207) or a legal status that prevents them from practicing a profession, they are not eligible for primary sector jobs. Inversely, secondary sector jobs (lower wages, few benefits, and undesirable working conditions) are assumed to be of no interest to native workers. This view regarding the lure of particular labor markets is driven by the nature of firms and the qualifications of the job seekers. The secondary sector typically is made up of workers (especially women and minorities in the past, immigrants in the present) who follow an arbitrary series of jobs rather than a career path and are generally denied opportunities for acquiring skills and advancement (Edwards 1973, 16).

In the immigrant-advocacy rendition of the U.S. segmented labor market, employment boundaries are assumed to be impenetrable; there will be no occupational mobility between "native jobs" and "immigrant jobs." If the boundary between the primary and secondary sectors is impenetrable, it follows that the immigrant labor will not displace native labor. Exceptions would include, for example, those skilled migrants to the United States who found high-skilled and well-paid primary sector jobs in the Texas oil tools and extraction industries (Hernandez-Leon 2004, 444).

In the "vacant jobs" debate, there is a further assumption that the boundary between the primary and secondary sector industries is immutable. In contrast to the primary sector—with its oligopolistic corporations and bureaucratic hierarchy, the secondary sector consists of industries that are more economically precarious and have lower profits and less advantageous working conditions (Edwards 1973, 16). Intentional or not, immigrant advocates describe the U.S. economy as though firms are still divided into primary and secondary sectors, as was the case in the 1960s. The incorrect conclusion drawn from this assumption is that industries located in one sector will not navigate to the other, meaning that there is little risk of an industry acquiring a new interest in secondary market workers.

If the U.S. economy is truly segmented, then the boundary between the primary and secondary labor market is impenetrable and the boundary between primary and secondary industries is immutable. In short: no occupational mobility for immigrants or displacement of native workers, and no sector shift for enterprises.[3]

Poultry Could Be a Secondary Labor Market

Poultry processing work is tough, dirty, dangerous, and poorly compensated. Government agencies such as OSHA and the U.S. Government Accounting Office (GAO), journalists, anthropologists, union organizers, and church organizations all concur. If poultry labor draws from the secondary labor market, then migrant labor has filled this niche, doing a job that native workers will not do. Both employers and workers suggest that the work is "undesirable." "No experience needed, we train" and "transportation provided and housing available. Good starting wages" read two ads placed by Hudson Foods in Rio Grande, Texas (Katz 1996).

Behar reports on the Duvalls, who lived in the central Arkansas town of Russellville. Poultry work allowed them to live at the subsistence level—and no better. Thomas Duvall, 50, quit his low-paying job at a nearby Tyson Foods plant after twenty years. He had emphysema and no savings. His wife left her job at Tyson in 1990 because of work injuries. After about fourteen years of pulling the intestines out of chickens, she no longer had any grip. She told the reporter, "The supervisors just got so nasty to me that I finally quit. . . . They would tell me to do work that I just couldn't do" (Behar 1992). Cobb (2004) provides a description of the "chicken hangers":

Chicken processing is a dirty business, but no job in a poultry plant is more dreaded than "live hang"—the first—and dirtiest—stage of processing. Here, workers known as "chicken hangers" grab birds by their feet and sling them onto fast-moving metal hooks. The birds, weighing approximately five pounds each, fight back by pecking, biting, and scratching the hangers, who wear plastic cones around their forearms to shield off chicken attacks. Then, as workers finally hoist the birds onto the hooks, the chickens urinate and defecate out of desperation, often hitting the workers below.

GAO (2005b) and others make clear how dirty and dangerous this work can be. The GAO reports that employees often work in extreme temperatures—such as in refrigeration units that range from below zero to 40 degrees Fahrenheit. Workers complain about "dizziness and fatigue" on the disassembly line. Many work in hazardous conditions involving loud noise, sharp tools, and dangerous machinery and must stand for long periods of time wielding knives and hooks to slaughter or process meat on a production line that moves very quickly. Those responsible for cleaning the plant must use strong chemicals and hot pressurized water. Workers complain of the heat and the malodorous gas that rises from gashed stomachs (Robbins 1987, 66, cited in Mason and Singer 1980, 5). As Fink described it, the production process moves from temperatures starting at 120 degrees Fahrenheit down to freezing, and the floors are slippery with chicken fat and wet from constant hosing down (2003, 17).

In addition to the job being unpleasant, unappealing, dirty, and difficult, it is one of the most dangerous industries. The GAO (2005b) lists the common injuries as cuts, strains, cumulative trauma, and injuries sustained from falls but also more serious injuries, such as fractures and amputations. Workers, who are crowded together and working with knives and scissors on a fast-moving line, often cut themselves and others. In 1994, poultry ranked third among the nation's industries for cumulative trauma injuries such as carpal tunnel syndrome, behind only meatpacking and car body assembly. In Mississippi in 1991, OSHA fined a company for an exposed drive shaft resulting in the amputation of a worker's legs (Horwitz 1994). In December 1997, OSHA proposed fines of $840,000 against Hudson's Noel plant for "willful safety and health violations" that led to three hundred cases of cumulative trauma disorder. OSHA had already fined Hudson for earlier violations. In 2004, Tyson received an OSHA citation and a $436,000 fine for alleged violations following the asphyxiation of an employee who had inhaled hydrogen sulfide, a gas produced by decaying organic matter (Parker 2006).

Metrics vary, but three separate reports have concluded that the injury rates are about twice those found in manufacturing. In 1994, Horwitz reported that "poultry processing ranked as the nation's 11th most dangerous industry, with an annual injury and illness incidence rate of 23.2 per 100 full-time workers, almost double that of trades such as coal mining and construction" (1994). In 1996, according to OSHA, workers in the poultry slaughtering and processing industry suffered 9.5 injuries and illnesses that caused lost workdays (for every 100 full-time workers), in contrast to all U.S. workers who experienced only 3.4 such injuries for every 100 full-time workers. The 2000 OSHA injury statistics reveal that one out of every seven poultry workers was injured on the job, more than double the average for all private industries (Stein 2002).

Unions allege that rates are higher, but because workers fear losing their jobs or work time they hesitate to declare their injuries. The GAO (2000) survey of OSHA inspections between 1994 and 1998 acknowledged the limitations of the OSHA data. It revealed that OSHA inspection rates averaged 8.6 percent for establishments with labor unrest, in contrast to 1.3 percent for with no labor unrest. The estimates are even more conservative because OSHA citations are a prerequisite for OSHA inspections, and citations are more likely to occur in cases that are complaint-driven, in unionized establishments with ongoing labor unrest.

There are other health-related risks. Due to the danger of contracting diseases from chickens, the Bureau of Labor has listed the poultry processing industry as one of the most hazardous of all occupations. Evidence of health and sanitary problems also comes from foreign countries that periodically suspend imports from certain plants. The Mexican government, for example, in December 1999 temporarily de-listed 17 U.S. meat plants (9 were poultry) because inspectors reported sanitary violations (USDA 2000). Russia did the same. The U.S.-Russia chicken wars started in 1996 when Russia banned imports due to claims that they were contaminated with chemicals and bacteria. In 2002, a Russian inspector gave one of Tyson's newest facilities a failing grade. Moscow demanded a host of new standards regarding worker gear and chlorine levels in the washing water.[4] The U.S. Undersecretary of Agriculture asserted that some of these violations might have been exaggerated. As quotas, tariffs, and other trade protections become less acceptable internationally, sanitary measures become the tactic used by developing nations to shield their domestic industries from international competition (White et al. 2004).

Plant rules also can be harmful. Poultry work is tough because of the harsh work rules associated with assembly line work—"machine-pacing" and "lack of control." The posted notice on bathroom trips reads, "Walking off the line without someone to relieve you is not allowed. This is considered a voluntary quit" (Horwitz 1994). At a De Queen, Arkansas, plant owned by Pilgrim's Pride Corp., where Horwitz later worked, unexcused bathroom trips were punishable by a three-day suspension. In a Mississippi plant, one worker told the reporter that her supervisor said, "The rule is, you can't go to the bathroom more than three times a week [beyond scheduled breaks], unless you got a doctor's permit." Other workers in Mississippi and Arkansas told the reporter that they have sometimes urinated on themselves because they were unable to locate a foreman for approval and were scared to leave the line.

Extremely low wages contribute to the unappealing nature of the job. Labor is low-paid in this industry because of its location in right-to-work states. Since 1972, the real wage in the industry had declined 10 percent (Guthey 2001, 63). Although the wage gap between poultry and other manufacturing has fluctuated over time, poultry work is one of the lowest in the entire food industry and one of the lowest in manufacturing. In 1994, "jobs on the poultry line pay less than in any other manufacturing industry, except apparel" (Horwitz 1994). According to the GAO (2005b), meat and poultry workers earn a median salary of about $21,320 per year, much less than the average for workers in all manufacturing industries, which is about $33,500. In 1980 poultry wages were only 55 percent of red meat wages; by 1992 they had risen to 78 percent of red meat wages and 63 percent of manufacturing wages (Hetrick 1994). The role of unions contributed significantly to these wage improvements.

If these are secondary labor market jobs, one would predict high turnover and vacancies—in short, support for the claim that immigrants take the jobs that nobody wants. Looking at the undesirable, dangerous, and low-paying nature of these jobs, one could reasonably conclude that there is an "impenetrable" occupational boundary that native workers are unlikely to cross. Such occupations appear suited for immigrants, and immigrants seem suitable for those jobs. Immigrants, especially illegal ones, are limited in their choice of employment and generally lack access to supplemental income activities, such as the informal economy or government aid.

Native workers have other options. The southeastern region has an active informal economy, and industries such as poultry typically drew from marginal workers with alternative sources of earned income. Griffith attributes the native workers' weak labor force attachment to poultry to the availability of informal, small-scale domestic production such as fishing, gardening, baking, honey sales, furniture repair, income tax preparation, and palm reading (1990, 162). The schedules for these informal activities sometimes conflict with routine plant work. In addition, if a spouse had regular employment, including health insurance, the labor force attachment to poultry would have been even weaker.

These two claims were made: (1) that immigrants filled jobs that nobody wanted; and (2) that native workers eschewed those jobs. A detained poultry processing worker opined, "We Hispanics do all the hard, disgusting work other people don't want" (Constable 1995). From the perspective of employers and hiring personnel, immigrants were a necessary and even preferred workforce. First, they were willing to work those unpleasant, dangerous, low-paid jobs. As sojourners or recent arrivals, they endured lower wages by sharing housing and transportation. Second—and to the advantage of employers—immigrant networks provided a reliable and continuous supply of workers to industries that otherwise suffered high turnover and labor vacuums.

Employers stressed the absence of native workers. One plant manager said that the difficulty in hiring local whites, blacks, and even Hmong refugees was due to "poor working conditions . . . would you rather go into a place that's clean and dry or wet and bloody and cool all day long?" (Fink 2003, 17). Plant managers cited labor turnover as a major problem; 48.1 percent said they perceived a worsening of the labor problem between 1985 and 1990 because "Ours aren't the best jobs—they would rather work at Westinghouse, DuPont, etc. Other plants moving in are getting our workers. Chamber of Commerce is partly at fault. They bring in new business, but no new workers. In this area, there's only 4.6 percent unemployment and 2 percent of those wouldn't work in a pie factory" (Griffith 1990, 164).

Reports of labor vacancies appeared with more frequency in the early 1990s. Fink suggests that employers faced a crucial labor shortage once the surplus labor of the depressed southern farming areas was exhausted and the booming sunbelt drew workers to more favorable employment (2003, 14). When there were vacancies in Burke County, North Carolina, the company would run buses to and from Cleveland, an adjacent county. Fink cites a Case Farms manager who reported that in the 1988–91 period, there was a struggle to find adequate labor to keep up with the production demands (2003). An employer at Showell Farms, a 400-employee plant in Maryland, told a similar story. When the INS raided the plant in 1995 and found twenty-seven illegal immigrants, the employer explained that it was difficult to hire U.S.-born workers because the local unemployment rate was low (Constable 1995).

When Tyson opened its Sedalia, Missouri, plant in 1993, it struggled to find local workers. It turned to the Pettis County Welfare office for participation in a plan to place welfare workers in Tyson plants. The state office, functioning like a "hiring hall," sent recipients on job interviews with Tyson. Recipients who declined the job or refused the interview with Tyson were removed from the agency's system or sanctioned with the denial of food stamps. Of the 195 welfare recipients sent for an interview with Tyson in 1998, 22 accepted the job, 30 were sanctioned, and the rest were no longer on county rolls (Murjada 2002, 5). Following a 2007 ICE raid on the Crider poultry plant in Stillman, Georgia, it turned to independent contractors to replace its lost Hispanic population. "Struggling to fill its ranks, Crider began busing in felons on probation from a state prison and residents of a homeless mission nearby Macon" (Perez and Dade 2007). Employers argued that the insufficiency of native workers had forced them to hire immigrants.

Was a southern industrial boom responsible for plant vacancies? The vacancy explanation is predicated on the dual notions of undesirable poultry work and more desirable alternatives. Employers might have found it necessary to seek new workers due to the skilling-up or upward mobility of the native population. Indeed, many industries in the region employed workers who had previously worked in poultry. In 2006, the condom factory in Eufaula, Alabama, experiencing smaller orders, foreign competition, and automation, was about to lay off half of its 260 workers. One worker at risk who had previously worked in a chicken processing plant worried about having to return to a place so cold and wet that she got sick a lot (Dugger 2006). Southern states began to receive substantial investment and experienced job growth in the mid-1980s. Alabama grew by over two hundred foreign companies and a capital investment of over $14.5 billion (Alabama Development Office 2007). From 1993 through 1998, Mercedes Benz (1993), Honda, Hyundai, Toyota, and Boeing (1997) were among the investors. By 2002, Alabama had about 84,000 jobs in the motor vehicle industry alone. Other companies that entered since 1990 include Daim-lerChrysler, Johnson Controls, Trico Steel, Ipsco Steel, and Navistar International. Caterpillar, which manufactured fuel systems parts, set up a plant in Georgia in 1994. Building on its existing manufacturing clusters, Georgia recruited new industrial tenants. One company established in 1999, Jefferson Blanking, stamped out metal parts for General Motors, BMW in South Carolina, and others. Georgia also became home to TD Automotive Compressor, a division of Toyota that makes variable speed compressors for air conditioning systems, and Kubota, which makes industrial tractors and lawn equipment (Young 2009). In 1993, Mississippi gained 850 new jobs with the Rocket Factory and 2,000 jobs with the 2000 startup of Nissan. In conclusion, it *is* plausible that new industrial investment offered upward mobility to local workers, created a tight labor market, and necessitated immigrant hiring.

Shortages: The Poultry Boom

While the vacancy explanation assumes a fixed quantity of unfilled disagreeable jobs, industry growth can create real shortages by altering the balance between labor demand and supply. If industry growth created labor shortages, the "apparent" ethnic succession was actually Hispanics supplementing, not substituting, the native labor force. The poultry industry expanded along with consumer demand (fig. 3.1). American yearly per capita chicken consumption rose from an average of 23.5 pounds in 1960 to 89.6 pounds in 2000. Sources attribute this 281 percent rise in consumption since the 1960s to several factors.[5] The chicken's nutritional profile and price are cited by industry analysts. Dietary studies and numerous concerns regarding meat led Americans to consume more poultry. "Americans increasingly view [chicken] as a healthier and safer alternative to red meat" and "have been forsaking pork and beef over the years" (Cobb 2004; Behar 1992). At the same time, poultry became

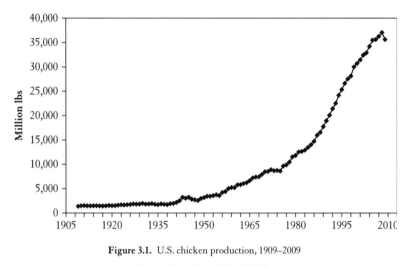

Figure 3.1. U.S. chicken production, 1909–2009

Source: Data from USDA (2009).

more affordable: "Chicken costs 50% less than it did three decades ago" (Behar 1992).

In addition, innovations like processed chicken, breaded chicken, and nuggets encouraged consumption. These innovations were accommodated by changes in the American lifestyle like the popularity of fast food restaurants. Tyson helped McDonald's develop the Chicken McNugget in the early 1980s. It was able to spin off this successful restaurant item for retail sale by creating its own frozen version for home use without costly test marketing and advertising. The fast food venue offers an opportunity for growth. Tyson executives see a future in areas such as chicken nuggets: the "hottest" trend is boneless, breaded chicken products that are available anytime and anywhere, from gas stations and kiosks to quick-service restaurants and retail stores (Smith 2002). The shift to processed chicken brought significant changes to the industry: by 2000 nearly 90 percent of chicken volume was sold as pieces (Fink 2003, 12).

International demand has also driven up chicken production. U.S. exports, which were essentially flat until 1975, increased from 1976 to 1989, and then took off (fig. 3.1). Export values grew from $630.7 million in 1990 to $2.4 billion in fiscal 1996. In 1997, exports siphoned off about 20 percent of U.S. poultry production (Reddington 1997). Some export growth was driven by sporadic epizootics (animal plagues), such as the late-1990s mad cow disease in Europe that led consumers to shift to poultry. And a highly contagious bird flu led the Chinese government to kill 9 million chicken and other poultry. Problems with Newcastle disease in northern Mexico decreased Mexican production and increased demand for U.S. exports.

Beyond epizootics, major changes in the international diet drove up demand. The international market is fortuitous for U.S. producers because those consumers prefer dark meat and parts of the chicken that Americans will not eat and because they have become receptive to mechanically deboned chicken. Japanese poultry consumption increased by a factor of ten between 1960 and 1980 and continued to grow until 1990. This market seems safe because the Japanese diet includes larger quantities of poultry than its domestic industry can provide. In the 1990s, exports climbed 500 percent, with China, Russia, and other FSU (former Soviet Union) countries leading the demand (Cobb 2004). In the first eight months of 1996, for example, the FSU countries (including Poland) accounted for 48 percent of all U.S. broiler exports (USDA 1996). Even Iraq imported American chicken. In 1996, Hudson shipped $250,000 worth of frozen chicken parts to Iraq through a broker in Jordan. Because this was in violation of the U.S. trade embargo with Iraq, Tyson Foods, which acquired the assets and liabilities of Hudson Foods in 1998, paid a fine of $150,000 to settle the allegations (Reddy 2002).

After the collapse of its collective farm system in the early 1990s, Russia opened up to food imports. In 2001, 8 percent of chicken meat produced in the United States was sold to Russia (White et al. 2004). According to *U.S. News and World Report* (2002), "Moscow alleges that food aid projects are flooding Russia with U.S.-made frozen chicken, leading Russians to develop a taste for "Bush legs," the Russian nickname for American chicken named for former President George H. W. Bush. The Peco Food website boasts of increasing exports of "jumbo wings" and "jumbo legs" to Indonesia, China, Spain, and Romania (Cobb 2004). All of these countries continue to be large importers. Tyson also followed fast food giants like McDonald's and Kentucky Fried Chicken and identified several potential foreign markets—Brazil, Mexico, India, Eastern Europe, and China—as the best bets for growth.

While this trend is certain to continue, exports are vulnerable to the vicissitudes of international political and trade conflicts. The aforementioned U.S.-Russia chicken wars created a glut of chicken meat in the U.S. market and havoc in the industry. Politics also threatened sales to Cuba. Poultry industry officials complained that their earlier surge in sales to Cuba could be halted by the George W. Bush administration's attempt to reinterpret a 2000 trade law covering payment for the U.S. shipments to Cuba. The 2000 law required Cuba's payments to be deposited in a bank before any merchandise could be unloaded from the vessels. Bush's proposed "reinterpretation" would have required payment even before shipments left U.S. ports for Havana. In 2003, companies such as Tyson Foods, Louis Dreyfus, and Gold Kist were shipping about fifteen thousand tons of Alabama-raised poultry to Cuba. Alabama Agriculture Commissioner Ron Sparks said that such a reinterpretation of the law would damage Alabama's poultry farmers and producers (Mitchell 2004).

Despite fluctuations, overall demand and production rose during this period. This fact would support the argument that the industry, having exhausted the local labor supply, hired immigrants to supplement its labor force. As Stein notes, "When Tyson food expanded into processed, branded chicken products in the late 1970s, the company developed an insatiable appetite for labor to perform the necessary cutting, deboning, and breading. Between 1980 and 1990, the company's national workforce increased from 8,000 to 44,000" (Stein 2002). In an article entitled "Why did employment expand in poultry processing plants?" Hetrick argues that the 96 percent increase in employment between 1972 and 1992 was the result of increased demand for chicken (1994). This demand was not met by investment in technology; rather, it was met with increased low-wage labor. Nationally, the number of poultry workers increased 19 percent between 1992 and 1997 (from 224,309 to 242,826). Between 1992 and 1997, Georgia and Mississippi had employee growth rates above 40 percent.[6] Using a slightly different time frame, Horwitz (1994) reports, "It is the second-fastest-growing factory job in America since 1980 and now [1994] has a work force of 221,000, roughly equal to that of steelworkers." Compared to other industries in the region, Bob Hall, a research director for the Institute for Southern Studies in Durham, North Carolina, said that in sales and employment, it is bigger than peanuts in Georgia, bigger than tobacco in North Carolina, bigger than cotton in Mississippi, and bigger than all crops combined in either Arkansas or Alabama (Horwitz 1994). So it would seem reasonable to conclude that increased domestic and international consumer demand led to an increased demand for labor and that these new shortages were filled by a new wave of immigrant workers. "Apparent ethnic succession" was really migrants supplementing the preexisting workforce.

Neither Vacancy Nor Shortage

Up to this point, I have offered the strongest case possible for two conventional explanations: immigrants, often illegal, took jobs that nobody wanted (vacancy); and firms supplemented their insufficient labor force with immigrant workers (shortage). The immigration literature delineates a number of ways that native working-age populations become unavailable (Enchautegui 1998). First, geographic relocation in search of better opportunities reduces native availability. Incarceration does the same. Second, the presence of immigrant labor induces native labor to invest in human capital, resulting in upward mobility (Reed 2001; Griffith 1990). Third, welfare, income transfers, or informal economy activities, including illegal ones, weaken labor force attachment and lower the unemployment and poverty rates. Fourth, new capital investment in the area offers alternative positions. To appraise the plausibility of the labor vacancy and shortage hypotheses, I draw from the U.S. Census population, unemployment, and poverty data. My logic involves answering four questions. Was there still an African American population in those counties when the shift to a Hispanic labor force was occurring? Did unemployment rates decrease overtime? Did the informal economy reduce the level of poverty for African Americans? And did new investments offer better-paying jobs?

Three facts are incontrovertible: (1) this is not a "dream" job; (2) managers complained about needing labor; and (3) the size of the poultry labor force was expanding (the last column in table 3.1). Nevertheless, substantial evidence challenges the adequacy of the "vacancy" and "shortage" explanations. Two pieces of evidence were presented in chapter 2. First, the U.S. Census data show that there were virtually no Hispanics in the five states in my sample (Alabama, Arkansas, Georgia, Mississippi, and North Carolina) in 1980. Those states were not traditional destinations for immigrants. Industries in those states must have operated with the native (black and white) labor force. Second, despite consensus among employees, OSHA, union organizers, and academic and journalistic muckrakers

TABLE 3.1. Population increases by state and county, 1990–2000

	State total*	Increase in black population state level	Median increase in black Population county level**	Median increase in black population in poultry counties***	Increase in black Population in poultry counties	Increase in poultry labor force in state (1992–2002) ****
Alabama	10.1%	14.53%	9.53%	17.87%	68,676	816
Arkansas	13.7%	14.24%	12.36%	30.25%	13,982	7136
Georgia	26.4%	37.04%	14.20%	17.88%	76,819	6995
Mississippi	10.5%	13.84%	10.71%	18.09%	36,617	8277
North Carolina	21.4%	21.97%	12.58%	10.16%	14,819	3096

* Data from Perry and Mackun (2001).

** Author's calculations based on census data. For the first time in 2000, respondents could identify themselves as "Black or African American alone," or "Black or African American in combination with one or more races." The U.S. total of the latter is 5 percent higher than "African American" alone, but only 2 percent higher in the five states. I used the total for 2000.

*** Author's calculations for counties based on data from the U.S. population and economic censuses.

**** Author's calculations based on U.S. Economic Census data, in 1992 using industry code SIC 2015 and in 2002 the NAICS 311615.

that the work was distasteful, stressful, and dangerous, African Americans continued to work those jobs (Schwartzman 2008). In the rest of this chapter, I present additional evidence suggesting that: (1) the labor market was not that tight; (2) native labor was not all siphoned off by geographic mobility or new investment; (3) levels of poverty did not significantly drop; and (4) native workers still wanted those jobs.

At times, even managers and industry representatives assumed sufficient local worker availability. In areas where options were limited, especially for the black women who made up the majority of the workers, poultry plants were the best-paying jobs (Applebome 1989). Early management actions reflected confidence in an adequate labor supply. In 1978, for example, when some two hundred mostly black workers organized a strike against a Mississippi plant, the plant remained open, and the company drew "on a labor pool that includes friends and relatives of the picketers" (McCarthy 1980). The reporter believed the new strategy against unions in the South, replacement hiring, was based on the unequivocal presence of a labor surplus. In response to the 1979 strike against Sanderson in Laurel, Mississippi, Chris Marston, a labor official in Mobile, Alabama, made it clear that there was no shortage: "The strike is not a union weapon anymore. . . . It's so easy to come up with workers now, because the economy is so bad. In many places, the strike is almost a management weapon. It gets rid of the so-called agitators and brings in the docile workers" (McCarthy 1980).

Even in 1991, areas in the poultry belt seemed to have labor surpluses. Choctaw Maid Farms made a decision not to hire back those employees in the evisceration and cut-up department who had walked off the job in a labor dispute regarding the plant heat, lack of fans, and long hours worked by employees. The plant manager told them, "If you walk out, don't come back." The personnel manager told his assistant to hire more people; by Monday morning, he decided that he had enough people to replace the walkouts and did not need to hire anymore. Some were hired the very Friday of the walkout; others were instructed to attend a mass orientation on Saturday. The company hired eighty-two new people that Saturday morning and compensated them for a one-hour group orientation. The names mentioned in the NLRB (1992) decision do not indicate a Latino presence.

There is no evidence that African Americans left states or counties with plants. The 1990–2000 median increase in the African American population in poultry counties ranged from 10 percent in North Carolina to 30 percent in Arkansas. Perhaps the most suggestive population counts are those that compare African Americans with the number of additions to the state-level poultry labor force. Between 1992 and 2002, the total number of poultry employees in the five states rose by 26,320, but this was dwarfed by the increases of the African American population in counties that had poultry plants (table 3.1). In Mississippi poultry counties, the 1990–2000 increase in the African American population was 36,617. The Mississippi poultry industry hired 4,852 additional employees. For Alabama, the African American population increase in poultry counties was 68,676, while the number of new employees in the whole state increased by 816 (1992–2002).[7] There is no evidence of geographic mobility in the African American population or the establishment of new plants in counties with radically different racial distributions.

Physical presence, of course, is hardly a sufficient condition for labor force attachment. Entry into the labor force is a geographic, demographic, and social process. If workers were present but underage or otherwise occupied, employers would have been compelled to seek alternatives. State-level unemployment data do suggest a tighter labor market by 2000 (table 3.2). In all five states, unemployment rates declined from 1980 to 2000. Although this drop in unemployment also holds for African Americans, their unemployment rates remained high, at about twice the state average. In Arkansas, the 1984 minority-youth unemployment rate was 32.4 percent.[8]

In support of the vacancy hypothesis, I noted the impressive number of heavy industries that moved into these five states with skilled jobs. However, at the same time, other plants were shedding workers and leaving the South (and the United States). Arkansas registered layoffs in metals, lumber and wood products, textiles, and stone and glass. In 1982, Alcoa moved its automotive wiring systems production from its two Mississippi factories to a new plant in Acuna, Mexico (Dillon 2001). In 1991, Goodyear cut six hundred employees and sold its Alabama plant to a Dutch chemical company.

Textile industries joined the global relocation. Between 1994 and 2000, Georgia lost 65,000 jobs in the textile industry (Hart 2004). In 1999, Forstmann & Co., a wool textile manufacturer, closed two plants in Georgia, displacing 730 employees. Another major textile producer, Fruit of the Loom, had subsidiaries in the South, including thirteen in Alabama and

TABLE 3.2. Unemployment rates

	1980 State*	1981 African American**	1990 State	1990 African American	2000 State	1998 African American
Alabama	8.4%	21.0%	6.3%	13.9%	4.1%	8.4%
Arkansas	7.5%	21.1%	6.8%	18.9%	4.2%	14.9%
Georgia	6.2%	12.1%	5.2%	9.6%	3.5%	8.2%
Mississippi	7.7%	16.9%	7.7%	15.4%	5.6%	9.9%
North Carolina	6.4%	12.1%	4.2%	7.9%	3.8%	6.9%
U. S.	7.1%	15.6%	5.6%	11.4%	4.0%	8.9%

* 12 month non-seasonally adjusted unemployment (U.S. Department of Labor, Bureau of Labor Statistics).
** 12 month unemployment rate for African Americans 16 years and over. For individual states, the series begins in 1981 and stops in 1998 (U.S. Department of Labor, Bureau of Labor Statistics).

five in Mississippi. Shortly after filing its 1994 SEC report, the stock value of this Chicago-based company with 40,000 employees worldwide started to tumble (SEC 1995). From 1995 onward, Fruit of the Loom embarked on cost-saving measures, notably closing its U.S. textile operations and moving them and thousands of jobs to Mexico, Central America, and the Caribbean. Alabama lost 350 jobs in 1995 when the Florence plant closed, 290 jobs in 2002 when the Fayette plant closed, and 450 in 2008 when half of the workers from the Wetumpka plant were laid off. In 2009, Fruit of the Loom closed two more plants in Alabama, affecting 270 workers. By December of 1999, when Fruit of the Loom declared Chapter 11 bankruptcy, it had also transferred its financial base to the Cayman Islands to minimize taxes (*New York Times* 1999).

In 2001, the *New York Times* reported that North Carolina had lost 28,000 jobs, the largest loss in the country. Halbfinger described job losses in rural South Carolina—a preferred destination of small and medium-sized factories in the 1950s and 1960s. They moved into former cotton, tobacco, and peanut fields to escape the unions and higher wages of the North. In 2000, a latex glove plant, following the path of others, moved to China where the finished product would cost less. This departure may have been a reaction to the recession, but it continued a trend that was felt most sharply by blacks living in the persistently poor coastal lowlands of the South (Halbfinger 2002). Therefore, while some businesses were moving in, others were moving out.

From 1991 to 1995, all five states experienced increases in the number of manufacturing jobs. Arkansas had the greatest growth (10.9%), but the other four states also grew. This should have translated into a tighter labor

TABLE 3.3. Change in manufacturing jobs: 1980–2000

	1980–1985	1986–1990	1991–1995	1996–2000
AL	−1.25%	6.28%	3.41%	−6.30%
AR	0.29%	10.31%	10.98%	−1.15%
GA	6.90%	−1.32%	9.24%	0.13%
MS	0.18%	8.52%	3.98%	−5.17%
NC	0.75%	2.68%	4.49%	−7.20%
United States	−4.82%	1.05%	0.85%	−0.40%

Source: Author's calculations from data of Regional Economic Information System, Bureau of Economic Analysis, U.S. Department of Commerce.

market, but after 1995–96, the number of manufacturing jobs stagnated or declined (table 3.3).

Furthermore, investment did not always lead to alternative employment opportunities for African Americans. If native workers had shifted to new emerging industries such as BMW, they would have left labor vacuums in less well-paid industries such as poultry. But in Alabama, for example, the new investment in the 1960s and 1970s was concentrated in white-majority counties—limiting opportunities for blacks. Breckenfeld (1977) reported that employers strategically avoid counties with African Americans because of their willingness to unionize. Northern Alabama experienced new investment growth, but many companies refused to relocate in heavily black counties and instead went to white-majority counties in the northern portion of the state (Schulman 1991, 9).

Keeping wages low was part of the investment recruitment strategy. In 1990, a group of North Carolina business leaders told United Airlines not to build a plant that would have brought high-paying jobs to the state because its union shop would not be welcome. Instead the airline built in Indianapolis. In general, investors hoped to avoid racial conflict, evade affirmative action strictures, and union organization (Schulman 1991, 161–79).

Other investors were reevaluating these states because of the workforce's inadequate human capital. In 2000, Nissan brought 4,000 new jobs to Mississippi and planned to employ approximately 5,300 by mid-2004. They had recruited in 78 of Mississippi's 82 counties but were concerned about the availability of qualified workers. Georgia had offered DaimlerChrysler $320 million to build a new factory outside of Savannah; the state had already bought a 1,500-acre site and set up a training program when the firm pulled out of the deal (*The Economist* 2003). A senior vice president of Nissan North America said that in Alabama, trainers had to use "pictorials" to teach some illiterate workers how to use high-tech plant equipment (Erwin 2005). In light of the difficulties with an untrained and often illiterate workforce that Nissan and Honda encountered, Toyota decided in 2008 to build 100,000 vehicles per year in Ontario. Despite generous state subsidy offers, the company worried that training costs would be higher than in Canada. Because of human capital deficits, established companies also feared competition for the limited trained labor force. When Mississippi courted Hyundai of South Korea, the Nissan company spokesman expressed a "hope"—given the low educational levels in Mississippi—that no new plant should be located within eighty miles of the existing Nissan plant.

Taken together, the data and the narratives produce a mixed employment profile. The region did experience capital investment and growth of higher-skilled and better-paying jobs. On the other hand, the labor force attachment of local residents (particularly African Americans) continued to be weak. Tomaskovic-Devy and Roscigno (1997) argue that greater employment in core sectors (durable manufacturing, transportation, utilities, wholesale trade, and construction) did not significantly reduce inequality or poverty in part because employers were seeking cheap, nonunion labor.

An additional way to evaluate the vacancy hypothesis is to consider measures of well-being. If native labor is employed either in informal activities or in upgraded employment, it should reduce the poverty rates. While it is difficult to measure total income streams (wages, income transfers, gains from illegal activities, and informal economy activities), we might expect to find lower poverty levels in poultry counties, particularly given the dropping levels of unemployment (table 3.4). In those counties with plants (poultry counties), the correlation between the number of plants and unemployment is more strongly negative in 2000 than it was in 1990. This suggests an improvement in employment and a possible tighter labor market. While not much of a factor in poverty reduction in 1990, the positive impact of poultry counties on the percentage living below the poverty line dropped slightly by 2000 (from –.133 to –.114). Poultry-county poverty rates in 2000 remained quite high, ranging from 15 percent of the population in North Carolina to 23.5 percent in Mississippi. Second, in all counties, the associations between percent African American and percent unemployed *and* percent African American and percent living in poverty were higher in 2000. These numbers suggest that poverty and unemployment were already prevalent but getting worse for African Americans. The poverty and unemployment trends for counties with higher percentages of a white population are in the opposite direction.[9]

What I hope to have shown is that while the testimonies support the vacancy and shortage hypotheses for ethnic succession, the data available at the county level put them into question, as they overlook the economic reality of African Americans.

TABLE 3.4. County correlations: 1990 and 2000

	1990	2000	1990-2000 Comparison
Number of poultry firms in county by	(1992)	(1997)	
Percent Latino	.163	.385**	More Latinos
Percent living below poverty line	−.133**	−.114**	About same
unemployment	−.080*	−.182**	Less unemployment
Percent black in county by			
Percent living below poverty line	.602**	.752**	More poverty
Percent unemployed	.363**	.583**	More unemployment
Percent white in county by			
Percent living below poverty line	−.584**	−.726**	Less poverty
unemployment	−.358**	−.551**	Less unemployment

* Significant correlations for all 483 counties in the 5 states (one-tailed test).
Source: Author's calculations from file created by merging data from the 1990 and 2000 U.S. Censuses with data from and the 1992 and 1997 U.S. Economic Censuses.

African Americans Never Fully Rejected These Jobs

The most direct evidence that challenges the vacancy and shortage hypotheses is that some African American workers did not reject those jobs and continued to seek employment in the poultry enterprises. A sampling of union and U.S. government documents confirms that from the mid-1990s to the present day, African American workers have maintained interest in these jobs. This was the case according to Carney, an African American, a former poultry worker, a Vietnam veteran, and a LIUNA Local 693 union representative who helped organize three Mississippi poultry plants in the early 1990s: two Sanderson Farms plants and one run by Peco Foods. He told the reporter that after tough union certification drives and harassment by plant managers, things started to look up for the union and its members. The poultry industry was booming, and the union had fought for and received wage hikes and other benefits. "Then, the immigrants began arriving. . . . [L]ine-speeds increased and new jobs were filled by workers from Mexican towns they had never heard of, like Oaxaca and Chiapas. The immigrants worked harder, faster, and never complained. Labor contractors brought in groups of immigrants and paid them separately from other workers, often deducting a cut for their 'services.' Seemingly overnight, immigrants became the majority on the line at Peco Foods and a significant part of the Sanderson Farms plant" (Cobb 2004, 6). Labor contractors fired them after exactly ninety days so that they would not be eligible under the union contract to join the union, only to rehire them the same day under a new name and Social Security number. He discovered that workers who complained about not receiving overtime were fired on the spot, but even after massive firings, the poultry plants were able to bring in new immigrant workers without missing production quotas. Carney said that he "fields calls daily from African-American job seekers who claim to have been turned away from plants even as more immigrants are brought on" (Cobb 2004, 4–6).

The Department of Labor's Office of Federal Contract Compliance Programs found that Tyson Foods had engaged in discriminatory hiring practices against qualified women who applied for entry-level laborer jobs and qualified African American applicants for craft positions at its Forest, Mississippi, poultry plant. The allegations of discriminatory hiring practices were made by the Labor Department following an investigation from January 1, 1996, through June 30, 1997. The DOL mandated that Tyson Foods to pay a fine of $230,000 to settle the allegations of the African American women who had filed the suit (*PR Newswire* 2000).

Another DOL news release (2006a) reported that more than 2,500 minorities and women would benefit from the Tyson Foods agreement to pay $1.5 million in back pay for hiring discrimination. The offenses transpired at a number of plants from 2002 through 2004. The OFCCP issued findings that Tyson had discriminated against 1,354 rejected female applicants for entry-level laborer positions at three Tyson chicken processing plants (Arkansas), rejected 998 minority applicants for entry-level laborer positions (Oklahoma), and rejected 225 minority applicants for long-haul driver positions at Tyson's terminal in Springdale, Arkansas.[10]

The Crider plant in Stillman, Georgia, described by Perez and Dade (2007) had a workforce that was 70 percent African American in 1996. By 2000 the 900-member workforce was mostly Latino migrant workers, and by 2006, blacks had dropped to about 14 percent of the workforce. In 2007, ICE suspected that 700 workers had false work documents. It arrested two employees who were among those accused of running a false-document mill. The company worked with ICE to weed out those who could not prove their legal status, and then ICE raided the plant and took away 120 mostly Mexican workers. Seeking replacement workers, Crider raised its starting wage and offered free transportation from nearby towns and free rooms in a company-owned dormitory. Many African Americans from the surrounding area applied; in fact, most of the 400 applicants were black. Subsequently, the company and replacement workers had disagreements over breaks, working conditions, and wages paid through the contractors. This led to the felon and homeless hires mentioned above.

Conclusion

"Vacancies" and "shortages" are frequently presented to justify employers' hiring of illegal immigrants. In this case, they cannot totally explain the ethnic succession. Depopulation, geographic mobility, and spatial mismatch can be rejected as explanations. To summarize briefly, the data that I have presented in chapters 2 and 3 establishes that (1) those jobs were once filled by African American workers; (2) African Americans continued to apply for those jobs; (3) African Americans had higher levels of unemployment and poverty; and (4) availability of and accessibility to new industry jobs were limited. Employers' needs were evident; they had difficulties constructing a stable, content, and cheap labor force. While labor shortages must remain in the analysis, this explanation rests completely on market forces. In so doing, it ignores crucial national and global dynamics.

4

Taylorism Invades the Hen House

Immigrants did not enter labor markets that were vacant or simply experiencing shortages. To the contrary, immigrant workers were recruited, frequently in competition with native workers. In this chapter I outline why I believe that the "vacancy" and "shortage" explanations are incomplete. By treating immigrant hiring as the outcome of market forces only, those explanations lack agency and are ahistorical; they leave unexamined those nonmarket agents and elements that also led to perceived vacancies or shortages. My argument is that ethnic succession was principally the by-product of labor-management conflict.

Industry Reorganization—Mass Production

During Herbert Hoover's 1928 presidential campaign, the Republican National Committee inserted an advertisement into a number of newspapers, suggesting that, as president, Hoover would work for continued prosperity, including "a chicken in every pot." In 1992, U.S. per capita chicken consumption surpassed beef; by 2005, it reached one hundred pounds a year. The rise in consumption could not have happened without the transformation of poultry production. Production and processing have changed a great deal since the 1930s. Production evolved from an informal and highly fragmented industry—millions of small backyard flocks, where meat was a byproduct of egg production—to a formal, highly specialized (and therefore measurable) agribusiness (USDA 2002). The restructuring of the industry involved geographic and firm concentration, technological upgrading, pharmaceutical innovations, vertical integration, intensive farming practices (warehousing), mergers and acquisitions, and U.S. government subsidies (table 4.1).

Geographic concentration was encouraged by the financial incentives and antiunion environment offered by southern states, and a shift toward vertical integration that placed a premium on proximity to growing-out farms. The unorganized market system of trading chicks, feed, and other inputs was replaced by a more systematic division between the processors and the independent contract "growers" who raise birds.[1] The contract system was pioneered in the 1940s by a feed store owner in Georgia who began selling chicks, feed, medicine, and equipment to growers and then buying back the grown chickens for processing and sale. The "integrators,"

TABLE 4.1. Selected U.S. industry characteristics: Comparisons over time

Total broilers produced (billion pounds)*	(1945) 1.11	(2001) 42.45
Broilers slaughtered (in millions)**	(1960) 1,534	(1998) 7,838
Number chick hatcheries. Average incubator capacity (number of eggs)*	(1934) 11,405 24,224	(2001) 323 2.7 million
Time to attain 3 lbs.***	(1940) 4 mos	(1990) 6 weeks
Sale of whole birds (as % of total slaughtered production)**	(1963) 84.8%	(1997) 13.1%
Top four firm share of market **	(1963) 14 %	(1992) 41 %
Chicken purchased by processer under grower contracts (in %)**	(1940) about 0%	(1994) 85%
Total electricity purchased for heat and power (1,000 kWh)****	(1997) 5,253, 749	(2002) 6,966,990

* USDA (2002a); ** Ollinger et al. (2000); *** Bruce (1990); **** Author's calculations based on U.S. Economic Census 1997, 2002.

the agribusiness firms that replaced the feed store owners and packers, consolidated and controlled the process (Starmer et al. 2006). Growers are paid a per-pound fee for the use of their grow-out houses and associated costs and must follow the contract's growing-out guidelines in order to produce birds of uniform size and quality. Production facilities are typically located within twenty-five miles of the processing plant (Griffith 1990, 160). Observers note that since the early 1990s, thousands of chicken houses (growers) have cropped up across the South (Parker 2006). Because the poultry industry consumes a large amount of soymeal, the successful introduction of soybeans to the Southeast in the 1950s—an alternative to cotton—also contributed to the industry's relocation and expansion. By the end of the 1990s, approximately half of all poultry processing was concentrated in four low-wage, antiunion states: Alabama, Arkansas, Georgia, and North Carolina (Fink 2003, 12).

High-speed technological innovations offered new possibilities for slaughtering, feather plucking, and entrail removal. The industries installed mechanical eviscerators after 1976; automatic slaughtering machines can process ninety-one birds a minute. The mass production "rivals anything Detroit has produced" (Serrin 1980). In 1992, Frances Ketcher, 63, an employee of twenty-four years at the Simmons poultry plant in Arkansas told a reporter that "the pace at the plant is so frantic that chickens sometimes spill onto the floor, where they lie for as long as an hour" (Behar 1992). As the industry continued to evolve, it consumed more and more energy in the production process.

Over the past twenty-five years, the meat and poultry industries consolidated. Vertical integration and concentration involved not only chick farmers but also, in some cases, feed, freezing and packaging plants, and distribution networks. For example, by vertically integrating its business and controlling every step of production, from the hatchery to the feed mill to the processing plant, Tyson protected itself from fluctuations in market prices. In 1981, ConAgra purchased river terminals, barges, and grain elevators and got involved in agricultural chemical distribution (*New York Times* 1981).

Leading firms built very large plants, while some independent firms disappeared or were bought by larger firms, leading to a handful of large companies controlling a great share of the market. Mergers contributed to growth. ConAgra, Tyson, and others were all actively buying up smaller establishments. A large part of Tyson's growth came through acquisition and diversification (McGraw and Simons 1994). From 1975 to 1995, Tyson made about thirty acquisitions. The top producers often competed with each other for acquisitions. For instance, Holly Farms, one of the top producers in 1968, had acquired at least twenty-five other companies (Striffler 2005, 60). In 1989, after a two-year struggle between ConAgra and Tyson to take over Holly Farms, Tyson won. Buy-outs and mergers did not stop there: in 2003, ConAgra Foods Inc., one of the nation's largest food companies, sold its chicken processing operations to Pilgrim's Pride Corp. for $590 million in cash and securities. As a result of the mergers of the 1980s, eight large processors controlled two-thirds of the market (Fink 2003, 12).[2] By 2005, the top five companies held 50 percent of the business. Technology and industry concentration contributed to productivity improvements, while antibiotics facilitated the raising of thousands of animals in a single building. Productivity per worker nearly tripled from 1960 to 1987. This restructuring had a positive effect on profit margins, which increased fourteen-fold from 1980 to 1990 (Behar 1992). In 1994, *Feedstuffs* reported that broiler companies experienced higher returns due to the increased domestic demand and export markets (Brown 1994, 21).

The final product was likewise transformed by all these changes. By switching to a higher proportion of convenient, prepared, and refrigerated foods, Tyson responded to consumer tastes and secured higher returns. By 1997 only 13.1 percent of the slaughtered production was sold as whole birds (table 4.1). Also by the mid-1990s, consumers were more likely to purchase chicken *outside* of the grocery store.

Poultry and Government Support

From the 1980s on, production and profits were bolstered through political influence. Continual lobbying with state and federal governments for special-interest legislation, subsidies, and tax relief formed part of industry's ongoing repertoire for creating and maintaining profits. At the request of the meat industry, for example, the Reagan administration altered the policy regarding the frequency of meat inspections conducted by the USDA Food Safety Inspection Service. And as of November 1984, poultry plants with suitable facilities and good inspection records were allowed to increase the line speed from a maximum of 70 to 91 birds a minute (Hughes 1983).[3]

The lobbying was not new, although some found it inappropriate. In describing its company perspectives, Pilgrim's Pride noted that the "only blemish for the company . . . was Pilgrim's involvement in a campaign contribution scandal with eight Texas lawmakers." In 1989, the CEO, Mr. Bo Pilgrim, had handed out $10,000 checks to Texas state senators (with the payee's name left blank) to help persuade them to gut the state's workers' compensation laws. He successfully defended himself before a grand jury and was not indicted (FundingUniverse n.d.). Accusations of corruption were likewise leveled against Mike Espy, President Clinton's first secretary of agriculture, who in 1997 was indicted for receiving about $34,000 worth of sports tickets and other favors from Tyson three years earlier. A federal jury acquitted Espy in 1998 after a lengthy investigation by an independent prosecutor initiated by U.S. Attorney General Janet Reno. Tyson Foods pleaded guilty to making illegal gifts to Espy and agreed to pay $6 million (a $4 million fine and a $2 million contribution to the investigation) (Lewis 1998).

Poultry lobbyists worked to secure tax exemptions. In 1977, in a classic special-interest case, the Senate voted tax relief for two large poultry operations. The case for Corbett Enterprises (Maine) and Hudson Foods, Inc. (Arkansas) was successfully presented by Senators Edmund S. Muskie (D-Me.), John L. McClellan (D-Ark.), and James B. Allen (D-Ala.) over the protests of Sen. Edward M. Kennedy (D-Mass.). Unincorporated businesses and incorporated businesses with less than $1 million in sales were already exempt from the 1976 law requiring farming enterprises to shift from the cash accounting method to the accrual method in tax computations.[4] In the 1986 Tax Reform Bill, total or partial exemptions were extended to farm corporations controlled by three or fewer families—the case for nearly all of the top twenty-five poultry firms. Exemptions would deprive the U.S. Treasury of an estimated $1 billion over five years (Uehling 1986). Tyson also benefited from about $12 million dollars in tax breaks for expansion projects during Clinton's governorship. Mr. Don Tyson, chairman of the firm founded by his father, denied any impropriety; rather, he argued, with 22,000 workers in Arkansas, the governor has to be willing to work with the state's largest employer (McGraw and Simons 1994). Always the pragmatist, Tyson Foods donated to the presidential inauguration funds of Clinton ($100,000 in 1993) and Bush ($100,000 in 2005) (Buncombe 2005).

The industry gained from both direct and indirect government assistance. In line with bilateral trade agreements and the General Agreement on Trade and Tariffs (GATT), the global norm has been to eliminate government subsidies to farmers. Nevertheless, U.S. poultry processors continued to benefit indirectly from government subsidies. From 1995 to 2004, a majority of U.S. agricultural subsidies went to producers of sugar, oils, meat, dairy, alcohol, and feed crops. Starmer et al. call the 1996 Federal Agriculture Improvement and Reform Act (FAIR) one of the most significant shifts in U.S. agricultural policy since the 1930s. It eliminated the remaining supply-price control programs, resulting in increased production and lower commodity prices. The authors find that between 1997 and 2005, the market prices of corn and soybeans were an average of 23 and 15 percent below production costs, respectively. Farm income was no longer supported by higher market prices, as it had been before the 1996 FAIR act; instead, farm income now was supported by government payments. In 2000 alone, government aid made up 100 percent of net farm income in eight states (Starmer et al. 2006). The Farm Security and Rural Investment Act of 2002 expanded the payments. Among those critical of this farm bill are domestic farmers who have experienced drops in farm income and farmers around the world who can no longer compete with low prices of U.S. producers. The broiler industry benefited. Because feed accounts for an estimated 60 percent of total poultry production costs, the industry was able to keep costs 13 percent lower than they would have been if they had paid full market price for corn and soybeans (Starmer et al. 2006, 4). The effect of subsidies was cogently captured in an op-ed entitled, "Why Does a Big Mac Cost $2.79 and a Caesar Salad $4.39?" (Yost 2007).

The industry also gained from direct assistance. In 2002 Virginia received $44,947,397 in USDA disaster relief for farmers. Over a third ($15,027,968) went to Pilgrim's Pride Virginia plants. From 1995 to 2005, Pilgrim's Pride was the top recipient of farm subsidies in Virginia (Rudeclerk 2007). Many poultry producers also received support for exporting. Based on authority granted in the 1978 Agricultural Trade Act, the U.S. government has promoted the export of U.S. commodities though a variety of programs. In 1986, Congress authorized the USDA to spend $870 million on export promotion (1987–91) and over $1 billion for bonus crop subsidies. Under the Targeted Export Assistance Program, producer groups like the Feed Grains Council receive grants in the form of certificates for their surplus grains that may be redeemed for dollars. In 1986, poultry producers received $6 million to expand poultry and egg exports in the Pacific Rim and the Middle East. In that year, they received grants, as did producers of wine, wood, canned peaches, Florida oranges, dried peas and lentils, and dried prunes (Dunne 1987). Another program, the Market Access Program (MAP) was created to expand and maintain foreign markets for U.S. agricultural commodities and products through cost-share assistance. Because the MAP is intended to supplement efforts of the U.S. private sector, an applicant must contribute resources to its proposed promotional activities (USDA 2007). In 2002, 37.2 percent of expenditures for market development came from the U.S. government, and 62.8 percent came from the industry (Hanrahan 2008, 44).

The U.S. government has defended the industry in international markets. In 1981, the National Broiler Council filed a trade complaint, saying it had been driven out of Middle East markets by French- and Brazilian-subsidized poultry. The complaint went to nonbinding arbitration under GATT but remained unresolved. The U.S. share of the Middle East poultry market fell from 50 percent to zero. The Export Enhancement Program (EEP), USDA's direct export subsidy program, was launched in 1985 after failing to convince the EU and Brazil to stop subsidizing their farm exports (Dunne 1987). EEP spending has been negligible since 1996, but in FY 1996, 11,125 tons of frozen poultry (the only commodity sold under the EEP) received bonuses totaling $5.15 million (Hanrahan 2008). In 1999, FAS worked to eliminate the EU ban on growth-promoting hormones and to improve Mexican market access for U.S. wheat, dry beans, and slaughtered hogs (Galvin 2000).

U.S. agricultural exporters to Mexico have benefited from USDA programs. Two Export Credit Guarantee Programs (GSM 102 and 103) provide loan guarantees for specific commodities and specific countries. Agricultural exports destined for Mexico received the highest share of GSM loans between 1980 and 1994, and in some years, such as 1983, more than half of the agricultural sales to Mexico were financed with these credits (GAO 1990, 34). On the buyers' side, the U.S. Export-Import Bank assists by offering credit insurance, long-term loans, and guarantees. In the event that a Mexican buyer goes bankrupt, is forced into default, or is otherwise unable to acquire U.S. dollars, the Ex-Im Bank protects the U.S. company. In 1994, "The Ex-Im Bank provided more services to U.S.

business selling to or investing in Mexico than in any other country in the world, and Ex-Im Bank remains open for cover in Mexico for all programs" (Detzner and Gonzalez 1995). Poultry products have been promoted by the USAPEEC's Mexico office.[5] It has participated in large retail and food service shows in Mexico, featuring products at in-store promotions at Walmart Supercenters (USDA 2000, 25). Space does not permit a thorough review of government assistance to poultry, but these examples demonstrate how the rise of poultry exports was due to more than simple changes in supply and demand.

Assembly Lines That Match Detroit

Taylorism involved the reorganization of both production and labor. Braverman described Taylorism as the management of work under capitalist conditions: management sets tasks and directs the way they are performed (1974, 90). Taylorism adapted the labor process to the technology. Taylorism invaded the hen house with new mass production methods that rivaled Detroit and new labor processes. Each workplace employed more workers, sped up processes, and urgently required workers to stay attached to the disassembly line. These changes are summarized in table 4.2.

Today's poultry factories have more employees and multiple shifts. OSHA's report on Hudson Food (regarding the $332,500 fine for safety violations) mentions that the Noel, Missouri, plant employed 1,400 people (1997). In his report on AFL-CIO's organizing campaign of Perdue's poultry workers, Hamilton (1980) notes that the plant in Accomack, Virginia, had about a thousand workers. Larger plants concentrated a larger market share and had larger workforces. Share of industry value shipped by plants with more than four hundred employees rose from 29 percent in 1967 to 88 percent in 1992 (Ollinger et al. 2000, 7). Plants were often described

TABLE 4.2. Selected labor process characteristics: Comparisons over time

Assembly line speed (birds/minute)*	(1970s) about 35	(1986) 91 allowed
Share of total industry value shipped by plants with more than 400 employees**	(1967) 29%	(1992) 88%
Production per worker (Index) ***	(1960) = 100	(1987) 300

* Bruce (1990); ** Ollinger (2000); *** Behar (1992).

as cramped and noisy. And they put some workers dangerously closer to knife-wielding co-workers. They also created possibilities for worker organization.

As described above, plants are factories with mechanized high-speed lines driven by increasing amounts of energy. The technology required constant attendance; workers had to remain on the line. Workers experienced this as bondage, because management had no compassion for human needs. "Down the chain, a worker named Jose yells and waves wildly, like a drowning man. Bathroom trips are discouraged and require approval. But the foreman can't hear because of the din, and Jose is left grimacing and crossing his legs. Finally, half an hour later, a weary cheer ripples along the line. 'The last bird's coming!' someone shouts. Jose sprints toward the bathroom" (Horwitz 1994). Automation's intrinsic dangers were evident in the previously mentioned 1991 Imperial Foods fire in Hamlet, North Carolina, that killed 25 and injured 56 out of a total worker population of 245 (Behar 1992). The plant fire was caused by the spontaneous rupture of a hydraulic line on a deep-fat fryer.

The technological capacity to debone chicken led to rising consumer demand for nuggets and fillets in fast food restaurants. Speed made the work more repetitive and more dangerous. Keeping up with the rapid line pace for eight hours or more resulted in injuries. In chapter 3, I presented some of the injury data that placed poultry processing high among the nation's industries. Hand ailments were so common that many plants routinely prescribed pain killers, vitamin B6, and hand wraps to help workers get through the day (Applebome 1989). Following the norms of Taylorism, work was divided into non-interchangeable parts. Since the 1990s, tasks have become more automated and compartmentalized, depriving workers the chance to develop additional skills. For example, workers on the "knife line" often are not allowed to sharpen their own knives—for "safety reasons" (Horwitz 1994).

Taylorism's invasion of the hen house brought profit to the owners and distress to the workers. Workers complained that work became increasingly difficult, dangerous, and underpaid. Taylorism led to a deterioration of working conditions, but it also concentrated the workforce geographically. This made the chicken industry a receptive environment for union organizing. Strikes and walkouts in the 1980s and early 1990s emphasized working conditions: the line, bathroom breaks, chemical spills, earnings, benefits, and hours. In 1979, for example, some two hundred workers struck against a plant in Laurel, Mississippi, because of ignored complaints regarding the dizzying pace on the production line (68 birds/minute) and the dangerous gases in the workplace (McCarthy 1980). Taylorism's triumph was increased production and enriched companies, but it simultaneously created objectionable working conditions, and energized unions to respond. These labor actions and companies' responses opened up a new chapter in labor-management conflict.

A New Labor-Management Regime

In the early 1980s, fewer than 10 percent of Arkansas poultry plants were unionized. In this period reporters began noting historic "firsts" in the South: a first strike on a particular company, a first strike in a particular town, the first unionization in decades, and, most notably, the first unionization of African American workers. These labor actions were unprecedented, as was the willingness of unions to transport the labor struggle beyond individual plants, either by organizing at the state level or by organizing national product boycotts.

I provide a small sample of early reports that document the poultry workers' concerns and the reporters' beliefs regarding the innovativeness of their labor actions. In the February 1979 strike, the two hundred women at the Sanderson chicken processing plant in Laurel, Mississippi, were represented by the International Chemical Workers Union (ICWU) (McCarthy 1980). Workers struck because the company ignored the complaints mentioned above (work pace, gases, heat, and limited bathroom breaks). The bitter strike lasted through December of 1980. By then, the ICWU had spent $130,000 on the strike and called for a boycott of Sanderson products. The strike proved difficult because of the "South's antiunion tradition and continuing surplus of willing workers (including white workers) ready to fill jobs in the midst of strike" (Brown 1979).

In 1980, the UFCW launched a nationwide boycott against Perdue as part of a campaign to organize the company's 3,500 poultry workers. This was a new effort to organize workers and win bargaining rights in Perdue's five plants. Complaints against the company focused on the harsh and unfair treatment of workers, and a lack of job security—Perdue had fired over four hundred people in its Accomack, Virginia, plant in a two-year period. The plant employed about a thousand workers and had been the center of the union's efforts (Hamilton 1980).

In June 1984, half of the nine hundred workers from Marval Turkey (the nation's largest turkey processor) in Harrisonburg, Virginia, struck. Strikers complained about dangerous and oppressive work conditions. The union wanted salary increases. The parent company sought a new contract provision that would make it easier for workers to quit the union. The union also contended that the plant imposed harsh working conditions by speeding up the turkey-killing lines and imposing stringent work rules. The strike was the first ever in Virginia's $250-million-a-year turkey industry. During the six-week strike, the AFL-CIO called for a boycott of Marval. After six weeks, roughly half of the 500 strikers had returned to work, and Marval's parent company, Rocco Enterprises, had hired about 250 replacement workers. The company considered them permanent employees and would not replace them with returning strikers. Although the company felt that after six weeks, it had ended the strike, the UFCW was prepared to spend $100,000 per month for advertising and promotion of the turkey boycott (Perl 1984).

In 1985, discontented with their working conditions and wages, the workers of Lumbee Farms Cooperative, Inc., in Lumber Bridge, North Carolina, formed a group called the Employees Concerns Council. Discussions with employers left some disagreements unresolved (such as a wage increase), and workers decided to strike (NLRB 1987).

The next year, 1986, was a momentous year for labor organizing in Mississippi. The UFCW successfully unionized the catfish processors working for Delta Pride. The organizers visited churches and homes in anticipation of the certification election (Gilliam 1986). Several years later, in September 1990, those unionized workers struck, in what was described as the largest strike by African American workers in the history of Mississippi (Dine 1990a). In their first contract negotiation following the 1986 union election, workers overwhelmingly rejected the company's proposed wage increases, and 1,200 walked off the job. There were incidents of violence, as striking workers were shot at and one was beaten by a policeman. The UFCW called for a national boycott (Dine 1990a, 1990b).

In 1988, about 1,000 (of the 1140 workers) walked out of the House of RaeFord Farms, Inc. plant in North Carolina. A majority of them were poor black women (Hetzer 1989). Unmet demands for better pay, better benefits, and shorter hours precipitated their wildcat strike (a worker action without union participation). In another case in 1989, workers represented by the Retail, Wholesale, Department Store Union (RWDSU) struck against Cagle's Inc. of Georgia. They demanded improved pay, benefits, and working conditions. And in 1990, when seventy-seven Holly Farms drivers joined the International Brotherhood of Teamsters and went on strike, it was the first time the Teamsters had tried to organize in Wilkes County, North Carolina, since the 1950s (Swoboda 1990).

Management used traditional tactics (some in violation of the NLRA) such as firing union organizers and members, discouraging new unions, and encouraging the decertification of existing unions. In one case, a worker testified to a conversation with plant manager that went as follows: "the Respondent was going to 'starve' the employees out to defeat the Union as they had done in a prior union campaign at another of Respondent's plants" (NLRB 1993a). They had accomplished this by substantially reducing the kill and therefore the number of employees. Management went on the offensive against employee resistance by bringing in antilabor consulting firms, promoting lengthy election delays, and initiating decertification elections. Regarding his twenty-three Arkansas plants and the absence of unions in all but two of them, John Tyson said it is the desire of the workers to not have unions. In 1984, when Tyson won a decertification election against the UFCW, a manager was reported as saying, "We bought a plant in Dardanelle [Arkansas]" and got rid of the union. "Last year [1991] 80% of the workers signed a petition to get rid of the union. They just didn't want it" (Behar 1992). In July 1992, a judge overturned that decertification because the employee who led the drive was an "agent" of Tyson who had "threatened" new hires into signing the petition. Similarly, Choctaw Maid Farms, Inc., which operated plants in Carthage, Forest, Crystal Springs, and Pelahatchie, Mississippi, informed employees that the annual wage raises were being withheld because of their activities and sympathies for the RWDSU/AFL-CIO. In an NLRB hearing, the "Respondent" admitted that "only the Pelahatchie employees did not receive the wage increase in 1991 . . . based solely on Respondent's potential bargaining obligation with the union" (NLRB 1992, 523).[6]

Management borrowed tactics from the meat business, such as selling or closing unionized plants (sometimes with bankruptcy filings) and opening new nonunionized ones in order to abrogate master wage agreements and to drop the compensation paid to nonunion or low-wage operators. In 1983, Armour Foods Co. closed most of its twenty packing plants before the Greyhound Corp., its parent, sold the business to ConAgra Inc., which immediately reopened the plants with nonunion labor (*Business Week* 1984). Also in 1983, even though the UFCW union accepted a 44-month wage freeze, Wilson Foods Corp in Oklahoma City filed for Chapter 11 reorganization and abrogated its union contract. One worker recalled the shock of hearing that wages would be cut by 40 percent. In a similar move, the "troubled" Dubuque Packing Co. sold three meat plants to a group of executives. Two weeks later, the executives reopened the plants under the name FDL Foods Inc.—at pay rates of $6.50 an hour instead of $10.69. FDL also did away with dozens of restrictive work rules.

An extremely unusual management response to labor organization was described in the 1986 report by the President's Commission on Organized Crime. The commissioner wrote, "It is a classic example of how a legitimate businessman can find himself drawn to mobster-run firms in an effort to beat his competitor" (*U.S. News and World Report* 1986). In the early 1970s, East Coast poultry producer Frank Perdue ("It takes a tough man to make a tender chicken") wanted to expand sales in New York. Initially he resisted offers from Dial Poultry—a New York firm owned by sons of Paul Castellano Sr., a boss in the Gambino crime family—to market his poultry. But in 1976, when he saw a competitor selling chickens through Dial, he too started selling to them. Perdue subsequently turned to Castellano for help with his labor problem, first in 1980 when the UFCW tried to unionize his plant at Accomac and again in 1981 when the union planned to picket a Perdue restaurant in New York. Perdue failed to enlist mob support in both cases. According to the commission's report, Perdue violated no law. Perdue said, "In hindsight, I should never have had the meetings" (*U.S. News and World Report* 1986). Such reports suggest a new labor-management regime. Unions were more militant, and management embarked upon more aggressive actions.

These ethnographies, media reports, and union and U.S. government publications chronicle the presence of a new labor-management conflict in the 1980s and early 1990s, a conflict precipitated by the rise of labor activity in the South. However, this assertion presents two paradoxes. First, it is at odds with the national trend, which showed declining union density; and second, it is at odds with the conventional wisdom regarding the antiunion South. Because the southern union story is an "outlier" to the national trend and because it is a crucial component of my analysis, I summarize some of the literature on national and southern union density.

Declining National Union Membership

National union membership has suffered a precipitous decline, from around 36 percent for private nonagricultural workers in 1950 (Dickens and Leonard 1985, 331) to 13.6 percent for the private and public work-force in 2000 (Hirsch et al. 2001) and 12.5 percent in 2005 (*The Economist* 2005).[7] Since the 1970s, there has been a general decline in the number of NLRB certification elections and a decline in the percentage of elections won.[8] In addition to an ebbing membership, the scope of coverage allowed by the NLRB and collective bargaining agreements has been shrinking (Goldfield 1987; Perusek and Worcester 1995; Stone 1992). This disintegration of the earlier national labor-management regime has been attributed to a number of factors, including (1) net job losses resulting from deindustrialization and globalization; (2) organizing failures of unions, due to poor strategies and overdeveloped bureaucracies; (3) challenges presented directly by business; and (4) the weakened national legal framework under which unions function. Each of these has diminished union density in the United States.

First and foremost, authors cite the profound economic transitions taking place in the United States. Union membership and institutional strength waned with the general shift from Taylorism to Toyotism, namely a shift from centralized to decentralized diversified production. Whereas unions had gained a stronghold under the first, with its hierarchically organized mass production, they lost under the second, with its plant closings, layoffs, and shifts in labor force composition. Union strongholds were also challenged by the globalization of manufacturing, which relocated traditional union sector jobs offshore in underdeveloped countries, where workers are cheaper, less militant, and more responsive to authority (Griffith 1990, 178). The economic transformations reduced the number of workers in previously heavily unionized sectors of the economy; when unions won, there were fewer newly organized workers. Even where production did not move offshore, employers have used it as a threat to extract more concessions from remaining unions. The rearrangement of U.S. industrial production does much to explain the current union decline.

But, as some authors observe (LRA 2005; Stone 1992), this does not explain why the employees in the new sectors such as the white collar or service sector unionize at a much lower rate, or why deunionization continues among the existing manufacturing jobs. The LRA does not think that job losses in heavily unionized sectors since the 2001 recession account for membership decline. The number of manufacturing jobs fell by 13.2 percent between 2001 and 2004, but the number of union members in manufacturing fell by 23.5 percent over the same period (LRA 2005). Rates, therefore, must be affected by more than the economic restructuring.

To understand the decline, scholars also have examined the organizing efforts of unions. Dickens and Leonard attribute the decline in membership from 1950 to 1980 to (1) a decline in the rate of organizing; (2) a decline in the success of certification elections; (3) a decline in the growth of jobs that would have been part of the already unionized sector; and (4) a rise in decertification elections (which they consider to have an insignificant impact on the percent organized). Controlling for cyclical variations in economy, they conclude that 30 percent of the drop in membership rates can be accounted for by union organizing rates, 17 percent by election success rates, and 35 percent by slowed economic growth (1985, 330, 332).

In a similar vein, Perusek and Worcester attribute the decline of organized labor to the bureaucratization of unions, which disconnected leaders from members. Union bureaucrats, in pursuit of their organizational interests (maintaining dues, conserving strike funds, and so forth), chose cautious strategies when facing challenges. And more specifically, in recent years they were passively acquiescent. Because they strove to restore full participation with the Democratic Party, they pursued a moderate legislative program rather than workplace strength (1995, 13). These two critiques, that unions have inadequately organized in the face of a changing economy and that they have been too concerned with their own bureaucracy survival, overlap with charges leveled by the unions that broke with the AFL-CIO in 2005. Have unions become less successful in organizing and representing workers because of changes in the economy and union hierarchies too concerned with their narrow corporate interests? The criticisms that unions have been ineffectual in improving wages and working conditions might be due to a third factor, namely constraints on union activities.

Roadblocks were put in labor's way. Unions have encountered direct assaults from employers and less protection from a weakened NLRB. In weighing the contribution of all factors, Goldfield (1987) argues that the decline, which has been steady since the 1950s, cannot be traced entirely to events in the 1970s and 1980s. He concludes that the changes in the occupational and industrial structures, along with recessions, play only a minor role in declining union density. Instead, he argues, the capitalist offensive has been continuous since the mid-1950s. Employers have been found guilty of engaging in unlawful activities prior to or during union election campaigns. During the 1970s, for example, the number unfair labor practice (ULPs) charges brought against employers by the NLRB doubled. Summarizing the NLRB data (1968–84), Goldfield notes the rise in frequency and success of decertification elections. This, he concludes, was part of the antiunion offensive and not a good sign for unions (1987, 52). Employers also expanded their regular corporate antagonism to include hiring antiunion consultants, supporting an antiunion research arm of the National Association of Manufactures, and supporting litigation that challenged protections enjoyed by some unions. Goldfield concludes that employer resistance (the capitalist offensive) was the major factor in union decline.

Bronfenbrenner and Juravich (1994) examine the contribution of these factors to the union election win rate. Sampling over two hundred elections held between 1991 and 1992, they find that the win rate for the public sector unions was 85 percent, in contrast to 48 percent in the private sector. Their analysis adjudicates among various explanations, because it includes a control group (the public sector). The 37-point public-private gap cannot be explained by inadequate union tactics, demographic traits of workers in the bargaining unit, size of plant, sector of economy, employer background, or NLRB practices and procedures, all of which are represented in their model. They attribute the gap to private sector employers' use of aggressive antiunion activities, including antiunion campaigns, captive audience meetings, leaflets, letters mailed to houses, firing workers for union activity, promising benefits in return for union opposition, and visiting employees at their homes (1994, 20). In short, their analysis supports the conclusion that employers' attacks on the union ethic have been most responsible for union decline.

At the national level, employers have worked to undermine and modify the labor-management regime in order to weaken union power. Laws construct the national framework that governs the union-employer struggle. As Stone argues, "Actual union effectiveness is, to a large extent, a product of the legal rules that determine what unions can and cannot do" (1992, 583). Since the 1980s, judicial and administrative decisions have transformed the institutional arrangements that regulate the labor-management conflict. They have resulted in the disappearance of many legal rights and of the very collective bargaining regime that was created during the New Deal and flourished in the post–World War II period (Stone 1992, 576). They have weakened union power and shifted the balance toward corporations. Unions lost power, for example, on the scope of mandatory bargaining. After a 1981 Supreme Court decision, both the NLRB and the Supreme Court agreed that employers' decisions made out of a concern for economic factors were exempt from the bargaining obligation. Stone identifies other instances, such as the dilution of the statutory protection governing union organizing campaigns. Since 1982, the NLRB no longer restricts an employer from making knowingly false and prejudicial statements about a union during its organizing campaign. And since 1984, employers are permitted to poll workers during union campaigns. Finally, Stone points to the growing NLRB's ineffectiveness in preventing or remedying unlawful employer conduct.

Another major institutional change was the 1986 interpretation of the Mackay doctrine. In the 1938 case *NLRB v. Mackay Radio & Telegraph Co.,* the Supreme Court held that employers were legally allowed to hire permanent replacements for strikers when business survival required it. This became known as the Mackay doctrine. Since 1938, neither unions nor supporters in the Democratic Party have been able to persuade Congress to limit or prohibit this practice. The 1986 NLRB ruling about Harter Equipment Inc., a manufacturing firm in New Jersey, and the International Union of Operating Engineers fortified the 1938 ruling. This ruling allowed companies to continue operating by hiring temporary replacement workers during a lockout. A Wharton labor relations expert commented that hiring replacements was no longer regarded as "particularly deviant behavior." The NLRB's decision permitting the hiring of temporary replacements "takes an area of the law which was uncertain,

and makes it crystal-clear"-- an employer can lock out workers and continue operating with temporary replacements (Serrin 1986). The Mackay
doctrine is an important tool used by employers to temper demands of
overzealous unions. *NLRB v. Mackay* contributed to the weakening of existing unions because employers could use it tactically to rid themselves of
unions. In negotiations, the employer can offer a wage below the market
rate, knowing that the workers will strike. They can then be replaced, and
after twelve months, the striking workers are no longer eligible to vote
in certifying elections. Employers can proceed with decertifying elections
(Weiler 1993, 674, 686).[9]

Branches of the U.S. government also have undertaken antiunion actions. In 1981, President Ronald Reagan attacked the union PATCO. He
continued his attack by appointing anti-NLRB members to the NLRB
and launching investigations of union presidents for violation of the 1939
Hatch Act, which forbade public unions to engage in political activity
(Goldfield 1987). As organized labor lost power, it has been replaced by
what Stone calls an "individual employment rights regime" (1992, 593).
She points out that individual employees may take recourse to the courts
on issues of firing, privacy on the job, freedom from drug testing and sexual
harassment, and the like because they now have more leverage there than
they do through unions. Unions may have shortcomings in their bureaucratic structure and organizing strategies, but the new labor-management
regime places major constraints on what unions may do. Collectively, these
processes have contributed to the decline of union strength and impaired
organizing. This is the national trend.

Southern Divergence

The South has diverged from the national trend since the New Deal. In
contrast to northern worksites, wages in the South and the percentage of
union shops have always been lower. "Operation Dixie," a post–World
War II unionization drive, was spearheaded by the Congress of Industrial
Organizations (CIO). Despite the early militancy of predominantly southern and black unions such as the Food, Tobacco and Agriculture Workers
Unions, they did not have a place in the post–World War II union consolidation. The failure to expand unionization into the South has been attributed to fratricide among union factions, concern for the survival of the

labor-Roosevelt coalition and unwillingness of the labor organizations to confront the "black question." Southern organizing proved to be difficult because the national office often supported local CIO officers whose position was antiblack and anti-Communist. The failure of "Operation Dixie" left the U.S. labor movement in a weakened position and the South without significant union presence.

Today, the overwhelming majority of southern states are right-to-work states.[10] Because of this, state development councils, chambers of commerce, and local politicians were successful in getting northern firms to relocate to Dixie." Diebel summarized it as follows: "Unions not welcome. That's the message workers get as they try to organize to North Carolina. With the lowest wages and worst working conditions in the United States, 'New South' states have become a haven for profit-hungry firms and hovel for workers" (1993).

In the 1970s, U.S. union membership dropped to its lowest levels since the postwar period, and the South followed this trend. In 1970, the national membership average (for nonagricultural, private and public, wage and salaried workers) was 27.8 percent. Alabama came closest with 22.8 percent; Arkansas was second-closest, at 15.7 percent. Georgia, Mississippi, and North Carolina registered far less, with 13.7 percent, 15 percent, and 8.8 percent respectively (Hirsch et al. 2001). Of course, these percentages are only rough approximations of labor activity. In their analysis of NLRB hospital data (1974–79), Becker and Delaney contrast three aspects of southern unionization: 6.8 percent fewer elections, 4.7 percent fewer negotiated collective bargaining agreements, but intriguingly, equal probability of union election victories (1983, 382).

Despite lower density levels, Goldfield thinks the "difficulty" of organizing the South is a misreading (1987, 140). Compared to the losses in the traditional industrial belt, for example, union density in the southern states held steady or gained slightly. Overall, the public and private union decline in the five southeastern states (1980 to 2000) was not as steep as the national decline.[11] Furthermore, the contrast is pronounced within the private sector, where, from 1985 to 2000, Alabama's union membership rates surpass the national average. Alabama retained the highest level of union density (with the greatest volatility) and North Carolina recorded the lowest (and the least volatility). The three other states had middle-level union density and volatility (fig. 4.1).

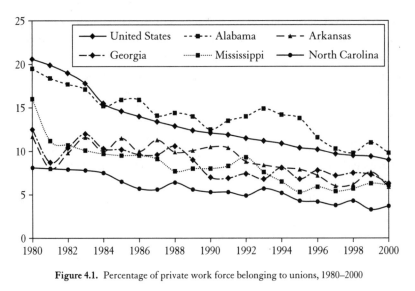

Figure 4.1. Percentage of private work force belonging to unions, 1980–2000

Source: Data from Hirsch et al. (2001).

New Unions and Social Movements in Poultry

I cited above some of the historic firsts for unionizing in the South. Two crucial factors contributed to the rise of labor activity in the 1980s. First, poultry workers were newly empowered as a result of recent union reorganization. Second, unions received significant support from civil rights and community groups.

Union mergers strengthened labor representation, which in turn contributed to the rise in labor-management conflict. In 1968, the Amalgamated Meat Cutters and Butcher Workmen merged with the United Packinghouse Workers of America. The new union, with about a half-million workers, was seen as powerful and progressive. In 1979, this union merged with the Retail Clerks International Union to form the UFCW. Although some judged the UFCW to be less aggressive and more cautious, the 1979 merger established one of the first modern multi-jurisdictional mega-unions. The UFCW represented more than one million workers in the food processing, retail, and commercial industries (Brueggemann and Brown 2003; *PR Newswire* 1995a) and gave workers a unified voice in the food industry, from the packing house to the grocery store. The RWDSU affiliated with UFCW in 1993, and in 1995, the UFCW and

LIUNA (Laborers' International Union of North America) joined forces with community and religious leaders to form the National Poultry Alliance. LIUNA represented nearly 750,000 workers in the United States and Canada in food processing, maintenance, clerical, construction, environmental remediation, the public sector, and the postal service. The 1995 organizing campaign against Perdue in Lewiston, North Carolina, was the first in which LIUNA and UFCW cooperated and shared resources through the National Poultry Alliance (PR Newswire 1995a). These union mergers led to an increase in labor activity. The UFCW claimed a 10 percent membership growth in the southern region in the late 1980s—three to four points higher than their nationwide growth (Greer 1992). Following its formation, the UFCW engaged in a number of prominent labor struggles in meat processing, including pork and turkey. Particularly noteworthy were the struggles against the large meat processors who were withdrawing from the master agreements that had created industry-wide benefit levels and wage rates. In beef and pork, unions were confronting the ascendancy of IBP (Iowa Beef Processors, Inc.) and the relocation of processing away from urban centers to rural areas, closer to the supply of feedlots, cattle herds, cheap labor, and the weak union tradition (Brueggemann and Brown 2003; Fink 2003; Horowitz 1997; Stull and Broadway 2004). Despite union losses, some foresaw those wage cuts in meat and pork helping to invigorate the union movement (*Business Week* 1983). The first-ever strike against the Virginia turkey processor Marval and the successful unionization of the Mississippi Delta Pride catfish workers are some examples of UFCW's efforts in the South.

My analysis of the NLRB data corroborates the role of the UFCW.[12] From 1985 to 1999, the UFCW was involved in an increasing percentage of all the NLRB elections held in four of the five states (Arkansas is the exception). A second finding is that there was an upward trend in the number of ULPs filed against employers by the UFCW after 1991. The main types of ULPs are CAs, a charge filed by workers that the employer committed an unfair labor practice in violation of the NLRA, and CBs, a charge filed by employers that a labor organization committed an unfair labor practice in violation of the NLRA. These practices violate the NLRA because they interfere with the rights of workers or employers in union organizing, collective bargaining, and the like. The data set only includes those ULPs that were filed and survived the initial investigation as being "in violation" of the NLRA.

In poultry, the UFCW, RWDSU, a union that merged with UFCW in 1993, and LIUNA, an affiliate were key players in contesting management's excesses. In fourteen of the fifteen years that I analyzed (1985–99) they were involved in at least 75 percent of NLRB poultry sector elections; in eight of the years, they were involved in all of the elections. The labor actions of the 1980s were focused on working conditions and employers' moves to abrogate wage contracts. Later, in the 1990s, there were more ULPs filed against employers for violation of the rights of labor to organize and be represented. Unions such as the International Brotherhood of Teamsters also dedicated time and financial resources to organizing poultry workers.

The second contribution to rising labor activity came from new support from civil rights and community activists. Historically, African Americans and southern unions had been antagonistic. This antagonism dissolved over time: organized labor actively fostered the civil rights movement and vice versa. In their study of intermovement revitalization between 1947 and 1981, Isaac and Christiansen (2002) found that the organizational militancy of the civil rights movement had a positive impact on labor activity. They concluded that the spillover was strongest from social movement organizations and that the impact was largest in public sector organizing. The growing receptivity to and the active leadership of African Americans in the labor movement both invigorated union activity. Whites' national union affiliation decreased by 9 percent in private sector unions from 1983 to 1991, but black union affiliation held steady (Greer 1992). Halpern and Horowitz (1996) report that the United Packinghouse Workers of America was the first union to join Martin Luther King Jr. and the Southern Christian Leadership Conference's drive for civil rights during the 1950s.

The southern labor movement received support from notable national civil rights leaders. When the aforementioned workers of Lumbee Farms met in 1985 to discuss a strike for better wages, they were joined by members of a group called the Robeson County Clergy and Laity Concerned in Lumberton, North Carolina. In 1986, the UFCW's dramatic and successful campaign at the Delta Pride catfish plant created the organizational capacity for subsequent strikes. In 1990, when these workers launched "the largest strike in the history of Mississippi," it benefited from the attention of the Congressional Black Caucus. Rep. Bill Clay (D-Mo.) went to Indianola, Mississippi, to hear the testimony of Delta Pride's striking workers.

In 1991, Rev. Jesse Jackson appeared in Hamlet, North Carolina, after the catastrophic Imperial Foods fire. In the aforementioned 1995 electoral campaign at the Lewiston, North Carolina, Perdue plant, the joint effort of LIUNA and UFCW was joined by Congressman John Lewis (D-Ga.), a participant in the original "Freedom Summer" some thirty years earlier, and Rev. Jackson. The National Poultry Alliance, headquartered in Lewiston, made plans to spearhead "Freedom Summer '95," a large and comprehensive organizing campaign. Describing the Alliance, Rev. Jackson said, "It's what the real 'New South' and a new labor movement are all about" (*PR Newswire* 1995a).

Both union consolidation and support from civil rights activists bolstered union success in the South. Some have described this as "social movement unionism" (Seidman 1994; Fantasia and Voss 2004). It differs from traditional business unionism in that social movement unionists attempt to build unions as organizational vehicles of social solidarity, to experiment with corporate campaigns as way to overcome the huge power disparity between employers and employees, and to adopt an orientation toward social justice, rhetorically connecting the labor movement revival to broader movements for democracy and social citizenship (Fantasia and Voss 2004, 127–29). In the mid-1990s, southern clergy reported that they joined with labor because the "movement is addressing the key ethnical issues of the day, including the growing gulf between the haves and have-nots."

During the 1995–96 labor conflict at the Case Farms poultry plant in Morganton, North Carolina, clergy prayed in front of the factory to urge management to sign a union contract and improve working conditions (Greenhouse 1986). The "citizen action" was an unprecedented alliance of poultry workers, growers, consumers, environmentalists, farmers, and religious leaders. It claimed to represent over fifty organizations, including Clean Water Action, the Community Nutrition Institute, the National Contract Poultry Growers Association, and the National Farmers Union. They kicked off a national campaign and sent a letter to Tom Shelton, CEO of Case Farms, urging him to negotiate with workers. At a press conference at a Methodist building in Washington, D.C., they called for an internal taskforce to review the poultry industry (*PR Newswire* 1996). In a similar case, striking Tyson workers in Corydon, Indiana, formed "truth squads" to speak the truth about the working conditions in many plants. They appeared at a Tyson Foods plant in Vienna, Georgia, to support workers who were organizing with UFCW Local 1996. The Corydon workers gained support from the National Baptist Convention, USA, Inc., the largest African American denomination, who asked their affiliates not to buy Tyson chicken for church functions. Social movement unionism brought together poultry workers and unions throughout the South with religious leaders and other social activists. Taylorism had transformed production, transformed work—and the labor-management regime.

Conclusion

In this chapter I provided a synopsis of the formidable transformations in the poultry industry that gave rise to automated processing and expanded production. The maturing industry garnered direct and indirect support from various branches of the U.S. government. Southern labor also underwent organizational maturation. Union mergers and reconuration brought new life to labor activity, and Taylorism presented labor with a new target. The next leg of the journey passes through the dual crisis of industry and ends with ethnic displacement.

5

Solving Industry Crises:
Pollos Y Polleros

Industry faced two crises in the mid-1990s.[1] In this chapter, I describe
the labor and profit crises. First, I develop a framework for conceptualiz-
ing and analyzing the labor-management regime. Then I draw from published reports and my own analysis of the NLRB data to identify changes
in that regime. Second, I offer a synopsis of the profit crisis that concerned
industry leaders. Third, in evaluating possible solutions, I conclude that
immigrant hiring addressed both crises. Hiring illegal immigrant workers
was a conscious strategy: it addressed the profit crisis by lowering labor
costs, and it addressed labor aggressiveness by substituting a docile labor
force. From this historical and conflict-focused perspective, immigrant
hiring takes on a different connotation than the one found in the current
immigration debate. While one does find "market-force" contributions
to ethnic succession, such as industry growth and technological transformations (chapter 4), one also finds "agents," such as industry recruiters,
unions, U.S. regulatory agencies, and the National Labor Relations Board.

A Framework for Analyzing Labor-Management Regimes

I conceptualize a labor-management regime as an interactive relationship between labor and management where either party could be totally dominant or completely dominated. Between those two extremes lies a zone of struggle where parties engage in militant/aggressive and defensive actions. Management aggressiveness and labor militancy are provoked by exogenous and endogenous conditions.[2] For management, exogenous conditions that foster aggressiveness against workers could be changes in the technology of production, changes in the structure of the poultry industry, or a profit crisis. By endogenous conditions I refer to management's attempt to minimize or eliminate those intra-firm labor actions guaranteed by the NLRA. For workers, exogenous conditions include changes in the nature of work (Taylorism) and changes in the union environment (for instance, a union commitment to organize a plant). By endogenous conditions I refer to labor's response to employer violations of NLRA-guaranteed rights. Reactions are interactive—defensive actions of one party might be animated by the previous aggressiveness of the other. The outcomes of management-labor struggles depended on the relative power of the actors.

I analyze the NLRB election and Unfair Labor Practices data sets from 1984 to 2000.[3] The frequency counts provide an opportunity to profile two decades of labor-management activity (as conceptualized above and in figure 5.1). Elections are classified as Certification of Representative (RCs) and Decertification (RDs). A RC election follows a petition, which is normally filed by a union seeking an election to determine whether employees wish to be represented for collective-bargaining purposes by a specific labor organization. An RD election follows a petition that can be filed by an employee, a group of employees, or any individual acting on their behalf, seeking to determine whether the current union should continue to act as a bargaining representative of employees. In my framework, I treat RCs as labor militancy and RDs as management aggressiveness.[4]

Unfair Labor Practices (ULPs) register complaints ranging from work environment to labor/management activities. These violations interfere with the rights of workers or employers in the process of union organizing, collective bargaining, and the like.[5] In my framework, I treat CAs as labor defensiveness and CBs as management defensiveness. I interpret a rise in CAs as a measure of union defensiveness against employer antiunion

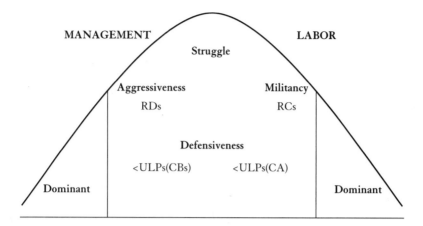

Figure 5.1. Labor-management regime schema

actions. A decline could indicate that labor and management had reached a compromise—employers felt no need to file grievances against unions, and unions had no reason to file against employers. Alternatively, a decline could mean that employers had successfully undermined union strength, the very agent needed for a CA filing. These are represented schematically in figure 5.1.[6]

In the early period, a fair number of CAs addressed working conditions: bathroom breaks, chemical spills, line speed, and gases as well as earnings, benefits, job security, and hours. For example, in November 1985 workers at Lumbee filed a CA after four workers had been fired. The complaint specified that workers were underpaid and had not received a wage increase for a number of years. The company argued that the discharge was lawful because workers were soliciting a strike based on the company's hiring of Koreans and foreigners: "too many Orientals and Koreans," according to one witness. The NLRB dismissed the company's claim—only 6 of the 450 workers were Korean (relatives of army personnel at nearby Fort Bragg)—and found that the discharged employees' concerns were economic, not racial. The NLRB required Lumbee to reinstate all strikers and pay lost earnings plus interest (NLRB 1987). Later CAs focused on employers' actions such as harassing or threatening union organizers, interfering with representation campaigns and elections (NLRB 1992), surveillance of employees, and company fraud in initiating decertification elections (NLRB 1993c).

For analytical purposes, I grouped the data into three periods: 1984–89, 1990–94, and 1995–2000. These periods match inferences that I drew from the qualitative data, namely that labor-management conflict increased in the late 1980s and early 1990s, and was followed by a period of management victory and labor retrenchment. In addition, the middle period coincides with the rise of immigrant-hiring.

Poultry Labor-Management Regimes

The poultry labor-management regime was shaped by the larger system described in chapter 4. In the five states (Alabama, Arkansas, Georgia, Mississippi, and North Carolina), public and private nonagricultural unions showed episodes of successful organizing at the end of the 1970s (up to a high of 24 percent of nonagricultural, private, and public workers unionized in Alabama in 1979). The post-1980 trend was volatile and does not lend itself to any clear interpretation (see fig. 4.1). It does seem, however, that union density declined more slowly than the national average (with the exception of Alabama, which had clear bursts of activity). For the three periods demarcated here, the five-state averages of private and public union density are 10.1, 8.7, and 6.9 percent, respectively.

Naturally there were far fewer elections in the poultry industry (a total of 91 from 1984 to 2000). Arkansas ranked highest with twenty-five elections and North Carolina lowest with six. RC elections made up 85.7 percent of all poultry-sector elections.[7] The RCs ranged from 100 percent of elections in North Carolina down to 72 percent in Arkansas. States vary in terms of labor militancy (initiating more RC elections) and success (winning RCs). Based on number of elections, unions in Alabama and Mississippi were the most militant and most successful, in Georgia and Arkansas more militant but less successful, and in North Carolina successful, but with fewer elections. Table 5.1 summarizes the labor-management activity of each of the five states.

The number of ULPs filed also indicates the level of labor-management activity. From 1984 to 2000, 93 percent of all ULPs filed in the five states were against employers (CAs). States vary in terms of labor defensiveness (initiating ULPs against management) and success (having them resolved in labor's favor). Using these indicators, labor in Alabama and Mississippi

TABLE 5.1 Poultry sector labor-management activity by state, 1984-2000

	Elections	RCs as % of all elections	Union wins as % of all elections	Total ULPs	CAs as % of total ULPs	% of CAs decided for union
AL	22	95.45%	40.91%	157	88.54%	30.94%
AR	25	72%	12%	127	89.76%	36.84%
GA	19	84.21%	36.84%	115	90.44%	18.27%
MS	19	89.47%	52.63%	196	98.98%	27.32%
NC	6	100%	66.67%	123	93.5%	28.70%
5 states	91	85.71%	36.26%	718	93.04%	28.44%

Source: Author's calculations based on analysis of the NLRB data set.

appeared more defensive and more successful. The others appeared somewhat less defensive, with mixed levels of success. There certainly is something worth pursing in the individual state stories, but the argument posited in this book revolves around the time periods. The labor-management regimes were not static: the number of elections declined across the three periods, and the number of ULP filings increased from 212 to 299 (table 5.2). From 1984 to 1989, there were more total elections, 76.5 percent of which were for certification. For example, in 1989, the Chauffeurs, Teamsters, and Helpers Local 391 filed an election petition with the NLRB in a proposed unit that included chicken-catchers, forklift operators, and live-haul employees. These employees work outside the processing plant, retrieving the seven-week-old broilers from the contracted growers and delivering them to the Holly Farm processing plant. Holly Farms contended, unsuccessfully, that because this work is incidental to agriculture and performed on a farm, not in the factory, it was exempt from NLRB protection. The NLRB approved the bargaining unit (1993), a decision that was confirmed in the U.S. Court of Appeals for the Fourth Circuit (1995). Finally, in 1996, the U.S. Supreme Court in *Holly Farms Corp. v. NLRB* affirmed the judgment of the Court of Appeals. During the 1984–89 period, management initiated the highest number and percent (23.5%) of decertification elections and engaged in the highest number of defensive ULP-CB filings (table 5.2).

The 1990–94 period stands out as the most militant for labor. Although there were fewer elections than in the previous period, 92.8 percent of

TABLE 5.2 Poultry sector labor-management regime: Comparisons over time

	1984–1989	1990–1994	1995–2000
Average U.S. union membership of all public and private nonagricultural workers	10.8% (17.65%)	8.7% (16.06%)	6.9% (14.28%)
Labor-management activity			
Elections (number)	34	28	29
ULPs (number)	212	207	299
Labor militancy			
% elections = RC	76.5% (24)	92.8% (26)	89.7% (27)
% RC wins /All elections	26.5%	46.4%	37.9%
Labor defensiveness			
% ULPs = CA	72.2% (189)	91.3% (189)	96.3% (288)
% CA wins [of all ULPs]	37.3%	30.0%	16.4%
Management aggressiveness			
% elections = RD	23.53% (10)	7.2% (2)	10.3% (2)
Management defensiveness			
% ULPs = CB	10.85% (23)	8.70% (18)	3.79% (11)

Source: Author's calculations based on data from Hirsch, et al. 2001. The rest are author's calculations of NLRB data set.

them were for union recognition, and unions were the most successful during this period. In the 1995–2000 period, labor was more defensive; 288 CAs were filed against employers, in contrast to 189 in each of the earlier periods. For labor, however, the success of the 1990–94 period was not sustainable. In that last period, union density was down, electoral victories dropped to 37.9 percent from their 1990–94 peak of 46.4 percent, and successful defensive actions (CAs) declined to 16.4 percent.

The conclusions that I draw from my analysis of the NLRB data are consistent with those portrayals drawn from various reports, namely that 1984 to 1989 were years of early labor mobilization, which provoked the highest levels of management reactions (RDs and CBs). The years between 1990 and 1994 were years of greater labor militancy, with the highest level of electoral success. In the last period, 1995–2000, labor's militancy and (greater) defensiveness were least successful. Despite filing many more CAs, only 16.4 percent were resolved in labor's favor. Table 5.1 summarizes most of these findings.

The new labor organizations described in chapter 4 were engaged in labor campaigns and disruptions. This put management on the defense. In addition, by the mid-1990s, industry was confronting a second crisis, also generated by Taylorism: overproduction and declining profits.

Industry Crisis

In the early stages, Taylorism promoted growth and profits. Between 1980 and 1990, Tyson's profits increased fourteen-fold, and growth in the company's per-share earnings ranked first among Fortune 500 companies (Behar 1992). By 1992, U.S. poultry consumption surpassed beef, productivity per worker was almost three times what it had been in the 1960s, and in 1988, the industry experienced record production. Producers eyed international markets and invested. Cagle's Inc. earnings increased because of a strong market price for broilers. Tyson Foods Inc. in 1994 planned to spend $400 million to build four new broiler complexes. In 1996, Simmons, the 19th-largest poultry processor, completed a $27 million construction program—increasing processing capacity 25 percent.

But poultry was not immune from business cycles. Reports suggest that good fortunes peaked somewhere in the mid-1990s. Around 1995, overproduction and rising expenses drove down prices (Tobler 1995). "In 1999, armed with breeding flocks rebuilt from the J-virus and more than a decade of profits, the chicken industry expanded two to four times as much as it should have, and companies lost money for two consecutive years, losses that were previously unimaginable" (Smith 2001). From 1995 to 2001 the industry had a rough time, as companies "struggled with overproduction, low pricing and minimal to negative returns" (Smith 2002). Rising grain prices also reduced industry profits. Executives speculated that production of breast meat had rushed ahead of demand, leading to consumer "chicken fatigue." Poultry executives pointed to overproduction, particularly on the part of smaller producers who did not pull back to the same extent that the major producers did. This produced difficulty in pricing, according to Gregg Lee and John Tyson at Tyson Foods Inc. "They don't have obligations to shareholders the way we . . . the public companies do, and their lifestyles haven't needed to change," Tyson said. The excess production was certainly a function of those processors that were not as disciplined,

Lee said, but it was also due to "genetic improvements . . . that led to improved breeder performance—more eggs to set and more chicks to place—and better commercial performance—more livability, more live-weight and more breast meat . . . the industry moved to a larger bird for deboning breast meat and value-added products and in absolute pounds, has produced too much breast meat" (Smith 2002). Smith reports that 2000 and 2001 were the worst since 1980–82. Some companies were selling off related businesses. Gold Kist Inc., for example, sold off its farm-supply operations in 1998. The executives of larger firms also told Smith that they expected smaller firms would exit the business, particularly family businesses that lacked adequate capital for technological upgrading.

Producers with an appreciable export market also were apprehensive about the volatility of their major international markets. Following Russia's call for additional testing of U.S. exported chicken in 1996, poultry producers cut back. This had been a prospering market. Hudson Foods Inc., Tyson Foods Inc., and Simmons Foods Inc. of Siloam Springs, Arkansas, all announced broiler chicken production cutbacks of 7 to 8 percent because of high feed prices and the loss of Russia as an export market (Stewart 1996a, 1996b). The drop in export prices for broiler meat to Russia resulted in razor-thin margins (USDA 1997). In the Russian market, the United States was increasingly challenged by France and the Netherlands, which were exporting broiler wings and legs (USDA 1998). In China, the USDA (1998) reported, "A decade of double digit growth in world poultry meat trade has come to a halt." Shipments to Japan dropped almost 20 percent as U.S. poultry encountered competition from Thailand and China. The decline in exports was attributed to the expansion in domestic broiler output (particularly in China), competitive suppliers, and the high value of the U.S. dollar. Certainly these markets were expected to rebound in the future, but the difficulties in the export environment from 1995 to 1999 concerned producers.

One Solution for Two Crises

The Holly Farms-Teamster conflict captures the calamitous mixture of the two crises, demonstrating the interactions among industry competition, mergers, working conditions, and labor activity. A worker told a reporter that until 1987, Holly Farms was the "best place to work in North Carolina" (Swoboda 1990). However, in 1988, Holly was financially weak and trying to avoid a takeover. Struggling to cut costs, it reduced the pay of three hundred drivers, who would no longer receive compensation for "waiting time" to unload cargo. Several drivers went to Greensboro and joined the International Brotherhood of Teamsters. By 1989, Local 391 had signed up enough drivers to force and win a union election. But in 1989, after the takeover, Tyson folded the Holly Farms transportation department into its own. Teamsters Local 391 no longer represented a majority of drivers. Tyson ordered further cuts in pay, required drivers either to sign a card agreeing to new conditions or be fired, and fired fifty workers. Drivers struck and the Teamsters attempted to organize four thousand production workers at three Holly Farms processing plants. A union activist complained that "ever since Tyson took over the company, it's been nothing but push, push, push on the assembly line . . . things have got worse and worse . . . it has reached the point where it gets harder and harder to get relief to go to the bathroom because of the push in production." The union charges that Tyson sent threatening letters to employees warning that the union was threatening their future.

Perhaps the 1980s labor-management struggle could have continued for another decade: management aggressively transforming production, labor militantly attempting to unionize and improve working conditions, and management resisting. This conflict, which began during periods of industry growth and profit, became increasingly costly by the mid-1990s, the period of industry crisis. Although the profit crisis was exogenous to the labor-management regime, it weighed heavily on its resolution.

Searching for Solutions

Abstracting from the plethora of media, industry, and research reports along with my own analysis, I infer that businesses required a solution that would simultaneously mitigate both crises. Solutions typically employed by industries in response to overproduction and profit would not adequately address the labor conflict. Likewise, some of the conventional responses to labor conflict would do little to resolve the profit crisis. I represent this dilemma and the payoff from alternative solutions in table 5.3.

TABLE 5.3 Schematic representation of alternative solutions

	Solve profit crisis	
Solve labor conflict	YES	NO
YES	Hire illegal immigrants	Mergers Bankruptcies Offshore production
NO	Tax relief Government subsidies New product lines Expand markets	

Businesses respond to falling profits in a number of ways. Sometimes they attempt to curb production. Poultry industry leaders perceived barriers to any industry-wide curb because small producers would not participate in reducing output. Another solution was product innovation. Tyson's business plan was to continue elevating its product mix to higher-quality, higher-value-added products. Chicken prices are always dependent on grain prices, but by producing novelty products (and increasing their value), grain prices become less of a factor. Such a solution might address the profit crisis, but would do little to mitigate the labor conflict.

A third possible solution was industry consolidation (mergers and takeovers), but as previously noted, aggressive consolidation had already taken place. These were typical headlines from the 1980s and early 1990s: "ConAgra Buys Out 50 Percent of Imperial Share of Country Poultry," "Simmons Foods Inc., the Country's 19th-Largest Poultry Processor, Has Agreed to Buy the Chicken-Growing Operations of Camden, N.J.-Based Campbell Soup Co.," and "Tyson Foods Splurges with Two Poultry Acquisitions." Toward the end of the 1980s, ConAgra and Tyson's were locked in a hostile battle to take over Holly Farms. In 1989, Tyson won that battle. John Tyson predicted that additional consolidation would take place as the single-process and family-run plants exit the industry, some selling to larger nearby plants. But consolidation would not solve the profit crisis; in fact, it had contributed to overproduction. In addition, because of mergers, takeovers, and expansion, "much of the industry has lost money and taken on considerable debt in the last 36 months . . . I haven't seen unbridled expansion . . . In an industry no more consolidated than ours, it took a kind of bloodbath for industrywide production restraint" (Smith 2002). Furthermore, the past consolidation had fueled the labor conflict. Additional consolidation did not seem like a timely panacea.

Bankruptcy, an anti-labor tool, was another option. For example, in 1983, Wilson Foods Corp. filed for Chapter 11 reorganization to abrogate its labor contracts. And Armour Food Co. in 1983 closed most of its plants before the Greyhound Corp., its parent, sold the business to ConAgra Inc., which immediately reopened the plants with nonunion labor (*Business Week* 1984). Pilgrim's Pride closed its Athens plant. As one of the hundreds of workers out of work said, "I lost all of my retirement that I had accumulated from Gold Kist when Pilgrim's filed bankruptcy" (Schultz 2009). The Hormel & Co. case is noteworthy because Hormel was trying to *avoid* the bankruptcy solution undertaken by other packers in the face of onerous labor contracts. The nation's number three pork processor struggled with a high wage bill negotiated with UFCW in 1981. Hormel managed to get UFCW leaders (representing more than three thousand Hormel workers) to put to a vote a wage-concession package that cut wages and benefits by about $6.50 per hour. *Business Week* (1984) estimates that, along with similar concessions won earlier from the rest of Hormel's union workers, the package could add at least $25 million annually to the company's pretax earnings. In short, the bankruptcy solution would eliminate labor conflict—by eliminating labor—but is potentially disruptive for a firm.

Some U.S. industries solved their profit crisis by offshoring. In response to the generalized profit squeeze of the 1970s and the refusal of the working class to absorb the costs of that crisis, businesses opted for geographic relocation to capitalize on lower labor costs. However, many were not simply relocating production; they were also fragmenting and decentralizing it, bringing an end to classic Taylorism. Global capitalism—the construction of "commodity chains"—was the solution for the structural crisis of the 1970s. Offshoring would mitigate the profit crisis by reducing labor costs and simultaneously eliminating the labor problem. Would it work for poultry? Two companies did enter into cross-border mergers and acquisitions in Mexico, but they produced mostly for Mexican consumption—they were decidedly not *maquiladoras* producing for export.

A number of factors have impeded widespread agricultural relocation. According to Cornelius, moving fresh fruit and vegetable production offshore was slow because they are both labor- and capital-intensive. Mexican agricultural producers have lower labor costs but also lower productivity. In addition, U.S. producers have advantages of superior cooling and handling facilities for perishable commodities and immediate access to the U.S. transport system without border delays (1993, 490).

A Pilgrim's Pride Corp. executive did not see any advantage to offshoring. New rules proposed by USDA would allow U.S. poultry companies to ship whole carcasses to Mexico for the labor-intensive cut-up and deboning operations (with cheaper labor costs) and re-export them back for sale in U.S. supermarkets. Pilgrim's Pride already had operations in both countries, but the spokesman said, "All you'd bring back is white meat. . . . You'd send down there a 4.5-pound chicken and you'd only bring back 10 to 12 ounces of boneless breast meat." Add import and export fees, plus transportation and refrigeration costs, he judged, it wouldn't be worth it (*Arkansas Democrat-Gazette* 1997). In contrast, a 2002 USDA report estimated that the "white meat" market was one possible niche for future growth of Mexican exports to the United States. The authors speculated that if Mexico's poultry industry expanded to meet the rising consumption patterns of a growing Mexican middle class, with its continued preference for dark meat, the white meat surplus could be exported to the United States (Salin et al. 2002, 2). Offshoring would eradicate the labor struggle but, at least in the 1990s, executives did not enthusiastically embrace it.

Market expansion could ameliorate the profit crises. Poultry lobbyists appealed to the U.S. government, which during this period worked to secure and expand export markets. One case became known as "Chechens for Chickens." By 1996 Russia was the single largest market for U.S. chicken, 90 percent of which came from Tyson Foods (Ireland 1998). When Russia moved to protect its own poultry industry by banning U.S. imports, claiming insufficient health and sanitary standards, the industry urged the Clinton administration to suspend aid to Russia unless it lifted the ban. In the end, an agreement called for exporters to test a 25-gram sample (less than an ounce) for salmonella from one chicken carcass out of every load bound for port or out of each ship bound for Russia. This agreement was to end the Russian embargo on U.S. imports (Stewart 1996a). In a March 1996 summit meeting in Egypt, President Bill Clinton agreed to give public support to Russian president Boris Yeltsin for his reelection, in exchange for Yeltsin agreeing to dissuade Moscow from banning U.S. chicken imports. In addition, Clinton would back the pending $10 billion loan from the International Monetary Fund along with other economic aid that might bolster Yeltsin's reelection chances (Atlas 1996). Because Yeltsin was becoming increasingly unpopular for his war against Chechnya, this "chicken diplomacy" became known as the "Chechens for Chickens" affair. Continued export promotion could help mitigate the profit crisis; however, it would have little impact on the ongoing labor-management conflict.

Poultry and Smugglers

In contrast to those solutions, immigrant hiring could potentially crush labor aggressiveness and extract more value from labor. Immigrants did not initially move into labor markets that had been vacated by native labor or were experiencing shortages. Two bodies of evidence support this explanation: the active immigrant recruitment by employers and the resistance of native workers.

This analysis is time-sensitive; it is essential to identify the reasons behind the *initial* hiring, because once hired, chain migration and networks provided the flow of additional workers. The use of networks has been well documented, for both job seekers and employers (Berg and Kallenberg 2001). Networks benefit employers by reducing the personnel costs. Waldinger (1997) found that employers use immigrant networks for recruiting to the exclusion of native-born workers. Others have found ethnic differences in network usage. While Hispanics use networks, scholars observe that African Americans are less likely to use them. For example, Aponte (1996) found that the black-immigrant differences in Chicago employment rates could be explained by the immigrants' use of social networks. In more recent work, Smith concludes that it is not simply the absence of this social capital (deficient networks) that prevents job acquisition; African Americans actually eschew the use of networks (2005, 44). Through networks, immigrants might well come to dominate an industry (Enchautegui 1998).

Massey et al. describe the network effect as follows: once a few immigrants are established in a new location, kin, friends, and fellow villagers follow. Each earlier act of migration lowers the costs and risks while raising the expected returns for subsequent immigrants (2002, 19). Recruitment was self-generating in Morganton, North Carolina, as word of jobs spread through family and friendship networks in Guatemala (Fink 2003). Griffith reports that network recruitment was a poultry-industry norm. He found that while whites seemed to use networks least and blacks a bit more, Hispanics used them the most (1990, 176).

Intentional and Active Hiring

Hiring was not merely employing immigrants who presented themselves at the factory door looking for a job. Companies were active in advertising, recruiting, transporting, assisting with documentation, and housing, sometimes legally and sometimes illegally. Labor recruitment is not novel. Briggs cites cases such as Carnegie Steel Corporation's 1892 importation of cheap labor in Homestead, Pennsylvania, to assure a surplus— a move attacked by the AFL for violation of the Alien Contract Law of 1885 (2001, 63).

The recruitment and hiring of "nonimmigrant alien workers" in agriculture are authorized under the H-2A visa program. The certificate is valid for up to 364 days and requires employers to provide free and approved housing to all workers who are not able to return to their residences the same day. In rural central Louisiana, agriculture work in sweet potato, poultry, and ornamental plant cultivation provides the largest source of employment for Hispanic workers. They are recruited by relatives or brought in by recruiters hired by local farmers and companies. One Louisiana farm owner, James Deshotel of Deshotel Farms, first began to use Mexican workers in 1986; by 1999 he was employing some thirty seasonal workers who stayed in several houses he had had constructed behind the farm's packing plant. Most workers came from the Mexican states of Nuevo León and San Luis Potosí. Deshotel hired a company called USAMEX Ltd. to take care of the paperwork involved in acquiring H-2A visas. The company picked up the workers each season in Monterrey, Mexico, in company-owned yellow school buses. Dawson, another farm in the area, began to employ Mexican workers around 1998 because they "couldn't get guaranteed attendance" from local workers. They also hired USAMEX Ltd. to recruit workers, to take care of visas, and to transport workers to and from Monterrey each season. Dawson Farms housed its workers in a rented former nursing home in Cheneyville, Louisiana, a nearby town, and each day transported them back and forth to the farm in school buses. Dawson Farms grows, packs, and ships sweet potatoes. They hired some three hundred Mexican workers for planting and harvesting (Manger 1999). In 1999, businesses in the state of North Carolina employed over ten thousand migrant workers with H-2A visas.

Agricultural companies have greater access to H-2A visa farm workers who come openly and legally. Although workers are to be covered by wage laws and other standards, critics note that H-2A workers are tied to the particular growers, so they have little opportunity to change employers or organize for improved conditions. And because farm workers are not covered by NLRA's provisions, they risk losing their contract and deportation by joining a union (Human Rights Watch 2000).

Companies that hired undocumented workers for nonagricultural work offered "services" similar to those of H-2A employers. One Tyson case demonstrates the intentional and active aspects of hiring, including advertising, using recruitment agents, providing fraudulent documentation, transporting, housing, and facilitating access to social services. Active hiring was documented in the Department of Justice indictment against Tyson unsealed in the Federal District Court in Chattanooga, Tennessee (December 2001). As the result of an INS undercover action referred to as Operation Everest, Tyson managers were accused of a seven-year scheme (1994 to 2001) to recruit and hire hundreds of illegal immigrants from Mexico and Guatemala. The indictment accused them of arranging counterfeit work papers for jobs at more than a dozen Tyson plants. The sting uncovered 154 illegal immigrants who were employed at Tyson plants in Oklahoma, Virginia, Arkansas, North Carolina, and Tennessee. The indictment claimed that Tyson paid smugglers $100 to $200 per head. One smuggler paid another $3,100 for delivering seven illegal immigrants from Guatemala to the Shelbyville plant. The government found documents that showed payments from Tyson to smugglers as well as indications that the company used temporary employment agencies to cover up its actions (Barboza 2001a, 2001b). No Tyson executives were convicted, but former employee Amador Anchondo-Rascoon was (he spent two and a half years in prison). He had entered illegally in 1979 and became a legal U.S. resident through marriage. By the mid-1990s he was recruiting and transporting illegal immigrants from Mexico to Shelbyville. He would take paid leaves of absence for two weeks and return with a dozen or so workers. After leaving his job at Tyson's Shelbyville plant, he worked as a local grocer and continued to recruit illegal workers for Tyson (Rosenbloom 2003). Prosecutors relied mostly on tapes of secretly recorded conversations between undercover agents who posed as smugglers and transporters of immigrants. Tyson attorneys argued that if the company hired illegal workers, it was a result of the huge underground market for phony immigration papers, the government's flawed system of screening immigrants, and Tyson's use of temporary employment agencies to find workers (Poovey 2006). The case was dismissed by a judge in 2002, and in March 2003, a federal jury acquitted the company and three former managers of conspiring to hire illegal immigrants from Mexico and Central America to boost profits. Two former managers who made plea deals were each sentenced to one year of probation. Following appeals, it was finally dismissed in a federal court in 2008. District Judge Curtis L. Collier said that the plaintiffs failed to show evidence that Tyson harbored illegal aliens at seven plants across the South (Irvin 2008). The UFCW described it as a massive ring to smuggle more than 2,000 illegal aliens into the United States (2001). Reporters noted that industry experts had long believed that American food companies recruited in Mexico and knowingly hired illegal workers.

Advertising in Mexico was an important element of hiring. Companies advertised on the radio in Mexico, distributed leaflets, showed videos, and hired immigrant smugglers ("coyotes") (Barboza 2001a). Poultry plants sought workers through a classified ad in *El Diario*, a newspaper published in Juarez, Mexico. These were placed by an employment agency based in Dallas that recruited about five hundred workers in Texas and Mexico for the Union City, Tennessee, plant. The ads promised $15,000 to $18,000 a year for working on the assembly line (Rosenbloom 2003). Griffith noted that plants expanded their recruitment efforts with bilingual poster campaigns and radio ads (1990). *Rural Migration News* reported in 1998 that an Arkansas labor recruiter was advertising a toll-free number on Spanish-language radio stations located along the border.

In this early period, companies used recruitment agents or paid existing employees to bring others. Griffith reported that 34.4 percent of the plants he surveyed provided bonuses to workers who recruited friends and kin (1990, 160). Some plants had a policy of paying for each worker that an existing Hispanic brought to the company: "I called my cousin; he called his cousin, his brother-in-law. . . ." (Guthey 2001, 64). In 1995, Hudson Foods paid employees $300 for bringing a friend to the job (Katz 1999). In 1998, *Rural Migration News* reported that many of the workers in midwestern meat and poultry processing were recruited along the Texas-Mexico border by "independent recruiters" who received a bonus of up to $300 for each referred worker who stayed on the job for thirty days.

Companies transported immigrants to plant locations and then back and forth from their residence to work. This was not unique to the poultry industry. In a U.S. House of Representatives hearing on "Immigrations Issues: Alien Smuggling and Visa Overstays" (Nardi 1999), the INS expressed particular concern about the flourishing organized trade in alien smuggling and visa fraud. It reported that "smuggling organizations, recognizing that some employers in the interior of the United States rely heavily on an unauthorized workforce, have responded by providing transportation directly to the work sites." INS intelligence determined that the majority of illegal aliens with prearranged employment entered the country by crossing the southern border.

In "Operation I-25 Confederation," the INS successfully investigated and prosecuted Fred Parrish, president and owner of Atlantic Finishing, for his involvement in the recruitment of illegal aliens to work in his company. He was sentenced to a ten-month jail term, and the company was fined a total of $84,000. U.S. agents were tipped off when they stopped a van crammed with eleven illegals at a New Mexico checkpoint. An investigation uncovered the scheme to smuggle, transport along interstate routes to Georgia, house, and assist illegals in obtaining employment with fraudulent documents (Seelye 1997).

In addition to transportation, companies sometimes assisted prospective employees with paperwork. Following the 2007 ICE raid, David Purtle, Crider's president, claimed that the rise in Hispanic workers was gradual over the decade without any encouragement by the company. He was unaware that Crider employed so many undocumented workers. He said that the company "never skewed our hiring toward any ethnic group." One employee, however, reported that she received help with her application. When this Ms. Sauceda tried to use her ITIN (individual taxpayer identification number) which begins with a nine and therefore does not entitle its holder to work, the clerk intervened, suggesting that she had meant to put down a four or a six (Perez and Dade 2007). The indictment against Tyson also cited company assistance with fraudulent papers.

Companies accommodated their illegal immigrant labor force with housing. A number of companies built or used nearby trailer parks to house Hispanic workers (Griffith 1990, 166). In North Carolina, Case Farms secured initial lodging for new workers in a trailer park and an old hotel revamped into apartments. It organized a vanpool, distributed bicycles, and provided a private postal service to send money home to families (Fink 2003, 18).

Companies also recruited refugees from nearby states. In 1989, the human resources manager at Case Farms heard from a church group about a new source of labor—Guatemalans. A Catholic church in West Palm Beach, Florida, was helping Guatemalan refugees working in the citrus belt around Indiantown, Florida. The human relations manager went to the church, attended mass, and with the help of a Catholic charities worker, signed up ten workers who agreed to ride up to Morganton in a pickup truck the following weekend. Three weeks later, he recruited twenty more (Fink 2003, 17–18).

The New Labor-Management Regime

Ethnic displacement contributed to declining unionism, deteriorating work conditions, and a downward pressure on wages. This inverse relationship is a product of worker competition, excess labor supply, and the difficulty of organizing immigrants. In his study of sixteen OECD countries, Lee observed an inverse relationship. He identified workforce heterogeneity (language and culture) due to immigration as a hindrance to the group solidarity necessary for union organizing (2005, 74). Briggs (2001) also documents the many historical moments in the United States when immigration was associated with declining union density. These authors are attentive to the methodological problem of overdetermining the phenomenon of declining union density. They all look at immigration along with other factors, such as deindustrialization. In the meat products industry union rates fell from 46 percent in 1980 to 21 percent by the end of the 1980s. The GAO associated this decline with "increases in the use of immigrant workers. . . . Immigrants make up large and growing shares of the workforces at many plants . . . limits the opportunities of unions to organize meat and poultry workers" (2005b, 12).

Claims regarding the immigrant challenges to poultry labor organization in the 1990s are found in individual testimonies and in government and academic reports. In a Shelbyville, Tennessee, plant in the 1990s, Local 900 succeeded in negotiating wage increases averaging about 2 percent a year, barely enough to cover inflation. Negotiating leverage depends on the size of membership, particularly in right-to-work states such as Tennessee. As the plant's workforce became predominantly Hispanic, union membership plummeted from about 400 to fewer than 100. The early efforts to organize illegal Hispanics met with little success because they were vulnerable to arrest and hobbled by language and cultural barriers (Rosenbloom 2003). In 1998, Case Farm was under a court order that mandated contract bargaining talks with union representatives. Case, not wanting to give much, announced in May 1999 that it was done bargaining. The union had a hard time getting workers to participate in a work stoppage; the "rapid turnover in the plant combined with the presence of an increasing number of immigrant workers without legal permits accentuated the organizers' problems" (Fink 2003, 132). One report, however, suggested that the UFCW in North Carolina did try to organize immigrants. Because it viewed the 35,000 unorganized poultry immigrant workers as potential members, they hosted English classes for the Asian and Hispanic community (Greer 1992).

Initially, many immigrants were uninterested or hesitant to join unions. "Target earners" focus on maximizing earnings in the short run. If plants have high turnover, it is difficult for strong social groups to develop; instead, the workplace is marked by more individualistic relations between labor and management. Chavez, in his interviews with undocumented workers in southern California, confirmed that many of the temporary farm workers, living in shelters in canyons, ravines, and shantytowns, were earning money for a target, such as helping elderly parents (1992, 25, 32). In Laurel, Mississippi, a Peco Foods poultry worker put it this way: "I came here [from Veracruz, Mexico] to work and I don't want any problems." In the summer of 2003 he was threatened with firing because his Social Security number duplicated the number of another worker. He lived in a run-down trailer park on the outskirts of Laurel and sent as much money home as he could. This worker claims that his manager offered to sell him a new Social Security number for $700 (Cobb 2004). A more commonly cited reason for the difficulty in unionizing immigrants is that those without documents fear the companies. In an internal memo made public in a Pennsylvania suit, Tyson explicitly encouraged the hiring of Hispanics because their lack of English competence and their immigration status meant they were less likely to take any action, legal or otherwise, against the company (Stein 2002).

Companies gained from this labor force. A 2000 U.S. Department of Labor (DOL) survey of fifty-one poultry processing plants found that every employer surveyed was violating federal wage and hour laws. The DOL reported widespread violations including undercounting hours worked, impermissible deductions from wages, failure to pay required overtime wages, and improper employee charges (e.g., workers had to pay for gloves) for required equipment. The DOL took a stand to recover back wages owed to workers and to insist on future compliance. Perdue agreed to pay over $10 million in back wages to approximately twenty-five thousand workers (an average of $400 per worker) (Bobo 2002). This was the result of a 1996 complaint to the DOL charging that eight minutes a day of "donning and doffing" (the time spent changing between street and work clothes at the start and end of shifts) had not been paid. Fact-finding delegations were sent to poultry plants from 1996 to 1998. In another case, a federal judge granted class-action status to a lawsuit that contended that Tyson Foods Inc. had depressed wages by hiring illegal immigrants at eight plants in Tennessee, Alabama, Indiana, Missouri, Texas, and Virginia. The original was suit was filed in 2002 in a Tennessee district court by four Shelbyville plant workers who claimed that Tyson had violated the Racketeer Influenced and Corrupt Organizations Act (RICO) by knowingly hiring illegal immigrants who were willing to work for wages below those acceptable to Americans.

Illegal immigrants told Nicholas Stein of *Fortune* magazine that their status was being used against them: "If we didn't do what they wanted, they would threaten to call immigration." Hispanics were forced to work harder than their American peers. Curiously, injury and illness rates in the poultry industry fluctuated between 22 and 27 percent in the 1990–94 period before dropping to 14 percent in 1995—the year that the larger Hispanic inflows began. This reduction, which Tyson attributed to improved safety measures, saved the company millions of dollars in workers' compensation and insurance claims. As Stein reported, "Workers say that these pressures, combined with a lack of understanding of U.S. employment practices, also made them far less likely to report injuries or file for workers' compensation." For a serious cut, the company infirmary provided a band-aid. Supervisors even carried band-aids with them so that workers would not lose time going to the infirmary (Stein 2002). According to Assistant Attorney General Michael Chertoff, "The INS charged that Tyson preferred hiring illegal immigrants [between 1994 and June 2001] because they were forced to be more productive and were less likely to complain to management about inhumane working conditions and lack of benefits" (Vicini 2001).

Overall, the union position on immigrants has changed. At the national level, the AFL-CIO shifted from supporting legislation that restricted immigration in the 1980s, to a hesitancy to support immigration reform in the 1990s, to supporting immigration and the special needs of immigrants in 2000 (Briggs 2001, 4). In 2008, the United Farm Workers (UFW) hoped to recruit foreign workers. The UFW president Arturo Rodriguez signed an agreement with the governor of the Mexican state of Michoacán to recruit temporary workers for U.S. farm jobs that would be covered under union contracts. The union planned to negotiate contracts with growers who were willing to guarantee their legal rights. Although the federal government has resisted this state-by-state approach to immigration and guest worker programs, it's clear that the position of unions has changed (Burke 2008).

Poultry unions have joined the national reversal on immigrant workers. Cobb reports that at Peco Foods in Laurel, Mississippi, in the mid-1990s, it was rare for an immigrant worker to talk to a union representative in the plant. Since then, however, Carney, the LIUNA union representative who had described the earlier Hispanic influx, told the reporter, "If I've learned one thing over the past ten years, it's if you can't beat 'em, join 'em" (Cobb 2004). Henry Jenkins, the RWDSU union representative with whom I spoke, told me that they had recently hired two Spanish translators for the poultry plants.[8]

Conclusion

Some scholars are already persuaded that immigrants have a negative consequence for low-skilled native workers.[9] My goal is to demonstrate the negative impact of immigration under certain circumstances, in certain industries, and at certain historical moments. I believe that the poultry industry—newer to Taylorism, located in a historically antiunion South, and facing two major crises—meets those conditions. I have evaluated the two most-cited explanations for ethnic succession—"jobs that nobody wants" and "need for additional labor"—and have argued instead that the real explanation was labor-management conflict.

In reference to low-skilled native workers, some authors cite another justification, namely that employers prefer not to hire blacks. Research confirms that "employers often take race and ethnicity quite explicitly into account in hiring decisions" (Waldinger 1997, 366). Statistical discrimination means using race as a proxy for productivity. Such "employer preference" explanations tend to focus on the human capital traits of work ethic, readiness for work, discipline, and adherence to work schedules. Waldinger cites employer rankings of groups on work ethic: whites were ranked most favorably and blacks least. Although, he adds, some employers were critical of white workers—always complaining that "they feel that they should not be doing this type of work [furniture] because they are Americans" (1997, 376). In their interviews with managers, Moss and Tilly found that black men were viewed as lacking "soft skills"—particularly motivation and ability to interact well with customers and coworkers (1996).

Soft skills are not needed on the chicken line, but numerous researchers conclude that discrimination generally is based on productivity and work readiness arguments (Enchautegui 1998; Kirschenman and Neckerman 1991; Moss and Tilly 1996; Waldinger 1997). Waldinger argues that Hispanic immigrants lacked access to alternative sources of employment or income, were willing to work hard long hours, are not litigious, were less likely to have baby sitter problems, and don't have attitude problem of entitlement (1997, 376–79). When faced with a choice, given the industry's high rates of absenteeism and turnover, employers expressed a preference for immigrant workers. We should acknowledge that some African American (and other) workers may fall short in work ethic, readiness for work, and work discipline. But then we should also ask—what were the incentive structures and subcultural influences that generated those behavioral profiles in the first instance? This is part of my "American Dilemma" perspective—how did we become a nation of jobs that "nobody wants"?

In short, immigrant hiring (ethnic displacement) provided a way to resolve the labor conflict without compromising the surplus value extracted from the production process. For immigrant hiring, the mid-1990s was a watershed. Employers were not passively "faced with a choice" of workers; they created that choice by the early active and intentional recruitment of immigrant workers. Ethnic succession was ethnic displacement. This completes the "demand" or "pull" side of the migration story. However, recruitment and subsequent chain migration could not have been so successful without corresponding transformations in, and "pushes" from Mexico.

6

SQUEEZING OUT MEXICAN CHICKEN

Crossing the Border

Chapters 1 through 5 described the immigration "pull" or the U.S. labor "demand" side of the immigration story. My objective was to demonstrate the whys and hows of the observed ethnic shift. Conventional explanations such as "job vacancy" or "job shortage" are based on the idea of a self-actuating market. Rather than the invisible hand of the market matching willing workers with vacant jobs, I argued that it was the visible hand of recruiters, acting on behalf of companies that funneled immigrants into jobs. However, both my "socially constructed" labor-conflict explanation and the conventional "market-driven" one recount only the U.S. "pull" side of the story. The analysis must cross the border. Neoliberalism transformed the U.S. industry and labor organization, but it also led to ongoing labor displacement in—and a new migratory push out of—Mexico.

The forces that unleashed the immigrant "pull" into the United States and the emigrant "push" from Mexico were not totally independent or coincidental. Although I focus on NAFTA in my analysis of import and price data, it was only one of several conduits. Mexico was already integrated into the global economy. In numerous international exchanges—beginning with the 1980s debt crisis—Mexico had accepted freer trade and some neoliberal reforms. The icon that I use to capture this connection is figure 1.1, which shows the astonishing parallel in the rise of U.S. poultry exports to Mexico and undocumented Mexican migration to the United States.

The following chapters demonstrate how the developments in the U.S. poultry industry described in chapter 4 boosted U.S. exports, which in turn contributed to the reorganization of the Mexican poultry sector. The argument—imports depress domestic prices, which in turn drive out domestic producers—is familiar to those who study developing economies. I treat "price" as the "conveyor belt" that links imports to changes in production. My analysis, the findings of other researchers, as well as my conversations in Mexico all support the conclusions that poultry imports had a negative effect. Both large commercial producers and small barnyard producers felt the shock. For both the commercial sector (chapter 7) and small barnyard producers (chapter 8), I describe the direct (prices) and indirect (structural reforms) pathways by which global integration transformed local production.

For these two principal stakeholders I include (1) an account of the adaptations; (2) references to relevant social science debates on the effects of capital and commodity flows; (3) reflections on Mexico's ongoing global integration using NAFTA as a main watershed but acknowledging the role of the earlier conduits of neoliberalism; and (4) Mexican reactions.

Global trade—"battering down all walls with cheap prices"—provoked protests. I treat the reactions of the stakeholders as evidence for the claim that NAFTA caused the changes and injuries unfolding in the commercial sector. Hirschman's (1970) framework is a fruitful way to label these reactions. Voice (protest) and exit (emigration) were both criticisms of the Mexican government for not defending domestic production. To document the most vocal protests, I draw from my conversations with former poultry entrepreneurs and the documents of UNA (Union Nacional de Avicultures), the peak organization representing the commercial producers. The trade flows also augmented the surplus labor in the rural sector. Peasants periodically used mass protests to express their dissatisfaction, but more typically, they resorted to "exit." To document the reactions of small landholders, I draw from government and academic studies and my own conversations. As production became more concentrated and capital intensive, peasants left the countryside, and then they left Mexico (chapter 8).

Poultry Goes Global

For centuries, poultry traveled only a couple of hundred feet from hatching to human consumption. Today poultry trading is global. Mexico eventually became the third-largest market for U.S. poultry.[1] Although Mexico continued to be the third destination for U.S. poultry exports, its share dropped from 11 percent in 1989 to 6.2 percent in 2002, reflecting the expanding markets in China and the FSU countries.

Mexico's rise in meat imports began in 1980. Following Mexico's accession to GATT in 1986, Mexico reduced tariffs on select commodities benefiting some U.S. exporters. Before NAFTA and absent a preferential arrangement such as that worked out with the United States, the Mexican tariff on global poultry imports at times was as high as 260 percent. NAFTA (effective January 1, 1994) changed this. Chapter 7 of the agreement laid out rules for agricultural trade among the three North American partners. Its goals were the liberalization of agricultural trade and the reduction, elimination, and harmonization of sanitary and phytosanitary measures.

NAFTA eliminated many tariff and nontariff barriers. Selected commodities, such as corn and other basic grains, were scheduled for a 10- to-15-year phaseout period to ensure a gradual Mexican adaptation to international competition. However, NAFTA advocates complained about those few exemptions that were targeted for "illiberal" treatment and benefited from recalcitrant protectionism. Miller argues that areas of Chapter Seven on Agriculture were so contentious that the market access provisions in the so-called 'Agricultural Chapter' are really three bilateral agreements (Miller 2002, 3). In a Mexico–United States bilateral agreement, poultry was accorded a ten-year phaseout. It was scheduled to drop to zero percent in January of 2003. The phaseout timetable underwent subsequent modification to delay tariff-free entry of some poultry parts. Even with deferments until January 2008 in portions of the tariff elimination, Mexico's imports of U.S. poultry rose (fig. 6.1).[2] Owing to superior technology and organization, U.S. producers were prepared to supply large volumes (table 6.1).

Imports rose in response to consumer demand and trade liberalization. Between 1989 and 2002, Mexican commercial statistics show an 806.9 percent increase in kilograms of imported poultry and poultry parts.[3] This is principally a one-way flow, because the export of poultry and egg products to the U.S. market is hampered by cumbersome and excessive regulations and procedures enforced by both the USDA and the Mexican Department of Agriculture. UNA acknowledges that Mexican producers have not made the investments and facility improvements required for compliance with USDA regulations (Engormix 2005).

Globalization brought advantages to Mexican consumers and advantages and disadvantages to Mexican poultry producers. One benefit of GATT and

TABLE 6.1. Productivity rates for poultry production

	Mexico	United States
Feed required per kg of meat (1993)	2.3	2
Produced kg of meat per bird (1989)	3.1	6.5
Number of cycles per year (1989)	4.5	6

Source: Data from Pesado (1996, 170–171).

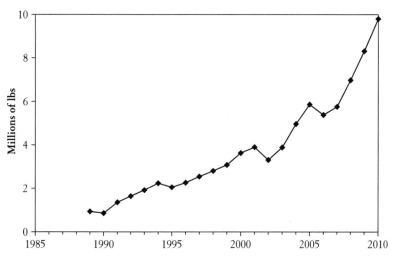

Figure 6.1. U.S. chicken exports to Mexico, 1989–2010

Source: Author's calculations based on data from USDA (2012).

then NAFTA was a drop in poultry prices. Consumers were able to purchase a greater variety at lower prices. By 1992 the price of chicken in Sonora, Mexico for example, was one-third of its price in 1989 (Hernandez et al. 1996, 2). Although the price of chicken breast increased slightly by 2002, the price of whole chicken and legs and hindquarters dropped. With the reduction of import tariffs, Mexican consumers had access to U.S. poultry that was produced with the benefits of advanced technologies, lower-costs inputs such as feed, and economies of scale. U.S. producers were able to ship the preferred dark meat at costs significantly below those of local producers (Sparshott 2002). In addition, the local supply was augmented by Mexican producers, who could now import cheaper feed.

Mexicans began eating more chicken: per capita poultry consumption rose from 5.4 kilograms in 1980 to 24.2 kilograms (about 54 pounds) in 2005 (SAGARPA 2007a), and somewhere between 26 (UNA) and 29 kilograms (USDA) in 2010. The Mexican government attributes this rise to an expansion of integrated companies, industrialization, and a low price relative to other meats. UNA points to more retail outlets located closer to consumers, confidence in the quality and freshness, the growth of fast food restaurants, the diversification of poultry products, and a desire to consume meats with lower levels of fat (2005). The recent availability of precooked chicken and fried chicken, or the trend of using chicken in sausage also boosted consumption (Villamar et al. 2004, 10). The USDA believes that Mexican aggregate demand grew due to improved consumer purchasing power and stable exchange rates (USDA 2000, 22). Import demand was boosted further by epizootics such as Newcastle disease, which destroyed Mexican flocks in the 2000–2002 period.

For Mexico's producers, the principle advantage of NAFTA was partnership in new institutional mechanisms in which the terms of international commodity trade could be negotiated. In this bureaucratic realm, Mexico could gain from technical committees and arbitrational tribunals, clear rules on hygiene standards, and ways to combat the practice of dumping, to name a few. Mexico also gained access to U.S. technological and pharmaceutical developments and cheaper producers' goods such as corn and sorghum. World sorghum trade, for example, was dominated by U.S. exports to Mexico. In 2003/2004, the U.S. share of world sorghum exports was 75 percent, and Mexico's share of world imports was 69 percent (U.S.

Grains Council 2010). The price decline of more than 50 percent between 1975 and 2000 benefited poultry producers.

The disadvantage was competition. Legal and illegal (clandestine) poultry imports were a continuous threat. Many predicted that the market opening would have negative consequences for Mexican producers. Analysts described it as a "crisis," a "debacle" (Hernandez et al. 1996). Commentators pointed out that producers had insufficient time to adjust, and even with the extended temporary tariff protection (1994–2003), the poultry industry would be a "losing activity." When the final import quotas and safeguard tariffs were removed in 2003 (revised to 2008), some predicted, the United States would export large quantities of processed poultry and byproducts into Mexico, provoking bankruptcies and unemployment (Pesado 1997, 151).

Between 1980 and 2000, the Mexican poultry market registered a rising demand and supply, and the supply, previously cornered by domestic producers large and small, now included imported poultry. Domestic production increased by a factor of five, but imports grew at a faster rate. Although Mexican producers still provided 87.1 percent of the poultry consumed in 2005, it was down from 95 percent in 1990 (Zarate 2003).

Price: A Conveyer Belt of Globalization

"Globalization" critics argue that imports cause or threaten to cause serious injury to competing domestic production and importing societies. Imports of corn, cotton, rice, hogs, and vegetable oils (palm, soy, and sunflower) are among the commodities commonly identified. Lower import prices benefit consumers, but they may force locals to abandon production. Analysts at the Food and Agriculture Organization of the United Nations (FAO), among others, see the 2008 collapse of the Doha Round of WTO negotiations as a defensive reaction of developing nations to this globalization phenomenon.

"Import surges" are one way to gauge the impact of imports. Both the FAO and the WTO define an import surge as a sudden and unanticipated or unusual increase in imports. The WTO detects surges when the import volume and the import price of a product deviate from established base-period values.[4] The WTO agreements outline trade remedies to be adopted in the face of import surges. The FAO defines a surge as a 30 percent positive deviation in a given year from the moving average of the previous three years (2006).

Import surges disrupt local markets through prices. Import prices affect wholesale prices, which in turn affect producer and consumer prices. Only producers who employ technology and have high food conversion efficiency (the feed required to produce one kilogram of meat) can survive a drop in wholesale prices. Furthermore, a drop in consumer prices will increase consumption, which in turn may boost imports. Thus, price is the mechanism that transforms import surges into injury for local producers. In 1960, developing countries had an agriculture surplus of $7 billion; by 2001, they had an agricultural deficit of $11 billion. Because their domestic production was wiped out by cheap imports, 70 percent of developing countries are now net food importers (KUNA 2008).

The FAO made the case for the injurious effect of global poultry trade. Poultry ranked third among commodities with a higher frequency of import surges between 1980 and 2003. The FAO estimates that developing countries have experienced 669 cases of poultry import surges between 1984 and 2003, the greatest frequency occurring over the 1999–2003 period. Approximately 50 percent of the surges were registered in Africa, although Africa received only 5 percent of the global poultry trade. The FAO studied the impact of import surges on local poultry industries. Cameroon, for example, had low levels of poultry imports until 1999, at which time poultry imports increased by 286.7 percent. Reports document a decline in retail poultry prices followed by lower domestic production and losses of rural jobs. Between 1999 and 2004, some 92 percent of poultry farmers abandoned the sector (Pingpoh and Senahoun 2007, 11–12). In Senegal, U.S. imports jumped from zero in 1999 to 639 tons in 2000. Poultry farmers complained about the flood of imported frozen chicken legs and parts—often hawked by street vendors or at markets for a fraction of the price of locally reared birds. Imports forced farmers to abandon their own production: chicken sheds went bare. One Senegalese farmer reported, "I used to have 1,000 chickens, now I've not even got 200." Another farmer with a backyard farm complained that he could not make ends meet: "If I bought a sack of chicken feed, I would have nothing to put on the table for my own children" (Massar 2005). Kwa (2008) cites the case of the Ivory Coast, where poultry imports increased 650 percent between 2001 and 2003 as prices dropped. This resulted in 1,500 producers ceasing production and the loss of 15,000 jobs. These studies all connect import surges to prices and labor displacements.

Mexico experienced poultry import surges similar to those described by the FAO.[5] In three periods (1991–94, 1997–98, and 2003), import volume was more than 25 percent higher than the average for the previous three years. The three-year moving average smooths out the year-to-year volatility. Imports dropped, for example, in 1995 because of the peso devaluation and in 2004 when poultry from several U.S. locations was banned because of avian influenza. Inversely, they rose following the 2000 outbreak of Newcastle disease and Mexico's destruction of millions of birds. Changes in the tariffs (particularly for leg quarters and thighs) also affected the flows. Whether one uses the previous three years or just the previous year, the import surge trends are similar.

Imports, even at only 15 percent of total consumption, modified the Mexican market by driving down prices. U.S. exporters were selling chicken pieces at 50 percent below the Mexican price (Hernandez et al. 1996, 2–7). Ramirez et al. report that from 1987 to 1998, the import price decreased 62.9 percent, causing producer and consumer prices to drop (2003, 82).

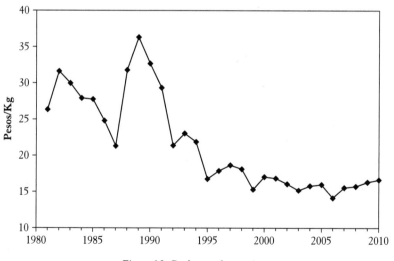

Figure 6.2. Poultry producer prices

Source: Author's calculations based on current poultry prices to producers (SAGARPA) converted to real prices based on the National Producers Price Index (in 2003 Prices) (Bank of Mexico).

UNA estimates that between 1989 and 1999, consumer prices declined an average of 6.7 percent per year and 33 percent for the whole period. The producer price decline during this period was 47 percent—advantageous for the consumer but not for producers (Zarate 2003). Overall, real poultry prices to producers declined after 1989 (fig. 6.2).

It is important to put the price declines in historical context. In their analysis, Ramirez-Gonzalez et al. (2003) report a general decline in consumer and producer prices from 1970 to 1998.[6] This makes it clear that even before the NAFTA-induced import surges, the increased supply, accessibility, and industry development described in chapter 7 exerted downward pressure on prices. They broke the series into two periods, classifying the 1970–86 period as "closed" (imports were insignificant) and 1987–98 as "open." They observe that wholesale prices rose in the first period and fell in the second period, a trend that was significantly related to import prices (2003, 79). In short, the open economy, with its higher volume of imports, lowered the wholesale price of poultry, which in turn lowered the consumer price. More poignantly, Ortiz-Hernández (2006) shows how poultry lost ground against the average price for all foods, including corn, which also suffered price declines (fig. 6.3).

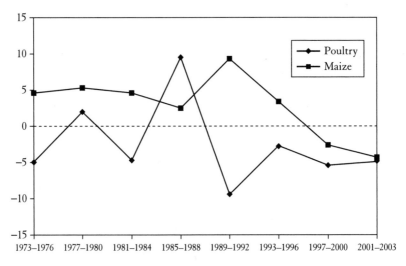

Figure 6.3. Maize and poultry prices compared with index for all food

Source: Data from Ortiz-Hernández 2006. The zero line represents the Consumer Price Index for the food group (food, drink, and tobacco) in 2002 prices. The data points for poultry and maize represent their respective divergence from the food group price.

A final corroboration comes from the relationship between the import surge index that I constructed and the consumer price data. In figure 6.4, I plot the size of the import surge against the percent change in the deflated producer prices. There is an overall negative association between the two. In conclusion, one can safely infer from this plethora of research findings that prices were affected by a number of factors, crucial among them being the volume of imports. There is a convergence in the scholarship on the claim that NAFTA increased imports and that imports affected market and producer prices.

To the extent that authors identify disadvantages of free trade for Mexico, the least developed of the three NAFTA signatories, they highlight the injurious effects that imports have had on prices. Put more poetically over 150 years ago, "The bourgeoisie, by the rapid improvement of all instruments of production, by the immensely facilitated means of communication, draws all, even the most barbarian nations into civilisation. The cheap prices of its commodities are the heavy artillery with which it batters down all Chinese walls, with which it forces the barbarians' intensely obstinate hatred of foreigners to capitulate" (Marx [1848] 1964, 64).

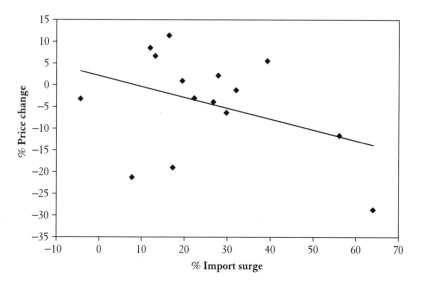

Figure 6.4. Import surges by rate of price changes, 1991–2005

Source: Author's calculations. Import surges = percentage increase (in tons imported) of a given year minus the average of the three previous years. Import data from SAGARPA. Rate of price changes = percentage change of real producer price for a given year from previous year divided by earlier year.

Transforming Mexican Production

Since their 1493 arrival in the New World, chickens have been part of the Mexican economy. On May 9, 1600, by Royal Order of the Viceroy of New Spain, the Count of Monterrey, Don Gaspar de Zúñiga y Acevedo, obligated the indigenous population to raise chickens with the objective of producing eggs and meat to guarantee their own maintenance and recuperation from the demographic catastrophe unleashed by conquest, colonization, and the *encomienda* system. Six hundred years later, FAO analysts insist that poultry has a vital role to play not only in providing nutrition but also for its contribution to rural incomes and employment opportunities (Pingpoh and Senahoun 2007). Mexican governments shared the sentiments of the viceroy and the FAO. Preoccupied with rural poverty, Mexican governments have promoted small- and large-scale agricultural and livestock production. By the end of the 1950s, Mexico had achieved self-sufficiency in poultry.

To what extent did globalization, in the form of NAFTA, transform, annihilate, or reconfigure poultry production in Mexico? The consequences of globalization vary by location in a multi-tiered production system. In developed countries, over 95 percent of poultry flocks are reared under intensive conditions. In contrast, in the developing world, flocks are typically reared under extensive conditions—barnyard or free range (Silverside and Jones 1992). Mexican poultry was produced by a heterogeneous group: flocks range from 52 million birds (Ruiz 2008, 237) down to 25 per year.[7] The Mexican Secretariat of Agriculture, Livestock, Rural Development, Fisheries, and Food (SAGARPA) delineates three levels of production. Large firms, domestic and foreign, are technologically intense (*tecnificado*)—using the most advanced technology and adapted to the necessities of production and the market. Typically, such firms are vertically integrated: many own slaughterhouses, processing plants, diagnostic labs, food supplies, transportation fleets, and distribution capacities. Their market niche is the large urban zones. They earn higher profits, offer lower prices, and continually gain market share. Firms classified as "semi-technified" (*semitecnificado*) are large but have deficiencies regarding sanitary conditions, feed acquisition, and economies of scale; their market niche is smaller regional markets. The smallest rural producers (*traspatio*) use traditional means without the benefits of modern technology. They produce for self-sufficiency and very local markets.

By 2000, all levels of Mexican poultry production had undergone change. The "industrial" branch was substantially reorganized (chapter 7), and the rural branch was essentially abandoned (chapter 8). Between 1980 and 2000, poultry production was transformed from a multi-tiered sustainable system to a bifurcated one with a small capital-intensive oligarchy (domestic and foreign) and an impoverished and diminished rural population. Shifts in the commercial domain included production increases, geographic relocation, concentration of market share by the larger producers, elimination through absorption or bankruptcy of many medium and small producers, the appearance of two U.S. subsidiaries producing for Mexican consumption, and a shift in state-industry relations from a state-nurtured and protected infant industry to one fully exposed to the global market. In the countryside, self-sufficient or *traspatio* production declined as rural survival became more precarious and peasant farmers embarked upon a rural exodus, first from the countryside and then from the country.

Using Emporiophobia (Blaming Trade) with Caution

In this chapter of the chicken trail, I have argued that free trade, prices, and markets were major conveyor belts "battering down all Chinese walls." Poultry production evolved from a stratified system (from large commercial to subsistence *traspatio*) to basically a single, modernized, capital-intensive one. The Mexican countryside, which had been dotted with family production systems, became a place of more and more abandoned villages. But were these changes just the result of trade? No, free trade, prices, and the market did not "act alone." Nor were they enforced coercively with the metal swords and guns of Hernán Cortés, the Spanish conqueror of Mexico.

First, I make the strongest possible case for the NAFTA effect, and then I expand the notion of globalization. To reiterate, NAFTA was only one milestone for Mexico that brought exogenously generated price changes. Prices were affected the 1982 debt renegotiation and currency devaluations. And Mexico's 1986 adherence to GATT led to tariff reductions and the introduction of limited, but cheaper, imported poultry. Neoliberalism is more than NAFTA, and NAFTA is more than trade.

Second, it was not just the invisible hand of the market that transported globalization into the heart of Mexican society. Other exogenous forces (under the stewardship of the United States, the IMF, the World Bank, and Wall Street) "coerced" a neoliberal restructuring of state–civil society relations. Acknowledging Mexico's more general integration into the global economy improves our understanding of production reorganization, and noting changes in the poultry sector improves our understanding of the ramifications of global integration.

7

Voice: Squawking at Globalization

From the 1950 to 2000, Mexico's commercial poultry production was transformed. My analysis of the commercial sector does not address directly the question of labor displacement and emigration, but it contributes to my project in three ways. First, it tracks the timing of poultry imports from the United States. Second, it clearly identifies the anticipated devastating consequences of NAFTA. Third, by tracing the evolution and transformation of the commercial sector, it offers a baseline of pre-NAFTA commercial production. Some transformations were due to natural industry maturation, but the industry clearly suffered from exogenous pressures on commodity prices and shifts in its state–civil society relations. To what extent did globalization in the form of NAFTA, transform, annihilate, or reconfigure commercial production in Mexico?

Reorganized Commercial Production

Mexican commercial production evolved from an infant industry in the 1950s—state-nurtured and state-protected—to one fully exposed to the global market in 2008. First, the geographic locus of commercial production shifted. From 1980 to 2002, the gains were greatest in those states closer to the principal consumer markets such as Mexico City. By 2004, 90 percent of chicken production was concentrated in ten states located near the center of the country (UNA 2005). The geographic shift meant that some states, such as Sonora, a dominant producer in the 1980s but farther from population centers, lost market share. Hernandez et al. report that Bachoco, for example, began its move out of Sonora in the 1980s. By 1994, they observed the closing of almost two hundred poultry farms (1996, 2). In addition to Sonora, the states of Tamaulipas and Baja California also suffered drastic drops in bird inventory between 1980 and 1993 (21.02%, 17.62%, and 18.6%, respectively). At the same time, the inventory in Puebla and Yucatan increased (12.5% and 13.7%, respectively) (Zarate 2003, 48–49). Relocations continued in the 1993–2002 period. Those states that lost market share from 1980 to 2002 often ended up in the "small producers" category (Zarate 2003, 54). The top twelve producer-states increased their share from 66.4 percent in 1980 to 79.4 percent in 2001 (UNA 2005), and the top five states increased their share from 36.9 percent in 1990 to 51 percent in 2005 (UNA 2007) (table 7.1).

Commercial poultry underwent enterprise concentration after 1980. It is natural that this sector would evolve and become more concentrated even without international integration. The commercialized process of fattening chicken was expensive: the fertilized eggs were imported from the United States; feed (sorghum and soy)—60 percent of the material inputs—was expensive and often imported, and the industry was struck by periodic epizootics such as Newcastle disease and avian influenza (Pesado 1996, 174). Those firms with larger profit margins, economies of scale, and easier access to credit could survive, often by displacing or absorbing others. The development toward more technified production was accompanied by a growth in monopolies and vertical integration. Pesado suggests that large firms could exercise control over the industry and the market by controlling strategic inputs, dominating the channels of distribution, managing the available capital, acquiring foreign technology, and defending policies that helped them conserve their position (1996, 151–55). This was a new type of firm for Mexico: the agroindustrial-commercial-financial conglomerate. These large firms, with new organizational forms

TABLE 7.1. Selected Mexican industry characteristics: Comparisons over time

	Earlier	**Later**
Consumption (kg per capita)	5.4 (1980)	24.2 (2005)
Domestic production (tons)	399,230 (1980)	2,500,000 (2005)
Poultry % of total GDP	0.273 (1994)	0.485 (2002)
% of agriculture & livestock GDP	4.130	9.526
% of livestock GDP	11.8	20.723
Imports as % domestic consumption	5% (1990)	13.3% (2002)
Consumption per capita	5.4 kg (1980)	21.8 kg (2007)
Import volume (tons)	43,469 (1989)	503,000 (2005)
	94,000 (1993)	
% produced by top 5 states	32.85% (1990)	51% (2005)
% market held by largest producers	33% (1996)	55% (2006)
Number of birds produced by Pilgrim's	0 (1985)	155,000,000 (2002)
% of Mexican market	0%	26.3% (2002)
Number of birds produced by Tyson	0 (1985)	85,000,000 (2001)
% of Mexican market	0% (1984)	14.4% (2002)
State-industry relationship	midwife	custodial

Source: Author's calculations taken from data available from USDA, SAGARPA, and UNA for various years.

including partners and stockholders, embarked on a path of more efficient production.

Poultry producers are categorized in a number of ways. Some classification systems refer to the level of technology embedded in the production (SAGARPA); some include only commercial producers (UNA 2008) or are limited to production partially prepared for consumption (ranging from "slaughtered"—whole or eviscerated—to value-added chicken "novelties"). Some count the number of birds per cycle (Real 1997). And some classifications include commercial as well as barnyard producers who sell live or untreated birds. These varying metrics generate noncomparable percentages, but the trends over time are similar: significant concentration well before the implementation of NAFTA. According to Zarate's enumeration, medium and small commercial producers had a modest market share in 1980 (27.3% and 5.8%, respectively), but by 2002 their joint share had dropped to below 18 percent (table 7.2). It also shows the dramatic producer concentration between 1980 and 1993—*before* NAFTA. Likewise, Pesado's analysis reveals a 27 percent drop in the number of producers from 1980 to 1989 (1997, 3). Hernandez et al. refer to this period as one of "industry consolidation" (1996, 4), a process that did not stop with NAFTA. According to UNA's enumeration, between 1996 and 2002 the smallest commercial producers dropped from 27 percent to 4 percent of the production, while the largest rose from 33 percent to 55 percent. All the classifications show the smallest producers losing market share throughout the whole period (table 7.2).

Among the largest producers, further concentration occurred as firms increased market share through mergers and acquisitions, particularly after the business failures associated with the 1995 economic crisis. In 1997, Bachoco listed its securities on the Mexican Stock Exchange (Bolsa Mexicana de Valores) as "Bachoco UBL" and on the New York Stock Exchange as "IBA" (Industrias Bachoco S.A. de C.V.). Bachoco attributes its increase in sales from 1997 to 1998 to investments in increased capacity, improved efficiency, and increased use of contract growers. In 1999, Bachoco bought out Group Campi, then the fourth-largest producer (SEC 1999); by 2000, it had captured an estimated 31.2 percent of all production (Zarate 2003, 21). By 2000, the top three firms controlled about 65 percent of the production (UNA n.d.). Clearly, commercial production underwent geographic relocation and concentration before NAFTA, and it continued after NAFTA.

TABLE 7.2. Percent distribution of Mexican commercial poultry

	Large producers	Medium producers	Small producers
1980	66.84	27.33	5.83
1986	72.71	22.91	4.38
1993	81.78	15.37	2.86
1994	81.41	16.04	2.55
1997	80.76	16.41	2.83
2002	82.40	16.06	1.53

Source: Data from Zarate (2003, 52–53). Excluding live animals and rural (traspatio) barnyard production.

Denationalized Commercial Production

Two U.S. subsidiaries producing in Mexico for Mexican consumption entered the country in the late 1980s. By 2000, they ranked second and third in production and market share: Bachoco (Mexican) had 41.2 percent of the bird inventory, and Pilgrim's Pride and Tyson had 18.2 and 10 percent, respectively.

Many critics of NAFTA highlighted the detrimental effects of trade. But NAFTA was really capital market liberalization masquerading as trade liberalization, a plan to facilitate the flow of investment capital. Foreign direct investment (FDI) is the movement of capital across national frontiers in a manner that grants the investors (multinational enterprises) control over their acquired asset. Production in the foreign country is financed— in principle—by the multinational, and profits accrue to the multinational through sales made by the foreign affiliate. Advocates of foreign capital investment flows extol the Mexican access to new capital, expanded capacity, access to global technological and pharmaceutical developments, cheaper producers' goods, and new jobs. Grappling with capital shortages (due in part to capital fight and a low savings rate), Mexico stood to benefit from FDI. In fact, Mexican governments regarded foreign industries as necessary for economic growth.

NAFTA was only one milestone in Mexico's implementation of neoliberal policies for foreign investors. In 1973, Mexico began to move away from regulated and state-owned industries. It opened investment to foreign enterprises. While still operating with an import-substitution-industrialization model, the 1973 Foreign Investment Law sought investment in areas that were underdeveloped or lacked technological capability. The law permitted foreign ownership up to 49 percent, but 160 arenas such as petroleum, mining, electricity, and transportation were excluded.[1] Under certain conditions, government approval was required, and negotiations could take four to sixteen months (Maviglia 1986, 292). Additional flexibility was granted in the 1983–88 National Industrial Development Plan, with the requirements, however, that FDI should complement existing industries; be ready to export; train Mexican personnel; create jobs; contribute to technological development; draw its financing from abroad; preserve cultural and social values; and be located in undeveloped geographic areas. In 1989, President Salinas de Gotari created the Committee for the Promotion of Foreign Investment, opened more sectors to foreign investment, and further liberalized the requirements. The 1993 Foreign Investment Law was drafted in anticipation of NAFTA and replaced earlier laws. It relaxed remaining restrictions on foreign investment and ownership. NAFTA (Chapter 11, Articles 1102 and 1109) stipulated that foreign investors and investment would be accorded treatment "no less favorable" than that given to domestic investors and that all transfers (profits, dividends, capital gains, royalty payments, management fees, technical assistance, and other fees derived from the investment) could be made to another territory freely and without delay. In 1994, Mexico accepted the OECD's Codes of Liberalization, removing all restrictions on international capital flows. Liberalization benefited the United States, which, in 1985, held about two-thirds of Mexico's $11.5 billion of foreign investment (Maviglia 1986, 282).

After 1987, broiler production was one of the preferred industries in which 100 percent foreign ownership was allowed (*PR Newswire* 1987). The USDA judged broiler production to be one sector where FDI was the most important source of Mexican market integration with the United States, adding that these large firms were capturing the lion's share of Mexico's rising poultry consumption (Hahn et al. 2005, 13). According to the USDA, "It is an important avenue through which U.S. food and beverage companies seek expansion in foreign markets" (USDA 2009).

With benefits of FDI come potential disadvantages. In his early work on Brazil, Frank (1969) identified five drawbacks. First, foreign investment did not bring new capacity; rather, it often bought out existing domestic enterprises. Second, foreign "investment" was not totally foreign; it received loans from Brazilian banks. In 1961, for example, the American firms SANBRA and Anderson & Clayton received 47 percent of the entire agricultural and industrial portfolio of Brazil's banks. These funds were re-loaned to Brazilian cotton wholesalers and producers at higher rates. Third, by vertically diversifying, firms ended up controlling additional areas of the economy. Fourth, investment decisions were dictated by corporations located in another country and based on strategies appropriate for their own corporate solvency. Fifth, profits were expatriated. Mayer raises a general concern regarding "unchecked" globalization (trade and investment liberalization), that domestic producers will be integrated with or bought up by foreign consortiums. As such expansion continues and more production is carried out by foreign firms, it would be "compatible with a poverty trap in which all domestic income accrues to low-skilled labor, any pre-existing domestic capital has been 'creatively destroyed' and domestic knowledge and technology receive no rents" (Mayer 2002, 20, 21). This scenario depicts one of the darker aspects of globalization.

Frank offers a useful checklist for assessing foreign investment. In poultry, there were some signs of this negative scenario—buying up existing Mexican plants, for one. Pilgrim's Pride Corp. acquired a Mexican poultry company in 1985. In FY 1988, it acquired four vertically integrated poultry production operations in Mexico for approximately $15.1 million. Its acquisitions included production and distribution facilities located in Mexico City and the states of Coahuila, San Luis Potosí, Querétaro, and Hidalgo. Pilgrim's said that the operations would produce about 600,000 broiler chickens a week to be sold in Mexico, representing about 12 percent of Pilgrim's total broiler production (*Wall Street Journal* 1987). Of this, about 3 percent was exported. Part of the acquired cooperatives had been developed with Mexican bank funds, although from the time of those acquisitions through FY 1994, the company made additional capital expenditures totaling $106 million. In 1994, the company took advantage of the economic crisis and purchased chicken farming facilities that had been built by the Union de Avicultores de Queretaro (Queretaro Chicken Farmers Union). The facilities included a feed processing plant, a slaughterhouse, and incubators. Local farmers had recently upgraded their facilities, but the peso devaluation made it impossible for them to repay their bank loans (Real 2003). "This strategic and synergistic acquisition of Union de Queretaro enables Pilgrim's Pride Corporation to enlarge its market share for chicken in Mexico . . . This purchase is consistent with our long-term strategy in Mexico," said Lonnie "Bo" Pilgrim, chairman of the board and chief executive officer of Pilgrim's Pride Corporation (*PR Newswire* 1995b). Pilgrim's was vertically integrated; it also produced table eggs, animal feeds, and ingredients (SEC 1994). As of January 1, 1994, Pilgrim's Pride was allowed to combine its previously taxed nonagricultural Mexican operations with existing agricultural operations and, as such, were not subject to taxes in Mexico. By December 1994, the company employed approximately 3,100 people in Mexico. Its total net sales of poultry and other domestic products rose from $721 million in FY 1990 and $921 million in FY 1994 to $1.4 billion in FY 1999 (SEC 1994).

Tyson entered Mexico in 1987 by forming a partnership with Grupo Trasgo, a Mexico-based poultry company. Initially it was to produce leg quarters and processed meats for export to Japan under Mexican-origin tariff conditions. In 1989, Tyson acquired preexisting *ejidal* groups[2] and counted on loans from Mexico's development bank.[3] The bank specialized in rural development, financing construction, and the supply of growing-out houses. In 1992 Tyson added thirty-two new groups with the support of a recently created fund to assist *ejidal* groups and small businesses involved with aviculture.[4] The Mexican fund provided the major part of the total investment costs (Garza et al. 1998). Tyson continued to work with "growers," some of whom had been associated with Grupo Trasgo at the time of the initial agreement, and in 1994, it bought up 95 percent of the stock. Some judge that this large-scale, cost-effective production helped transform Mexico's poultry industry. According to the U.S.-Mexico Chamber of Commerce, because the Mexican government had protected its poultry industry through subsidies and guaranteed prices, local producers had profited from inefficient production (1999a). Although trade flows became the "poster child" of NAFTA, FDI also profoundly denationalized the poultry sector.

Severing the State–Civil Society Ties

The industry's relationship with the state underwent major changes. For much of the twentieth century, the Mexican government was a "midwife" for industry. A midwife state "tries to assist in the emergence of new entrepreneurial groups. . . . A variety of techniques and policies may be utilized . . . erecting . . . tariffs . . . is one. Providing subsidies and incentives is another" (Evans 1995, 13–14, 78–80). From a modest commercial beginning in 1928, when the government founded the Escuela Nacional de Avicultura (National Poultry School), through the 1940s, when the early incubator and balanced food plants were installed, large-scale and vertically integrated firms grew alongside small-scale traditional production. Early government programs fostered industry concentration. The economic development program of President Adolfo Ruiz Cortines (1952–58) included new programs for rural producers. In 1954, the government, through the Bank of Mexico, created a program to fund the development of agriculture, livestock, and aviculture.[5] Its objective was antimarket and countercyclical. To address shortcomings in the market, it authorized credits that would diminish the financial risks associated with farming and livestock (FIRA 2007). The goals were to modernize the rural sector, to achieve self-sufficiency in eggs and fresh poultry, and to encourage export capacity (Hernandez and Maya 2002). Continued support came from President Adolfo López Mateos's Campana Nacional de Repoblacion Avicola (National Poultry Recuperation Campaign). This was in response to difficulties such as the 1957 flock devastation caused by the Newcastle disease outbreak, the subsequent dependence on foreign sources, and a sector-level commercial deficit. The program offered technical assistance, soft credits, protection from foreign imports (but tariff-free entry for newborn chicks), and guaranteed prices (Mayer 2002, 6; Hernandez et al. 1996, 2).

The 1966–70 economic development program promoted by President Gustavo Díaz Ordaz (1964–70) continued the "midwife" model and gave priority to the grain and livestock sectors. Further, Hernandez estimates that in 1973–82 period, public investment in the poultry sector was double that of the 1963–73 period (2001, 28). These programs successfully promoted technological advances: the bird population increased by a factor of three between 1960 and 1982 (Pesado 1996, 153). Founded in 1952 as a small table-egg operation in the state of Sonora, Industrias Bachoco—still the largest producer—benefited from these programs. In the twenty years after its founding, it expanded its operations to the nearby states of Sinaloa and Baja California and then to others such as Guanajuato to capture the major markets further south (Bachoco 2007).

By the 1980s, this state–civil society relationship was drifting toward a "custodian" role, in which the poultry industry was forsaken by the state. Evans defines this as industry regulation without promotion (1995, 13). It began in the late 1980s with the withdrawal of agriculture support and continued in the 1990s with the dismantling of major government agricultural subsidy programs such as the National Company of Popular Subsidies (CONASUPO).[6] The poultry sector first lost its subsidies. In January 2008, it lost the last of its tariff protection.

In conclusion, between 1980 and 2000, poultry registered growing levels of supply and demand. It experienced geographic and firm concentration, and domestic producers increasingly had to share their market with imported poultry and with poultry produced by U.S. subsidiaries on Mexican soil. On top of that, the nurturing state-industry relationship was severed. These shifts are all summarized in table 7.2.

Squawking

Large producers protested the market opening mandated by NAFTA and were successful in gaining some temporary safeguards. The last remaining quotas and import taxes on U.S. poultry legs and quarters were finally eliminated on January 1, 2008—fourteen years after NAFTA. This is an example of producer-driven protection. Based on his analysis of examples of NAFTA derogation, Miller concludes that producer-driven protection (in all three countries) was most successful when the producers were well organized, geographically concentrated (such as orange growers in Florida), traditional recipients of protection, and likely to face stiff competition with trade liberalization (2002, 1). UNA featured many of these elements. But as Krau observed in his study of Africa, "Externally generated economic liberalization has stimulated higher levels of business association activity, but not necessarily the political space for business association autonomy" (2002, 395).

Commercial poultry producers, represented by UNA, predicted that trade liberalization would injure their industry. Pointing out their complaints is extremely useful because they identify objectionable aspects of globalization and specify the anticipated negative repercussions. When UNA's predecessor organization, founded in 1958, began to dissolve, the Mexican government issued a decree (April 27, 1962) mandating its reorganization as UNA.[7] Since its founding in November 1962, UNA has worked to represent and develop the industry. It addresses sanitary issues, developments in technology, and domestic and international poultry policies. Along with SAGARPA, UNA has responsibility for collecting statistics on the poultry sector. Various UNA administrations devoted significant effort to recruiting individual producers into this peak organization. And UNA fortified its position with legal and economic consultants, particularly in the post-NAFTA period (Ruiz 2008, 189).[8] I divide the UNA complaints and actions into three broad categories: those dealing with international competition, those dealing with Mexican government's responses to the global neoliberal pressures, and those dealing with domestic policies.

Protesting Foreign Competition

UNA protested trade policies that exposed them to foreign competition. The early phase of trade opening followed the debt renegotiations of 1982.

In order to gain access to international markets, and thus the foreign currency needed to service its debt, Mexico had to open its own markets to foreign goods. This drastically changed the market environment for domestic producers. The USDA in turn "encouraged" U.S. exporters by offering financing through various agricultural export credit guarantees and programs (see chapter 4). As Mexico moved from a protected to a more open market, UNA voiced its preoccupation regarding U.S. poultry imports and Mexico's customs regulations. Six key protests are described below.

Following its 1986 adherence to GATT, Mexico reduced import tariffs and eliminated many nontariff barriers such as import licensing requirements. Pesado (1997) judges that Mexico's commercial opening in 1986 had a negative impact on national aviculture, in part because the United States subsidized input factors and had more advanced technology and higher productivity. Following complaints, Mexico reinstalled some license restrictions on imported poultry, but in 1988, a Mexico-U.S. bilateral agreement again suspended licensing requirements for fresh and frozen poultry. Imports rose from 14 million tons in 1987 to 56 million tons in 1988. Noting the big jump, UNA requested a (re-)suspension of "imports without licenses." Its request was honored and in 1989, the secretary of agriculture temporarily reinstated the licensing regulations (Hernandez et al. 1996, 6).

UNA successfully lobbied for exemption from NAFTA. It won an extremely significant concession—rather than the import tariff dropping immediately to zero in 1994, poultry was among those commodities granted a ten-year extension. The revised tariff was scheduled to drop from 260 percent to zero in January 2003, decreasing by 10.4 percent annually (Zarate 2003, 20). This provided the industry an opportunity to prepare for international competition.

Third, UNA expressed discontent about the flood of "above-quota" mechanically deboned chicken that entered duty-free, but it was unsuccessful in getting the Mexican government to stop issuing waivers. The bulk (84%) went to sausage companies and cold meat producers for whom domestic production had fallen short (USDA 2000, 9). Mexican sausage producers pressed for the additional duty-free quantities above the tariff-rate quotas (TRQs).[9] Duty-free imports continued to surpass the allocated quota. In 1999, the allowed imports were almost four times the official quota. Although the Mexican government published an announcement in 2000 that imposed a minimum 30 percent duty for imports in excess of NAFTA TRQs, it continued to waive enforcement of the original TRQs.

Fourth, in 2002, UNA requested that the secretary of commerce investigate the flood of cheap imported leg and hindquarters that was likely to enter duty-free after January 2003. The industry wanted additional time to adjust. Without safeguards for chicken legs and thighs, they estimated that imports would deprive local producers of 30 percent of the market. As a result of UNA's successful intervention, new customs categories and new tariff quotas were created for those poultry parts (USDA 2003, 2). This revised tariff offered protection until January 1, 2008, when it would (and did) drop to zero.

During the 2003–2008 period, UNA complained about meats entering clandestinely—either outright illegally or as "contrabando tecnico," technical contraband. This latter referred to meat that avoided higher import duties by intentionally getting misclassified, either camouflaged as fresh meat packed in brine or connected to other broiler parts. UNA was unsuccessful in mobilizing serious government enforcement against this illegal poultry.

Lastly, in December of 2007, the president of UNA began negotiations to extend the safeguards on chicken legs and hindquarters, requesting a reestablishment of the 2007 level (19.7%) for three to five years beyond the scheduled January 1, 2008, termination date. UNA predicted that the opening would cost Mexican producers 35 percent of the market. This request went unheeded. These examples capture UNA's objections and actions. Resistance to U.S. exports is certainly not unique to Mexico. The U.S.-Russia Cold War was followed, somewhat less grandiosely, by the U.S.-Russia Chicken Wars, a conflict that continued intermittently into 2010. With Russia's anticipated 2012 entry into the WTO, such trade conflicts will be arbitrated using the WTO settlement procedures.

UNA Reactions to Global Integration and Domestic Policies

Narrowing "globalization" to NAFTA commodity flows leads to an underestimation of the globalization effect. I have modified this to say that NAFTA was only one milestone in the global integration of Mexico that brought exogenously generated price changes. A second modification is to include certain policies that some might classify as narrowly "domestic" but were reactions to early stages of global integration. UNA protested other global integration policies as well as domestic policies of the Mexican government.

Global integration involved more than commodity competition. Mexican administrations implemented other policies that ushered globalization into the heart of Mexican society. Since the 1980s, when the IMF began restructuring debts and micro-managing economies, governments have faced pressure to embrace and implement reforms. These nonmarket pressures, initiated under the stewardship of the United States, the IMF, the World Bank, and Wall Street, transmitted neoliberal reforms into the fabric of emerging markets. From 1980 to 1998, Mexico was frequently the largest recipient of IMF credits, and the amount received by Mexico in 1995 was unprecedented—far out of proportion to any prior disbursement to Mexico or, indeed, IMF funding to any other country up to that time (O'Driscoll 1999). Such credit flows set the stage for the pressures of globalization that affected foreign investment, currency policies, and state–civil society relations.

UNA and commentators complained about those policies, referred to as "structural adjustment programs" (SAPs) in the 1980s and neoliberal programs after the mid-1990s. These policies were responses to exogenous pressures first in exchange for debt renegotiations following the debt crisis in the 1980s and then as a precondition for FDI and capital flows in the 1990s. Currency devaluation was key to both reform packages.

Monetary policies of the 1980s and 1990s threatened the survival of the farming and livestock industries. In pursuit of debt renegotiations, Mexico's reforms included peso devaluation. Poultry producers suffered from the 1982 devaluation; workers suffered from limited wage increases; and businesses suffered from increased interest rates on farm, business, and consumer loans. The 1982 devaluation made imports from the United States more costly. While this offered a slight protectionist benefit to Mexican agribusiness (GAO 1990, 26), the accompanying austerity measures had overall adverse effects. The 1985 suspension of subsidies to producers of sorghum, for example, led to a drastic rise in feed costs (Pesado 1996, 156). Those needing dollars for importing inputs (such as feed and machinery) were driven into bankruptcy.

Poultry producers (among others) suffered greatly from the 1994 peso devaluation, which was linked to NAFTA trade negotiations.[10] This devaluation, charitably referred to as the "December error," provoked what a former UNA president Jaime Yesaki Cavazos described as the most distressing economic crisis ever confronted. As an entrepreneur, he found himself several times at the point of almost losing everything (Ruiz 2008, 162). Because interest rates had been pegged to the dollar, the devaluation meant a rise in the "real" interest rate. Businesses were driven into insolvency when they were unable to repay existing loans or get new credit. I spoke with a former poultry plant owner in Hermosillo, Mexico who suffered this fate.[11] Virgilio had started his Sonora installation in 1990, hired a hundred or so workers, and produced table eggs and broilers. Despite SAGARPA's classification as "medium-size," such an operation still required substantial investment in incubators, vaccines, and other inputs. The peso devaluation destroyed his enterprise, he said, because repaying the dollar-debts became impossible. Owners experienced foreclosure and moved into other economic activities. Some small and medium poultry producers became affiliated with (or absorbed by) larger producers under partnerships (*aparcerias*). The currency devaluation limited the affordability of imported producers' goods such as grains, pharmaceuticals, and machinery. Between 1995 and 1997, over twenty thousand small and medium-sized businesses of all sorts declared bankruptcy (Development Gap 1998). NAFTA, devaluation, inflation, slower economic growth, and high interest rates all raised the cost of production (Mayer 2002, 8), which in turn inhibited investment. Research programs to create new domestic genetic breeding lines were neglected (Pesado 1996, 184). In addition, UNA blamed the Mexican government, which, as part of its anti-inflationary controls, had lax border policies, permitting the flow of the clandestine (and therefore untaxed and cheaper) poultry and eggs into Mexico. These policies all were a product of Mexico's global integration. UNA also sharply criticized what some might classify as purely "domestic" policies. Two domestic policy arenas were particularly troublesome and provoked periodic appeals and complaints to the Mexican government: price controls and certain import restrictions. The secretary of commerce controlled commodity prices and the importation of grains and seed oil plants—inputs for poultry. Producers were squeezed between declining revenue and rising input costs. UNA, under the presidency of Zaragoza Ibbery (1978–83), highlighted this plight with a staged "chicken giveaway" in front of the offices of the secretary of commerce in Mexico City. Recounting the event,

Ibbery told me that he personally gave away approximately 150,000 birds from his enterprise (pers. com. 2009). His successor as UNA president, Castro Sanchez (1983–87), continued to fight price controls. Although the principal target was government-controlled egg prices, UNA also objected to controls on poultry. Striving to combat crippling inflation of 100 percent, the Mexican government controlled prices on commodities (tortilla, eggs, milk, meat, and so on) that made up the "Basket of Goods." UNA struggled against the anti-inflationary policies of Miguel de la Madrid's administration (1982 to 1988), which forced UNA to accept the "infamous pacts" of not increasing prices (Ruiz 2008, 127). Under the presidency of Martinez Landa (1991–93), UNA continued to plead for better poultry and egg prices (Ruiz 2008, 147). Occasionally UNA's appeals for price increases were granted, but the organization repeatedly had to turn to the government for price relaxation. Overall, these consumer price controls seem to belong to Miller's classification of government-driven protection derived from a fear of significant negative popular social dislocations that could have threatened the overall political stability. Controls were subsidies for consumers but painful for producers.

The second source of domestic policy grievances concerned certain import restrictions. Many of the production inputs had to be imported, but individual poultry producers were not authorized to import them directly. Import licenses for oilseed plants, grains, soy, and other components of animal feed typically were not granted to poultry producers. Ibbery successfully petitioned the secretary of commerce for a one-time import permission. In anticipation of a shortage of sorghum and maize for the following year, UNA appealed to CONASUPO and the secretary of commerce for urgent action. Imported grains were necessary to avoid the collapse of chicken and egg production (Ruiz 2008, 88). Another complaint involved methionine, an amino acid important for egg-laying hens. The government price was significantly above the market price, and UNA petitioned to import it directly (Ruiz 2008, 93). Conflicts over import permissions required for grains, machinery, tractor trucks, equipment for incubators and slaughterhouses, and other inputs continued throughout the 1980s and 1990s. UNA found itself in constant battle with CONASUPO over its monthly allocation, the timeliness of delivery, and the poor quality of the sorghum. This situation improved after NAFTA went into effect.

Many might suppose that restrictions on imported producers' goods and price controls were strictly domestic policies. From a world-systems perspective, however, it would be erroneous to isolate Mexico's domestic policies from its global integration. As a "developing" or "semiperipheral" country, Mexico had embraced an ISI (import-substitution-industrialization) strategy beginning in the 1930s with an eye toward achieving economic independence. Import restrictions constituted a mechanism for shielding domestic producers, benefiting some more than others. Price controls on food constituted a mechanism for improving the well-being of workers as well as subsidizing nonagricultural employers. While not as directly or transparently linked to global changes as commodity flows or neoliberal adjustment programs, they were, nevertheless, outgrowths of Mexico's location in the global order.

Conclusion

What was the NAFTA effect, on balance? The commercial poultry sector was no stranger to market risks and natural plights. Poultry has experienced a crisis almost every five years since 1980. Each one promoted industry concentration because only larger firms, with their access to credit, higher profit margins, and advantages of scale in technology, production, and marketing, were resilient (Mayer 2002, 10). Also, there were trade openings before NAFTA. Pre-NAFTA industry changes were under way as a result of GATT and the SAPs. As foreshadowed in the beginning of this chapter, the analysis of the commercial sector does not address directly the question of rural labor displacement and emigration. In fact, the rationalization of poultry production and increased consumer demand offered new job opportunities. UNA (2007) reports a 70 percent increase in the total number of employees (direct and indirect) from 1991 to 2003.[12] Although, as Pesado points out, owing to increased mechanization, direct-employment jobs were low in proportion to the national bird inventory (1996).

The value of tracking the commercial sector over these years is that it documents the negative impact of imports on commercial production. Government programs, periodic economic crises, GATT, SAPs, and epizootics had already fostered industry concentration, but NAFTA had a notable effect beyond all of these. NAFTA combined the total elimination of trade protection with the dismantling of major government agricultural subsidy programs such as CONASUPO. For commercial producers, NAFTA rearranged the relationships within the triad of the Mexican government, commercial producers, and trade partners.

8

EXIT MEXICO: "SI MUERO LEJOS DE TI"

Emigration from Mexico is not new.[1] Numerous researchers have identified the U.S.-Mexico wage differential as the major factor, even more than joblessness. As Huntington (2004) argues, with a five-to-one income differential between the United States and Mexico (in 2003), migration is inevitable. Beyond the customary cost-benefit analysis that drives migrants, specific historical factors have affected the flow. In addition, improved transportation networks make travel easier for individuals of varying ages and physical capabilities. By the 1990s, many more people could exercise their "exit" option.

I return to the original question: To what extent did globalization in the form of NAFTA transform, annihilate, or reconfigure poultry production and fuel emigration? As with the commercial producers, the NAFTA effect on rural barnyard producers can be traced through direct (prices) and indirect (reform) paths. My argument is not that NAFTA-mandated poultry imports led to a rural exodus solely because imports undermined the backyard production of poultry. Rather, it is that poultry was part of rural survival—one that was becoming less sustainable.

Highlighting poultry adds one more component to the scholarly work demonstrating the injurious effects of commodity imports.[2] The study of poultry production demonstrates the local consequences of globalization. To connect globalization, poultry, and migration, I use the following syllogism: imported foodstuffs contributed to the impoverishment and nonsustainability of rural production systems; the rural economy was dominated by "family production units" (*unidades de produccion familiar*) employed in diverse agricultural and livestock production, including poultry; and many of those experienced impoverishment and were forced to abandon their traditional agricultural activities.

In this chapter, I describe how trade and Mexican government policy shifts contributed to rural impoverishment and the responses of those affected. "Exit" was a widespread response, but certainly there were noteworthy cases of small-producer organized protests. In July 2000, for example, five thousand sugar cane farmers converged on the capital to protest imports. In January 2001, protesters in the state of Sinaloa demanded that the government impose higher import tariffs on U.S. corn. In July 2001, farmers gathered at the customs station in Chihuahua to turn back U.S. grain shipments. In July 2001, rice farmers in Campeche took control of two cereal plants and demanded that the government renegotiate their loans (Thompson 2001). Fearing a crisis, hog farmers asked the federal government to save the sector by demanding that importers consume a fixed percentage of the national production. That sector, which employed some three hundred thousand people, was suffering, they said, from massive imports and declining prices, scarce financing from the public sector, corrupt customs rules, and a lack of necessary infrastructure (Espinosa 2003). In 2003, hog farmers from central Mexico, angry over NAFTA, protested imported meat. In 2008, about a hundred Mexican farmers partially blocked the border crossing between El Paso, Texas, and Ciudad Juárez, carrying signs that read, "Without Corn There Is No Country" (Tobar 2008). Overall, protesters were unsuccessful in obtaining trade protection or regaining state assistance. Miller, whose analysis regarding commodity protectionism was noted earlier, hypothesized that government-driven remedies (for instance, protection for corn in Mexico or culture in Canada) were most likely to ensue only when the government feared that the social disruptions could threaten the trade policy agenda (2002, 29). The Mexican government apparently felt that the protests did not rise to this level.

Some engaged in protest, but many exercised "exit." President Vicente Fox was quoted as saying that Mexico lacked the resources for such trade protection and that producers would have to be creative ("que se tendria que usa la creatividad") (Espinosa 2003). They were creative; they abandoned their nonsustainable agricultural activities and emigrated.

The Countryside

The rural population (around 20 million) makes up from one-fifth to one-fourth of Mexico (Abundis 2003; Burstein 2007, 7; DeWalt and Rees 1994; Fleck and Sorriento 1994, 9; Huerta 2001; Rosenberg 2003, and Wise 2004). Rural workers made up 27 percent of the Mexican labor force in the 1990s, in contrast to about 3 percent in the United States in 1993 (Fleck and Sorriento 1994, 9). Historically, the Mexican countryside was typified by less efficient and more self-sufficient farming providing a precarious source of income. Naturally, portraits of small landholders vary by region, but authors typically describe production units as small plots with a prevalence of cows, corn, and hogs. Private land holdings were unevenly distributed. In 1990, 67 percent of all private property holders collectively had less than 1.1 percent of the total area, whereas the top 1 percent held more than 75 percent of the area. The majority of the holdings were small. In the early 1990s, 59.5 percent of farmers cultivated less than 5 hectares, and 32.7 percent cultivated between 5 and 20 hectares (Zepeda 2000, 13). For maize, 49 percent of the nearly three million producers worked between 4 and 8 hectares, and productivity levels were low. Small corn farmers grew for home consumption or for sale in a local or regional market, often used manual and animal traction, and applied as much fertilizers and pesticides as household incomes would allow (King 2006, 1). In northern rural areas of Sonora, those without land worked as day laborers and supplemented their diet with home-reared chicken, fruit, and vegetables. The small holders had some cows that were used for producing beef and milk. Acuna described a Michoacán village of two thousand people in the 1970s as having slightly larger production units. In addition to growing sorghum and other commercial crops, those *ejidatarios* operated a pig farm with about seven hundred animals and were contemplating a poultry industry (1981, 14).

Poultry was an integral part of this rural life. In Chihuahua, SAGAR-PA's 2003 census registered 101,811 rural households with chickens (a total of 509,111 birds—an average of five per household). In the state of Michoacán, where SAGARPA was combating avian influenza, its technicians identified the target area of 40,000 rural households with a total of 6 million birds, an average of 25 birds per household. This small number of birds per household was in contrast to forty-seven large establishments in Michoacán with an average of 321,447 birds each (SAGARPA 2005). Family poultry production for subsistence (*traspatio*) could be found in practically all rural areas.[3]

The Mexican government recognizes the importance of traditional poultry production as part of overall rural subsistence. The *traspatio* system provides needed nutrition to rural residents in zones where formal markets are absent (Villamar 2001, 16). Although the meat may be of minimal quality and not particularly profitable, its rustic nature and suitability to local conditions permit its survival. The Ministry of Agriculture, Livestock, Rural Development, Fisheries, and Food stressed the importance of the high protein levels of chicken and eggs for the dietary well-being of rural residents and, in the event of a small surplus, the possibility of a modest income from sales. Rural enterprises also take maximum advantage of household labor. Under the umbrella of SAGARPA, the subsecretary for rural development produced pamphlets providing details on topics like how to construct chicken coops and how to feed and attend to the sanitary conditions of hens and chickens.[4] SAGARPA also praised the French system, where 30 percent of the market is supplied by small-scale organic farmers (2007b, 26).

Maria Jesus, now in her 80s, resident of a village of about a thousand inhabitants in the Yaqui Valley outside of Hermosillo, Son., recalled poultry's place in the family diet.[5] They used their *ejido* and small plot of land for cattle grazing and growing grains for feed. They sold milk and calves. Typically there were about a dozen hens in the yard, which provided eggs for daily consumption and, periodically, meat.[6] Until the 1970s, eggs were occasionally exchanged for other local commodities in a barter system called *tenda de raya*. Only in the 1990s did they regularly purchase poultry from a local outlet. Carmen, from the same village, remembered that in the 1970s, they had about fifteen hens, one rooster, and an average of ten chicks.[7] The family ate eggs daily, and chicken two to three times a week.

Her mother killed and cleaned the birds. As a child, she and three friends partook of the *tenda de raya* system. They would wait until about one o'clock in the afternoon, when her grandmother was napping, take some eggs from the hen house, and exchange them for candies at the village store. On special occasions, such as a birthday party, the family would buy chicken from other residents in the village. In the early 1970s, on the village outskirts, Gilberto operated a poultry farm with about three hundred chickens. He would kill about twenty-five at a time and deliver them to a local store. They had to be bought immediately. He died around 1978, and his farm closed. Carmen's recollection is that somewhere in the early 1980s, the backyard supply was supplemented by a vendor who brought chickens from Hermosillo, about two hours away.

This village portrait is similar to what I heard from Rosario (pseud.), who had lived in a town near Magdalena de Kino in Sonora. She told me that in the 1960s and 1970s, her family had about thirty hens and two roosters in the yard. It was part of their *milpa* (farm) operation, which included fruits and vegetables for home consumption. They sold calves for income. They ate eggs every morning and sometimes in the evening, and they ate chicken about twice a week. When there was a surplus (eggs or chicken), it was sold, exchanged, or given away. Children also exchanged surplus eggs for candies brought by a vendor who came around in a truck. In 1975, as her father aged, they started buying poultry from a local producer in Magdalena whose operation had about five hundred broilers. He closed around 1995. Rosario also described the "illegal" or "contraband" chicken (*pollo americano*) that was available in the 1980s. She recalled that it was brought from the United States at night on trucks, transferred to cars, and sold at the local stores. It came in a large box and included whole chickens and parts. She remembers asking the store owner, "Do you have *pollo americano?*" The owner would go to the back of the store to fetch it. She thought it was better quality than the local chicken. She also remembers that people thought that they had stomach ailments from *lombrizes* (worms) because local farmers let chickens roam freely, and they often ate human waste (pers. comm. 2008).

The presence of poultry was also recorded in the Mexican Migration Project data (MMP118). The MMP employs an ethnosurvey, combining techniques of ethnographic fieldwork and representative sampling to gather qualitative and quantitative data.[8] The data provide a profile of 118 Mexican communities over roughly fifteen years located in twenty-one states. The database contains 18,804 household interviews conducted in Mexico between 1982 and 2007. The survey was administered to households located in ranches (*ranchos* with fewer than 2,500 inhabitants); towns (*pueblos* having 2,500 to 10,000 inhabitants); mid-sized cities (10,000 to 100,000 inhabitants); and metropolitan areas. Interviewers inquired about the number of chickens that bring some income to the household (table 8.1). Only 14.3 percent of the 19,000 households reported having chickens, but it is higher in *pueblos* and *ranchos* (17.1% and 33.9%, respectively). This may be an underestimation of the actual bird count, because the interviewer asks for information about "non-domestic animals" that bring "some income" to the household (Durand et al. 2005, 27). My own conversations in the Sonoran village (in the MMP classification, a *rancho*) indicate that the primary function of the backyard stock was household consumption. Such poultry would have escaped the MMP count. Of MMP households that reported having chicken, 80.5 percent had fifteen or fewer, a number suggesting self-sufficiency. I divided their sample into two time periods: 1982–96 and 1997–2007. In comparing those time periods for the *pueblos* and the *ranchos*, it appears that the percentage of households having chickens in the *pueblos* did not change, but in the *ranchos*, the percentage dropped from 38 percent to 30 percent. In both cases, the average number of chickens remained about the same between the two periods (table 8.1). My analysis of these data produces a portrait that coincides with one drawn from other data: poultry had a presence in the most rural areas, and its presence declined after 1996.

Transformations

NAFTA brought an end to this rural life. Imports and increasing industrialization of domestically produced poultry changed the life of small rural producers. If they could afford to, those who had maintained backyard hens for home consumption increasingly found it more convenient to purchase poultry "parts." The low price of poultry and eggs led to a reduction in the number of households with chickens and hens. Small

TABLE 8.1. Mexican rural distribution of poultry

	% of households that have chickens	Average number of chickens per household of those that have chickens
Pueblos (category 3)		
1982–1996 (N = 467)	16.91%	12.91
1997–2002 (N = 492)	17.25%	13.23
Ranches (category 4)		
1982–1996 (N = 700)	38.19%	10.92
1997–2002 (N = 637)	30.29%	10.38

Source: Author's calculations based on data from MMP file (MMP118).

commercial producers of fresh and perishable whole chickens were unable to compete with frozen or chilled poultry parts. Nevertheless, as late as 2007, SAGARPA reports that while industrial poultry production met the demands of large urban areas, it generated no benefits for rural communities. Because small producers have been less and less able to compete with industrialized chicken (foreign or domestic), they abandoned their traditional poultry activities. SAGARPA judged this lamentable because rural enterprises require minimum capital investment yet occupy an important niche in rural community survival (2007b, 26–27).

Several case studies have documented the negative effects of trade on Mexican production. Oxfam describes a corn producer in Chiapas who had a crop that guaranteed a minimum income and some surplus for family consumption throughout the year. In last few years, he reported, while the price of corn fell, production costs hit the roof (2003, 5). Thompson (2001) estimates that there are 3.5 million corn growers and that imports have left them with 2.4 million tons of unsold corn. Pickard (2005) estimated that roughly 15 percent of the population depended on growing corn; when the Mexican government chose to forego collecting the allowed import tariffs on corn and beans, farmers were unable to compete with the cheaper U.S. corn. So too with imported U.S. pork, which in 2003 sold for about two-thirds the price of Mexican pork. As Tayler writes, "One-third of Mexico's hog farmers have gone out of business since NAFTA dropped tariffs on U.S. pork from 80 percent in 1994 to zero in 2001" (2003). Mexico's negative agricultural balance of trade with the United States was growing. The average agricultural trade deficit between Mexico and NAFTA partners grew during the 1990s. Mexico's agricultural exports to NAFTA partners rose, but food imports from NAFTA partners rose much more, generating a growing commercial deficit (Rosenzweig 2005). Millions of small farmers suffered.

Neoliberal Shifts in State–Civil Society Relationships

Mexicans are fleeing livelihoods devastated by the shift from a regulated and protected system of rural production to one open to the global market. A single trade agreement, of course, cannot be held solely responsible for Mexico's rural collapse. As was the case with the commercial producers, the state–civil society relationship changed radically for *traspatio* producers. Agricultural production is always vulnerable to the vicissitudes of nature and the market, but historically, the government had modulated such fluctuations through subsidized inputs, credits, and price guarantees. Most Mexican farmers were never rich, but rural households were becoming even less sustainable, and those renting land had a hard time accessing state-funded support programs (Oxfam 2003, 9).

Narrowing "globalization" to NAFTA-only commodity flows would lead to an underestimation of the true effect of globalization. Here, as above, I expand the model to include other global events that brought labor displacement to the *traspatios*: the 1982 debt renegotiations, the 1986 adherence to GATT, and domestic policies that were reactions to earlier stages of global integration. Once again, it was not only the invisible hand of the market that brought globalization to Mexico's small landholders; it was also exogenous agents (such as the Wall Street Bond raters and the IMF) that pressured Mexico to restructure its state–civil society relations.

In 1991, Mexico's undersecretary of agriculture, Luis Téllez, predicted dramatic changes in agriculture. He estimated that, within the following decade, the share of Mexico's economically active population in agriculture would drop from 26 to 16 percent, thanks to President Salinas's three rural reforms, "the North American Free Trade Agreement, the withdrawal of government subsidized production supports for family farming and a

Constitutional reform that encouraged individual titling of agrarian reform lands" (Fox and Bada 2008, 437).

Otero (2004) divides Mexico's politics of production into three periods: 1940 to 1983 (the commitment to ISI), 1985 to 1995 (the move toward a neoliberal political economy); and post-1995 (post-NAFTA). These also correspond to the major shifts in the state–civil society relationship for small farmers. During the first period, agriculture might have been inefficient, but efficiency was not the priority. The objectives of the *ejidal* system were subsistence and employment in exchange for political support. Agrarian policies also assisted the post–World War II industrial push by guaranteeing foodstuffs for the growing urban industrial population (Alonso 2002). Programs embodied the gains of the Mexican Revolution (1917) and their reaffirmation under Cardenas, the populist president (1934–40). The rural peasantry benefited from the agrarian reforms and unprecedented land distribution programs that Cardenas imposed. Their political support was organized in the National Peasant Confederation (Confederación Nacional Campesina). Land redistribution continued under President Gustavo Díaz Ordaz (1964–70) and President Luis Echeverría (1970–76), who together divided 32.9 percent of *all* hectares ever distributed from 1917 to 1976. The land redistribution system met its demise in 1992.

In the early period, development programs along with capital infusions attended to the vitality of this sector and the prosperity of its workers. Government rural assistance encouraged capitalization (technical support, subsidies for fertilizer and electricity, marketing) and provided countercyclical assistance (price controls, import barriers, credit, insurance) along with safety-net programs. CONASUPO, the state-owned enterprise, was committed to maintaining the purchasing power of low-income consumers and the income of small "basic crop" producers. Pursuant to the first goal, its stores sold basic products at lower prices. To small producers, it sold fertilizer and seeds at low prices and promoted domestic commerce and distribution of goods.

Guaranteed price supports contributed to rural survival. From 1965 to 1988 (with a few exceptions), prices paid by the government to the producers of commodities such as corn, wheat, sorghum, and soy were above international levels. Between 1980 and 1988, corn prices were at least double the international price (Huerta 2001, 147). Despite this, some rural workers were displaced. In the earlier period, however, they were absorbed into the growing industrial and service sectors (first the Mexican and later the

Border Industrial Program and *maquiladora* programs). Before NAFTA, rural sustainability depended on government assistance.

Faced with the 1982 debt crisis, Mexico accepted the structural adjustment programs outlined by the IMF as a condition for acquiring short-term financing and a renegotiated debt. The SAPs necessitated privatizing, reducing the size of the government, and consenting to foreign investment. In order to acquire the foreign currency needed for debt service, Mexico had to allow the entry of foreign goods. In reality, what appeared as "domestic policies" of the 1990s were prerequisites or byproducts of Mexico's global integration. The neoliberal agenda, continuing the pattern established by the SAPs in the 1980s, took the form of exhorting emerging markets to privatize and open up to direct and portfolio equity investment (Schwartzman 2006). In Mexico, this was accompanied, in December 1994, by a currency devaluation that led to high interest rates, in turn restricting domestic investment and employment.

These neoliberal reforms, starting during the "lost decade" of the 1980s and continuing into the 1990s, unleashed changes that contributed to the poverty that large segments of the countryside experienced. They did away with protections from global competition and many of the countercyclical and safety-net programs, while modernizing very little of the countryside. The Mexican government reduced spending on rural development; by 1993, the credit granted through the FIRA and Banrural (Banco De Crédito Rural State financial institution that provided low-interest credits in support of rural development) was slightly more than 50 percent of what it had been in 1980 (Huerta 2001). Perhaps the most notable domestic policy was the 1992 land reform (the revision to Article 27 of the 1917 Mexican Constitution), which envisioned larger-scale, modernized agricultural production through private land ownership, as opposed to guaranteed intergenerational usufruct of small *ejidos*. From that time forward, what had once been *ejidal* land could be bought and sold.

Some new policies of the 1990s did provide funding and a safety net. PROCAMPO provided direct payments to farmers who had produced maize, beans, wheat, and other grains. This temporary domestic assistance program (1993–2008) was to help modernize the rural sector by giving farmers an incentive to increase the local production of grains.[9] It was estimated to reach about 40 percent of those employed in farming and livestock activities. Critics noted, however, that the payments were not tied to actual production. The ALIANZA program also provided funding for rural producers. SAGARPA judged that it accomplished its goals of increasing productivity, improving production quality, and raising employment and producer revenue (2002, 14). However, the main beneficiaries were those with entrepreneurial capacity and the modest amount of required matching capital, that is to say, those who were relatively well off. Cord and Quentin (2001) find that participation in PROCAMPO significantly reduced the likelihood that a ejido household was poor (in 1997) but Alianza had no significant impact on poverty reduction.

A peasant from the state of Guanajato expressed his view that his class had been abandoned by the government (Ortiz 2008). Peasants complained that PROCAMPO did not cover the cost of inputs or the transportation needed to move commodities to market. The reporter noted that in the state of Morelos, 75 percent of the families depended on agricultural production; farmers in Quintana Roo felt totally abandoned; and those in states such as Campeche and the Yucatán lacked the resources to develop infrastructure or to mechanize irrigation systems. Farmers from Sonora (Valle de Guaymas) went to Mexico City hoping for financial support to plant vegetables, watermelons, and wheat. Despite their complaints regarding PROCAMPO's inadequacy, they advocated for its continuation. Overall reductions in government spending were disproportionately felt in the countryside (table 8.2).

The Mexican government was certainly responsible for the neoliberal shift; however, that decision was connected to international integration. From a world-systems perspective, even those "purely domestic" policies of nurturing and subsidizing rural production in the early period (before 1983) were, as I argued in the case of commercial producers, the response to Mexico's semiperipheral position in the world system. The goal of populist regimes was to sever dependency relations with the developed countries

TABLE 8.2. Mexican government expenditures

	1980	1996
Total expenditures as % of GDP	25.95%	17.57%
Expenditures destined to rural development as % of GDP	12.04%	7.51%

Source: Huerta (2001, 160).

and to promote national development. It is therefore inappropriate to consider these policies as principally "domestic."

Poverty and Labor Displacement

Both trade and transformations of state–civil society relations undermined household sustainability and to increased impoverishment in the countryside. The subsecretary of rural development classified 71 percent of rural inhabitants in 1980 and 81.5 percent in 1999 as moderately poor.[10] In 2002, 34.8 percent were judged to have an income insufficient for nutrition, and 67.5 percent had incomes insufficient for nutrition plus education, health, clothing, shoes, housing, and transportation (SAGARPA 2003). Mexico made progress in closing the rural-urban household income gap from 1992 to 2002 (the rural/urban ratio rose from 39.9 in 1992 to 47.1 in 2002), but poverty was still greater in the rural areas. Furthermore, despite improvements, the 2000 household income (in 1993 pesos) was the same as the 1989 level (SAGARPA 2003). And the safety net was now gone. Between 1994 and 1999, only 5.4 percent of the rural population was covered by Mexico's social security system (Huerta 2001, 55).

The growth in rural income was unevenly distributed. I have summarized SAGARPA's (2003) findings in table 8.3. They delineate the plight of the poorest. Between 1989 and 2002, rural income grew an average of 6.6 percent for the highest two income deciles, but only 3.3 percent for the lowest four. The wealthier 20 percent derived the greatest part of their monetary wealth from work and business income (60% and 24%, respectively). The lower 80 percent derived their monetary income first from work, and second from transfers. Transfers, in the form of remittances, pensions, and retirement funds, constituted 13 percent of the monetary income for the top two deciles, 26 percent for the fifth and sixth deciles, and 33 percent for the lowest four deciles. The nonmonetary sources constituted 19.6 percent of total household wealth for the top two deciles, but 27.6 percent for the lowest four. These differences in income streams are magnified by the fact that within the nonmonetary component, 21 percent came from subsistence farming for the top two deciles, compared to 43 percent for the bottom four quartiles. In short, the survival of the poorest rural households depended a great deal on transfers and subsistence production.

TABLE 8.3. Sources of Mexican rural income

Income deciles	% of nonmonetary contribution to total rural income 2000	% of rural nonmonetary income derived from subsistence farming	% of total rural monetary income derived from transfers 2002
9th–10th (top)	19.60%	21%	13%
5th–8th	24.54%	36%	26%
1st–4th (bottom)	27.64%	**43%**	33%

Source: Data from SAGARPA (2003, 45).

Reduced household sustainability and growing impoverishment contributed to labor displacement and rural flight. Reflecting on the nonsustainability of the small family production units, Otero bade farewell to the small farmer. He attributed the rural crisis and the destruction of the peasant economy to the rise of capitalist agriculture. Rather than bringing jobs either to the countryside or to the city, it created a large semi-proletariat that fell somewhere between salaried workers and peasant production. The rural economy continued to deteriorate, leading to more and more lost access to the land, but neither industrialists nor agrocapitalists were able to absorb that surplus labor (Otero 2004).

Not all scholars blame global integration for rural labor displacement. Mexico was in the paradoxical position of having both insufficient agricultural production and poor farmers. Government statistics underscore the low levels of productivity and lack of competitiveness. In 2002, farming, livestock, forestry, and fishing contributed only 5.7 percent to the Mexican GDP and 17.9 percent to the labor force (Rosenzweig 2005, 10). Mexican agricultural production was significantly less efficient than U.S. production. Mexico could produce 1.7 tons of corn per hectare, using 18 labor days to produce each ton, while the United States produced 7 tons per hectare, using 1.2 hours per ton (DeWalt and Rees 1994) (see also table 6.1 for poultry). Abundis estimates that in 2002, only three out of a thousand farmers or ranchers had any possibility of exporting (2003, 3).

For Zepeda (2000), the poverty and economic exhaustion of Mexican agriculture derives from the inefficiency of small holdings. Such extensions are insufficient for commercial competition or even for profitable exploitation. Zepeda's list of inadequacies includes insufficient financing, credit, and insurance; scare infrastructure (irrigation and electrification); inadequate marketing networks; poor quality inputs; inadequate management;

and irrational use of natural resources (deforestation, overfishing). Small plots neither merit nor produce adequate capital to buy a tractor or insure crops.[11] In 1991, for example, only 1.4 percent of the area planted with corn was insured. "Why isn't Mexico Rich?" asks Hanson (2010). He shares Zepeda's assessment of the inefficiency of the informal economy and criticizes romantic notions held by those who claim that small producers are vibrant contributors to economic growth. For Hanson, informal economic organization is inferior; it disperses resources excessively and tends to keep those in production who are poor managers or use outdated technology. Informality, Hanson argues, creates distortions in the economy that prevent naturally occurring reallocations of resources. In the end, for these authors, it is the organization of agriculture that perpetuates poverty.

Zepeda and others argue that inefficient producers should stop being farmers. They see the *minifundio* (small holdings) as an institutional obstacle to the development of agricultural wealth. It only persisted for many years because of Mexican government policies and, according to Alonso (2002), created economic distortions and deterioration in the terms of trade between agriculture and other sectors. Because *minifundio* were nonsustainable, they became increasingly vulnerable with the post-1982 precipitous drop in public investment, the removal of price supports, and the end of government subsidies.

Peasants were leaving the farms and farming as a way of life in Mexico was disappearing. A Michoacán *ejidatario* reported that he had produced commercial surpluses in the past but now was producing for subsistence and striving to hang in there while the children migrated (Gledhill 1995, 37). A sugar farmer lamented, "There is almost no place left in the country where a small farmer can make a good living." Thousands of peasants were abandoning small plots (Thompson 2001). Poultry production had existed on multiple tracks since 1955, but global economic integration affected rural producers, including those who used traditional means of raising poultry, either for self-sufficiency or for sale at informal local markets.

Changing Sentiments: From "Se Muero Lejos De Ti" to "Por Qué Nací Yo Del Lado Equivocado?"

The changing nature of Mexican emigration is captured in these two Spanish phrases. The song lyric "Beautiful Mexico, if I die far from you" captures the sentiment of early migrants, yearning for their country of birth. The second "Why was I was born on the wrong side?" captures the sentiment of a high school student in Tucson lamenting that she was born in Mexico and brought to the United States by her undocumented parents (Bagley and Castro-Salazar 2009). For voices of the displaced that went unheard by the Mexican government, either because they lacked the organization capacity of UNA or because their leverage in the face of global neoliberal pressures was weak, they exercised "exit."

Having followed the trail from trade and neoliberal reforms to rural immiseration, I now turn to the path from immiseration to emigration. NAFTA reinvigorated the longstanding debates about the benefits of global economic integration. To what extent can the rise in illegal immigration be understood as a consequence of market adjustments and the competitive disadvantages with which Mexico entered the NAFTA agreement? To argue that immiseration led to migration contradicts the predictions that NAFTA would ameliorate Mexican unemployment and poverty, thereby minimizing emigration.

Researchers have used different approaches to establish the rural poverty-displacement-emigration linkages. Some deduce the causal linkage from a national-level data set over time that shows an inverse relationship between per capita GDP and migration rates. Others have inferred causality based on Mexican state-level data showing a negative association between per capita income and remittances from the United States or between state-level poverty and emigration. This includes the governors of Veracruz, Oaxaca, and Nayarit, who pointed out that the crises in their states had generated new waves of migrants to the United States (Thompson 2001). Still others have sampled municipalities and drawn inferences based on migration rates, the importance of basic crops production, and the degree of Mexican government support (Fox and Bada 2008; Martinez 2007). In addition, the MMP interviews (sampled from municipalities known for migration) provide demographic detail on individual migrants (Massey et al. 1994). Collectively, the research findings depict impoverished rural environments that drive out their residents.

As I did with the discussion of commercial production, I first make the strongest possible case for a NAFTA effect, and then I expand the notion of globalization. In connecting trade-induced immiseration to migration,

I reiterate Przeworski's lemma—"the motor of History is endogeneity" (2007, 168). This methodological warning (that there may be unobserved covariates determining the outcomes) actually creates space for the world-systems paradigm since both the trade liberalization and emigration encouraged by the WTO were more likely to be associated with developing countries.

Trade, Rural Immiseration, and No Alternatives

The village of Comalapas in Chiapas, one of the poorest in the country, saw the rise of travel agencies on Main Street, offering just one destination—Tijuana. Agencies offered a range of services from bus tickets to plane tickets with a U.S. job thrown in (Oxfam 2003, 6). Former president Carlos Salinas de Gortari blamed former presidents Ernesto Zedillo and Vicente Fox for allowing Mexico to wallow in economic stagnation between 1995 and 2005. He said, "Five million compatriots left the country in search of a future in order to respond to their own expectations and those of their families. . . . It's difficult to encounter a country in times of peace that has a migratory phenomenon of this magnitude" (FNS 2008).

Martinez analyzed the net impact of market liberalization on migration. He studied small basic crops producers in 744 migrant-sending municipalities and tested the effects of the removal of price supports and input subsidies, the 1992 land reform that granted property rights, and NAFTA. He concluded that for the 1992–97 period, the negative effect of international integration and domestic reforms was strongest for basic crop producers. In other words, a rise in exposure to basic crop production led to a rise in the percentage of households with migrants. This was in contrast to the insignificant effect of the level of foreign direct investment or of imports and *maquiladora* exports (2007, 95–101). Being a basic crop producer is what mattered.

Was emigration the only alternative? Poverty and emigration certainly were an integral part of Mexican history. Undercapitalization of the countryside had historically contributed to the rural immiseration and displacement as well as internal migration. Mexico City grew from 1.8 million in 1940 to 18 million 1987. The challenge is to explain the new wave of labor displacement, rural expulsion, and emigration. The first factor was that rural immiseration led to labor displacement because alternative rural employment had stagnated over the past thirty years. The rural stagnation worsened after the trade opening in the mid-1980s, which resulted in lower prices for domestically produced agricultural goods (Ros and Rodriguez 1987).

During the growth period of the 1970s, displaced rural labor was absorbed into Mexico's urban areas and industrial zones. During the pre-NAFTA waves of international integration (such as GATT), some displaced rural population was absorbed in construction, commercial agriculture, or the growing export assembly industry. Moreno-Brid et al. describe the 1950–90 period as one in which per capita GDP grew at an annual average rate of over 3 percent and the dynamism of the manufacturing industry transformed Mexico "from an agrarian to an urban, semi-industrial society, and the incidence and depth of poverty decreased" (2009, 157).

In contrast, Moreno-Brid et al. write, the real GDP expansion in 1990–2006 was less than the 1950–80 average. By 2000, a weak U.S. economy and growing competition from China had reduced such job options. Lynch (2006) writes that only a sliver of new jobs are created for the about one million Mexicans who enter the labor pool annually, and according to the IMF, just 12.8 million of the country's 43 million working-age population have jobs in the formal sector. This was aggravated with the demographic increase in the relative size of Mexico's working-age population (Hanson 2006).

The export assembly industry has proven a weak engine for driving the Mexican economy, and the *maquiladoras* have lost step with the rising demand for employment. In 2003, the Carnegie Endowment for International Peace wrote that while FDI in Mexico led to the creation of 500,000 manufacturing jobs from 1994 to 2002, the country lost at least 1.3 million jobs in the agricultural sector alone, where one-fifth of Mexicans still work (Mekay 2003). Furthermore, in the export/*maquiladora* manufacturing sector, jobs have below-poverty wages—typically between one-quarter and one-half what it costs to provide basic necessities (Rosales 2006). Workers in the informal sector have even lower wages and no benefits, and many find themselves in unstable marginal jobs. There is no unemployment compensation, and only slightly more than half of the population had benefit coverage for health services, old age pensions, and disability and widowhood through the public social security system (Fleck and Sorrentino 1994, 28).

NAFTA and its interconnected reforms (currency devaluation, inflation, slower economic growth, high interest rates, and the withdrawal of
government support) created irreparable damage. For the commercial
sector (chapter 7), the devaluation affected the capacity to import and
bankrupted thousands of farms and businesses. For workers, the 1994 devaluation destroyed an estimated 1 million formal sector jobs; destroyed
low-wage jobs, causing millions of layoffs (Mayer 2002, 8); and diminished
domestic alternatives for displaced rural workers. These were the final
blow to a precarious and inefficient, but functioning, rural system.

The reforms created a pool of unemployed workers, further exacer-
bating the U.S.-Mexico wage gap. Migration to the United States became
a more attractive option. These factors propelled migrants first out of
rural areas and then out of the country; labor dislocation became rural
dislocation and then national dislocation.

Migrant Origins and Characteristics

For most of the twentieth century, migration involved predominantly agricultural labor from rural Mexico (Fussell 2004, 937). Migrants tended to be
male and relatively uneducated. The Bracero Program (1942–64) created
migration paths from rural central-western Mexico. The social networks
established in that period continue to fuel migrants in the contemporary
period.

Based on their data set of twenty-five Mexican communities (1987–92),
Massey and Espinosa (1997) find that economic deprivation and residence in
an agrarian community are strong predictors for the first migration trip to
the United States of undocumented workers. This "rural poor–emigration"
link requires at least two qualifications. First, the most destitute rural
workers are less likely to migrate. The mid-1990s migration from Zacate-
cas, for example, appeared to be of small landholders. They saw migration
as a better option than the corn production in which they were engaged
and were more likely to migrate than the extremely poor or better-off
rural residents (quoted in Lugo 2007b). Fox and Bada also find that the
more economically marginal have a lower probability of migration (2008,
441). These conclusions replicate earlier migration studies that found that
the first transnational labor migrants usually did not come from the very
bottom of the socioeconomic hierarchy but from the lower middle ranges

(Portes 1979; Portes and Rumbaut 1990). More recent research finds lower migration rates from rural municipalities with indigenous speaking residents (Martinez 2007). Individuals in the middle range have enough resources to absorb the costs and risks of the trip but are not so affluent to find foreign labor unattractive. Of course there are exceptions to these generalizations, such as the estimated twenty thousand primary school teachers who had left Mexico by 1996, had acquired work permits, but were working as unskilled laborers (Lugo 2006).

Second, we must be cautious in attributing motives based on just demographic and human capital characteristics. The longitudinal and comparative perspective developed by Massey in the MMP presents a multitude of significant findings. One is that the typical cost-benefit calculation of the migration decision ignores the role of accumulated social capital. Massey and colleagues have documented that increased out-migration makes subsequent migration more likely by reducing the risk and cost for later migrants who can benefit from the knowledge, assistance, and community organizations of those who went before them regarding the journey, work, and housing options at the place of destination. Thus, the experience of early migrants differs significantly from that of later migrants. Accumulated social capital contributes to the diversity of the migrant stream, making it "increasingly independent of the conditions that originally caused it" (1994, 1496). As the qualities (and quantities) of the migrant streams change, so too do the networks and institutions in the United States.

The classic rural stream has been diversified with skilled migrants and migrants of urban origin. More recently, displaced urban workers from Nezahualcoyotl (Mexico City region), Guadalajara, Monterrey, Toluca, Puebla, Morelia, León, Acapulco, and Veracruz have joined the migratory streams. Many moved from the primary industrial cities to northern export-oriented industrial cities or coastal cities specializing in tourism and trade (Fussell 2004). The stream of migrants to the northern Mexican border is demographically similar to the new urban stream of migrants to the United States (Roberts et al. 1999). Hernandez-Leon's case study of the industrial center of Monterrey demonstrates how skilled and semi-skilled urban workers came to join migrant streams. The neoliberal reforms in Mexico in the 1990s involved industrial restructuring, creating unemployment. They also transformed the traditional social welfare and labor guarantees, removing Mexico's safety net. Many of those trained and skilled displaced workers migrated to Texas, where they acquired jobs in the oil tools and technology industry (2004, 426–27).

Several factors have boosted the demographic diversity of migrant flow, which now includes children, the elderly, women, various social classes, the unmarried, and linguistically and culturally distinct ethnic groups (Hanson 2006). Consequently, migrants have a wider range of intentions, such as staying rather than returning or seeking year-long urban employment not seasonal agricultural work typical of former rural migrants (Fussell 2004, 939). While the number of urban-origin migrants is growing, a majority still comes from rural areas (Durand et al. 2001; Fox and Bada 2008; Marcelli and Cornelius 2001; Roberts et al. 1999). As the president of a producers' association in Sabino Cepeda, Puebla said, "Until we are offered a price which we can live off, people will continue going to the U.S. It is not possible to live in the countryside without decent prices for our production" (Oxfam 2003, 6).

Migrant Flows: Volume

In chapter 1, I argued that the central theme of this book is time-sensitive—the 1990s is the crucial decade. The thesis of dual labor displacement highlights the interaction of volume and timing of migration. The Mexican-origin population living in the United States is estimated to be around 30 million. I offer five comparisons that contextualize the estimated size of the migratory flow. For example, the total population of Mexico in 1955 was 30 million. The Mexican population receiving U.S. permanent residency in 1986 was estimated to equal 17 percent of all adult men in rural Mexico at the time (Fox and Bada 2008, 437).[12] NAFTA did nothing to reduce this number: in 2002, 14 percent of all people born in Mexican villages were living in the United States (Goodman 2007). Martin wrote that the number of Mexican-born workers in the U.S. labor force in 1997 was the equivalent of one-eighth of Mexico's total labor force and one-half of its formal sector private jobs (1998–1999, 419). A 1992 Mexican government survey found that 8 percent of the Mexican respondents had been to the United States and 17 percent had a household member there. By 1997, these numbers had risen to 9 percent and 21 percent, respectively

(Massey and Zenteno 2000). It is clear that U.S. migration has seized a significant fraction of the Mexican population.

Migrant remittances (dollars) also permit a rough (albeit methodologically problematic) estimation of the foreign-born.[13] Mexico is among the top three remittance recipients in the world. The amount rose from about $3.67 billion in 1995 to nearly $24 billion in 2006. As Wise (2003) has estimated, "One out of five Mexican households depends to some extent on wage remittances sent by family members working in the United States." Meanwhile, an IDB survey found that the average remittance to Mexico supported a family of 4.5 people (2007). In 1998, remittances equaled 63.3 percent of tourist expenditures and 38.5 percent of foreign direct investment. By 2003, they were 138.9 and 124.2 percent, respectively. And, in 2003, remittances ranked only second to crude oil exports as a source of foreign exchange (Hernandez-Coss 2005).

In global migration, demand (pulls) and supply (pushes) are rarely synchronized. For the United States, the "social organization of U.S. labor markets had been changed permanently so as to create a built-in, structural demand for immigrant workers" (Massey et al. 2002, 41). This shifting structural demand for labor is reminiscent of the nineteenth century, when the conjuncture of plentiful capital (both for farming and railroad construction) and cheap labor transformed the agricultural system from small plots to expansive commercial farms. West Coast farming was irrevocably reconstructed and became perpetually dependent upon cheap immigrant labor.

The Mexican crisis of the 1990s generated a potential migrant push that exceeded the number of visas allotted under the U.S. Immigration and Nationality Act of 1965. The established quota limit of 120,000 per year for the entire Western Hemisphere required Mexicans to compete with other Latin Americans. The number pales in comparison to the more than 3.6 million people waiting to receive an immigrant visa (as of January 1997). These visa-seekers already had approved petitions on file but were waiting because of limits on most categories of immigration and per-country levels. Mexico topped the approved-but-waiting list with 1,020,823 (Vaughan 1997, 5–6). The quota simply could not accommodate everyone who wanted to migrate. Without the prospect of receiving visas for work or family reunification, many opted to enter illegally and became undocumented immigrants.[14]

Estimates of the number of undocumented Mexicans vary widely and are calculated several different ways. The U.S. Census bases its estimate on the gap between visas awarded and foreign-born respondents (citizens and noncitizens). Martin uses the number of apprehensions to plot the flow over time (Martin 1998–1999). To show the rise in flows in the 1990s, I use the number of mismatches in the Social Security files. The INS estimated that in 1975, there were as many as 10 to 12 million aliens illegally in the country (with 85 percent from Mexico). More recently, Passel and Cohn (2011) have estimated the 2010 illegal population at 11.2 million (with 58 percent from Mexico). By 2007, according to the U.S. Census Current Population Survey (CPS) and the Department of Homeland Security (DHS), the number had stabilized or even begun to decline. This could have been due to the U.S. economic downturn as well as increased border enforcement.

Migrant Flows: Timing

The migratory flow was not evenly distributed over time; it grew substantially in the 1990s. A survey of a sample of Mexican-born individuals living in the United States finds that almost 50 percent arrived in the 1990–2000 period (fig. 8.1). In chapter 2, I presented my analysis of the Census data for the five states, the findings from the Dalton survey, and anecdotal evidence such as the rise in asylum applications and the increase in Mexican consulates. Even the Mexican government acknowledged the decade of soaring migration and in 2000 established Grupo Beta—a program to protect migrants (during their journey in Mexico) from transnational smuggling cartels. These sources all point to a similar conclusion: migration rose significantly after 1990.

The Social Security Administration (SSA) data reflects the number of undocumented workers who have acquired employment using a fraudulent social security number. I draw this inference from the number of wage items entered into the Earnings Suspense File (ESF). The SSA creates a social security number (SSN) for new employees and payroll funds go into the Master Earnings File. If the W-2 contains erroneous information, the funds are placed into the ESF. Since its inception in 1937, bookkeeping errors have always added to the number of units in the ESF, but they are

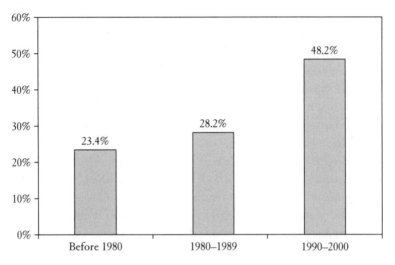

Figure. 8.1. Mexican-born residents living in the United States in 2000 by date of entry

Source: Author's calculations based on U.S. Census Bureau (2002) data. For each period, I combined the naturalized and non-U.S. citizens (22.5% and 77.5%, respectively).

removed once found. In other words, it is doubtful that the sharp rise of erroneous SSNs in the 1990s is due to bookkeeping. In light of the labor displacement transpiring in Mexico, it is reasonable to assume that many in the ESF are undocumented.

SSN "misuse" refers to situations in which individuals illegally use SSNs to obtain employment. An SSA analysis of employer's suspended wage items for a three-year period (TYs [tax years] 1996 through 1998) showed that approximately 96 percent of the reported items contained "irregularities" such as: (1) SSNs that were unassigned; (2) SSNs that were assigned to different individuals; and (3) SSNs simultaneously used two or more times (SSA 2001a). The ESF data show the number of mismatches growing at an accelerated rate (see fig. 1.1). A 2002 SSA report indicated that *96 percent* of ESF wages currently in the file had been posted since TY 1970. The number shot up after the 1986 Immigration Reform and Control Act (IRCA), which mandated that employers verify an employee's work status by examining a passport, birth certificate, SSN card, or alien documentation papers. This increase ensued despite the removal from the file workers who were "regularized" under the same law, having received amnesty, a path to citizenship, and a claim on their previous earnings. This measure, as is true of most, certainly underestimates the number of illegal aliens: some employers hire workers off the books without a W-2; some workers borrow or rent authentic social security cards; and others use an ITIN.[15] Hernandez-Leon, for example, describes a skilled worker from Monterrey who entered the United States legally on a tourist visa and then borrowed employment documents to get a job (2004, 442). I treat the ESF numbers as indicating a trend: the rise in the 1990s.

In 1995, the number of new wage items placed into the ESF overtook the all-time high of 1986 and continued its steep climb. Since 1990, the ESF has grown by an average of 5 million items per year, and the annual increase reached a high of 8.4 million in TY 1999. In that year, the ESF held a total of 212 million suspended wage items (SSA 2001a). A relatively small number of employers account for a disproportionate share of the suspended items and dollars. In 1996, for example, about three thousand employers (one twentieth of 1 percent of all employers) accounted for 30 percent of all suspended wage items. In analyzing the service sector, a SSA OIG study found one Chicago employer who issued over 17,400 W-2 wage reports in 1996. This employer supplied temporary labor to approximately 150 client companies in the Chicago metropolitan area and hired up to 300 temporary workers on a daily basis to perform light industrial work such as packing and assembly work and loading and unloading trucks. The employer had a 367 percent increase in suspended W-2s between TY 1993 and TY 1996.

In addition to the temporary work and service industries, OIG confirmed that the "Unauthorized Noncitizen Workforce" in the agricultural sector was a major contributor to SSN misuse. Several of the agricultural employers interviewed by OIG acknowledged that large numbers of their workers were unauthorized noncitizens. The employers told OIG that they examined various types of employment eligibility documents, but they knew many of them might be fraudulent (SSA 1999). In 2001, the SSA reported on California and Florida employers who deposited 100 or more wage units into the ESF between 1996 and 1998 (SSA 2001b). Looking at the top ten agricultural employers from each state, the SSA concluded that SSN misuse in the agricultural industry was widespread. About six of every ten wage items submitted did not match: two employers submitted over 7,000 SSNs that the SSA had never issued; another submitted over

900 duplicates in the three-year period. In chapter 2, I presented some of the SSA's findings for the five states in my sample. As one of the detained poultry-processing workers said, "They ask for your papers, but they don't look at them very hard" (Constable 1995).

Conclusion

The vertiginous rise in illegal immigration occurs at the conjuncture of a socially constructed pull from the U.S. and a crisis- and reform-induced push from Mexico. The migrant pull into the United States has some market-driven elements ("jobs that nobody wants"); it also has industry-driven, socially constructed elements (profit and labor crises). The economic crises and reforms in Mexico and their associated migratory push continue to distort the U.S. labor market.

My research suggests two conceptual shifts, introduced in chapter 3. First, the historical boundary of the segmented labor market is no longer impenetrable. Immigrants do continue to occupy secondary-sector jobs (lower wages, few benefits, and undesirable working conditions) such as agriculture, construction, and housekeeping, but they also acquire primary sector jobs in trucking (Milkman 2006), in factories, and elsewhere. Second, the boundary dividing primary- and secondary-sector firms is no longer immutable. Firms that historically belonged to the primary sector have restructured under globalization and crossed the boundary to become secondary-sector firms. The stable arrangements of firms and labor markets under monopoly capitalism weakened with the demise of Fordism. Kallenberg (2003) describes the changes in industrial societies and characterizes the variety of transformations that firms undertook in pursuit of flexibility in both the production and employment systems. He focuses on the firms that increasingly reassign a portion of their employment to nonstandard work. But clearly some firms desire to locate their *entire* employment system within the realm of nonstandard work arrangements. As immigration increased in the 1990s, those preexisting and new secondary-sector industries could draw on an immigrant labor force. Globalization and the increased labor supply provided firms the possibility of shifting their production processes and becoming secondary-sector firms.

And for Mexico, the economic reforms generated additional migratory pushes. Emigrants who made their way to the United States sometimes found themselves without access to public social services and under legal and societal scrutiny. For Mexican-born undocumented emigrants, the distress is captured in the comment of the young woman "Por qué nací yo del lado equivocado?"[16] This is the story of how Mexico, the beautiful, became Mexico, the wrong side.

This brings us close to the end of the chicken trail. My examination of Mexican commercialized poultry production (chapter 7) sheds light on the globalization/free trade debate in a number of ways. The industry data demonstrate the importance of using a more encompassing concept of globalization. It must include, as others have, the 1982 debt crisis and the subsequent pressures for neoliberal reforms. In describing the commercial sector, however, I have argued that it must be expanded further to include those "domestic policies" that resulted from Mexico's attempts to traverse earlier phases of globalization. Using a world-systems/dependency perspective, it is easier to understand how industry and the *traspatios* were first created and then transformed. NAFTA provided the final blow because it simultaneously eliminated trade protection, guaranteed prices, and sponsored subsidies in a way that had not occurred before. And by severing the traditional relationships between the Mexican government and rural producers, NAFTA also severed the relationship between Mexico and its citizens.

9

The Global Dilemma: Summary and Reflections

Although this book has analyzed only one commodity, it was with the promise that the poultry trail would synthesize the complex processes associated with the recent wave of globalization. Since 1980, poultry production has been altered by U.S. industrial changes, U.S. labor displacement, global trade relations, Mexican industrial changes, Mexican labor displacement, and Mexican emigration. I began with ethnic succession in the southeastern United States. Historically there had been few Hispanics in the five states which now lead in poultry production—Alabama, Arkansas, Georgia, Mississippi, and North Carolina. In the 1990s, industries in these five states became new destinations for Hispanic (and other) immigrants.

The changes in the U.S. poultry industry in the 1980s and 1990s reflected processes unfolding in the United States. In response to earlier declining rates of profit, many manufacturers already had switched to offshore production. The remaining firms shifted to restructuring their labor pool through temporary, part-time, and subcontracted workers. These variants of labor flexibility involved an unraveling of the labor-capital pact constructed after World War II. I argued that transformations in the U.S. poultry industry created conditions of labor conflict that were ameliorated by hiring immigrants. If illegal immigrants moved into an "occupational vacuum," it was a vacuum created by industry restructuring and labor conflict. Immigration eviscerated and gutted more than poultry, it eviscerated labor organization and employment opportunities for African Americans.

In addition to creating a new environment for labor conflict, industry transformations significantly augmented production and exports. Free trade did more than introduce U.S. poultry to Mexican markets; it contributed to a transformation of Mexican production. What had been a multitiered system, ranging from commercial to barnyard production, was converted into an oligopolistic system. Free trade fostered the end of the Mexican rural subsistence system. Surplus labor was pushed out of rural areas and into the northbound migrant stream.

The theories of comparative advantage and free trade have been promoted since the nineteenth century. But as early as 1841, the economist Friedrich List criticized the Law of Comparative Advantage as nothing more than a British doctrine designed to prevent the growth of other nations that might be potential competitors. Since then, many others have criticized free trade as a hegemonic ideology that falsely posits the universal and democratic benefits of free trade. It is undeniably the case that free trade is capable of contributing to the general good. It is also capable of producing what economists call externalities or what the military calls collateral damage. Regrettably, the "externalities" of economic theory become the social problems of nations and the tragedies of individuals. What free trade and neoliberal restructuring take away, individuals seek to regain through migration. And, what the WTO takes away, emigrants now seek to recoup through national and international conventions on migrants' rights.

The Externalities of Immigration

By 2000, there was a steady stream of migrants moving north. The flow of Mexican migrants to the United States violated early expectations about NAFTA that predicted little or no effect on immigration. Pro-immigrant advocates, both in the United States and in Mexico, endorse the migrant flow under the banner "they take the jobs that nobody wants." The first underlying assumption is that immigrants are entering a segmented labor market that is impenetrable. This means that those immigrants, without human capital, language, or legal status, will remain confined to certain occupational niches and therefore will not be in competition with native labor. The second underlying assumption is that the landscape for firms is immutable: only those industries that lie outside of the monopolist sector will hire principally from the secondary labor market. The poster highlighting these two premises could read, "Do *you* want to work on the poultry disassembly line?"

The notion of a segmented labor market was a corollary of the analysis of the interaction between monopoly capital and internal labor markets. Edwards (1973) linked the macroeconomic dynamics to the specifics of labor markets. During the phase of monopoly capitalism, the two sectors, with their corresponding labor markets, seemed relatively stable. Little cross-sector mobility was observed for either industries or workers. The post-Fordist period, however, brought radical shifts in both production and employment. In pursuit of flexibility, industries that historically had been part of the monopoly sector, with its well-endowed labor contracts, turned to the informal sector and secondary labor markets. They abandoned internal labor market mechanisms and embraced nonstandard work arrangements such as temporary and part-time work (Kallenberg 2003).

In pursuit of flexibility, the industry described in this book opted for insourcing (migrants). The two underlying assumptions of the justification "they take the jobs that nobody wants" are at odds with today's reality. First, migrants are not confined to the secondary sector; they have entered multiple occupational niches beyond agriculture. Second, recent economic shifts have driven industries out of the monopoly sector. In other words, the landscape for firms is no longer immutable. The restructured U.S. economy no longer has industries cleanly divided into those strata: what used to be thought of as the monopoly capital sector has eroded, and industries have outsourced and insourced. Globalization changed the nature of industries and their labor markets.

"Who Speaks for the Negro?" In 1965, Robert Penn Warren asked this question in the face of the split in the African American community and the continuing struggle for civil rights. The South has changed. Historically the South hosted a secondary labor market. The majority of jobs were secondary-market jobs, where most southern blacks worked. Immigration altered the occupational opportunities for African Americans. Theorists take it as a given that during major economic transitions, particularly cycles of creative destruction, certain occupations, certain communities, and even certain racial groups may be displaced. When NAFTA advocates identified new types of agricultural production in Mexico, for example, they also contemplated the annihilation of existing modes of rural production. But the ethnic succession in the southeastern United States was socially constructed, not just the result of creative destruction coming from the invisible hand of the market.

This was not the first time that African Americans workers have found their place in the occupational hierarchy challenged by immigrant labor. In 1895, Booker T. Washington spoke to the assembly of industrialists at the Atlanta Exposition. He counseled them not to look "to the incoming of those of foreign birth and strange tongues and habits for the prosperity of the South" but instead to "cast down your bucket among these people who have, without strikes and labour wars, tilled your fields, cleared your forests, built your railroads and cities, and brought forth treasures from the bowels of the earth, and helped make possible this magnificent representation of the progress of the South" ([1895] 1974).

Philip Randolph, a prominent black leader and president of the Brotherhood of Sleeping Car Porters, supported the passage of the Immigration Act of 1924 even though he preferred *complete* immigration restriction: "Instead of reducing immigration to 2 percent of the 1890 quota, we favor reducing it to nothing. . . . [T]his country is suffering from immigrant indigestion" (Briggs 2001, 120).

Many authors have lamented the deepening plight of African American men, for whom they foresee a depressing future. The U.S. Census counted 4,878,047 black men aged 20 to 39 in 1990 and 5,060,445 in 2000. Researchers conclude that black men are not doing well; the huge pool of poorly educated black men are more disconnected from the mainstream than Hispanics or whites; finishing high school is the exception in the inner cities; even when the economy was growing in the 1990s, young black men made little improvement; and incarceration rates keep rising.[1] Jobless levels are high, and trends are worsening. In 2000, 65 percent of black male high school dropouts in their twenties were jobless (that is, unemployed, not looking, or incarcerated). That figure rose to 72 percent in 2004. Having a high school degree reduced that rate only slightly.

The Census estimate of around 5 million black men aged 20 to 39 is less than the 2010 estimate of 11.2 million illegal immigrants in the United States. It is generally believed, however, that these groups are *not* labor-market equivalents and that the absence of legal and illegal immigrants would do little to solve the unemployment problem of African American men. In addressing the nonsubstitutability of these two populations (as well as that of white teens), scholars enumerate several job-labor force mismatches: geographic location, labor market information, human capital, and job desirability. In addition, scholars point to other mutually reinforcing processes such as network hiring, employer stereotypes about differential productivity, and African Americans' loss of interest in those jobs.

In general, these explanations may hold some truth, but this thought experiment leads to a problematic conclusion for the society at large. As Borjas reflects on the immigrant harm to the employment opportunities of native workers, "The dramatic increase in wage inequality that occurred in the 1980s and the 1990s raises serious social, economic, and political concerns for the United States. And the fact that part of this increased can be linked to immigration raises equally serious concerns amount immigration policy" (1999, 63). I join Borjas and others in situating the immigration process in a wider historical context.

Even Cesar Chavez, subsequently raised to the iconic status of patron saint of "La Raza," knew that the threat of immigration was fear not of another race but of job competition. In 1969, Chavez, along with Sen. Walter Mondale (D-Minn.) and Ralph Abernathy, head of the Southern Christian Leadership Conference, led a march to the Mexican border to protest illegal immigration. Chavez's fight was for the labor rights of agricultural workers—"la lucha" not for just for the civil rights of the Mexican minority.

And who speaks for workers? Historically, Taylorism was associated with union strength, primary labor markets, and an oligopolistic economy. In this story, Taylorism is associated with union weakness. Historically, Taylorism was associated with a tight labor market. In this story, legal and illegal migrants augment the labor supply. In addition, structural changes in the labor-management regime were accompanied by ideological shifts. The legal shift from "workers' rights" to "individual rights" has brought about an asymmetry in organizational power between management and labor. Firms and industries still organize as collectivities; workers present themselves as individuals.

The Externalities of Free Trade

U.S. producers benefited from the North American Free Trade Agreement in a number of ways. They benefited from a drop in Mexican tariffs. Because U.S. producers were technologically and organizationally more advanced, they were well positioned to supply large quantities to the Mexican market. In Mexico, imports affected large and small producers. The protests of UNA identified the impact. UNA delineated industry damages resulting from the trade openings. In tracing the effects of global integration on Mexico poultry production, I argued that free trade, prices, and markets were major conveyor belts "battering down all Chinese walls." The Mexican poultry sector had a difficult time competing with U.S. production, not only because it lacked the capital investment and technology and also because it was not the beneficiary of a parallel level of subsidized inputs available to U.S. producers (for example, the assistance the USDA offered U.S. exporters).

In addition there is the concern regarding FDI. Mayer raises a basic concern regarding the process of "unchecked" investment liberalization. When investment rules were liberalized, foreign firms entered into domestic production. The impact of foreign firms, however, is greater than that suggested by their sheer market share. Industry concentration and firm annihilation are two consequences. Mayer's concern (described in chapter 7) is that as such expansion continues, all production would be carried out by foreign firms (2002, 20). I would describe this scenario as the dark side of globalization.

Trade and capital openings transformed the producers' environment, resulting in an incremental loss of the domestic market; the elimination of the middle stratum; and the entry of two foreign subsidiaries, which became the second- and third-largest producers for the domestic market. These transformations did not lead to massive labor displacement and cannot be tied directly to migration; nevertheless, UNA complaints substantiate the nature of the trade impact. UNA was vocal; it exercised "voice," as Hirschman called it. Peasants more typically resorted to what Hirschman called "exit"—they emigrated.

SAGARPA (2007b) describes the role of poultry in the rural areas as part of a bundle of activities contributing to rural survival. Between 1980 and 2000, poultry production was transformed from a stratified yet sustainable system (ranging from large to *traspatio*) to basically a modernized, capital-intensive one. In this process, the Mexican countryside, which had been dotted with self-sufficient but not very efficient family production units, increasingly became a place of impoverished and abandoned villages. Small farmers left the countryside; then they left the country.

The post-NAFTA labor displacement was unlike earlier ones in two important regards. This time, no new low-skilled jobs were being created in the countryside, and the domestic and export assembly industries were weak engines of growth. They could not absorb the rising demand for employment. As subsistence producers, rural households were only a minor link in the poultry production chain. Nevertheless, for the first time, they were exposed to market forces without the buffer of government subsidies. In this way, NAFTA did more than create free trade and capital flows; it undermined rural subsistence.

Emporiophobia and Migration

The interaction between trade and immigration continues to be an important and contentious topic. I have addressed the connections between globalization and labor displacement in and across two countries. The mechanisms that bind trade and immigration are neither straightforward nor singular. Many scholars have worked to disentangle the effects of NAFTA on Mexico's development; I have endeavored to do this by following the trail of chicken. To what extent can production transformations, annihilations, and reconfigurations be attributed to NAFTA?

Supporters of NAFTA in particular and neoliberalism in general have been critical of analysts who blame globalization for Mexico's ills. It is true that free trade, prices, and markets did not act in isolation: Mexican leaders were active participants in this integration. Even the Mexican government, which endorsed the idea that if agricultural producers are inefficient they should stop being farmers, encouraged more efficient agricultural production so that Mexico could export "tomatoes, not tomato pickers." But now Mexico exports both.

NAFTA and its trade-induced price drops cannot totally explain migration. Likewise, poultry cannot carry all the explanatory weight for rural displacement. To understand labor displacement in Mexico fully, I have expanded the analysis. First, in describing the shifts in industry and *traspatios,* I included three major moments of global insertion—earlier debt renegotiations, GATT, and NAFTA. They all opened Mexico to foreign trade. Second, I noted, as have others, the need to include a discussion of the pressures on Mexico to adopt neoliberal reforms. They affected Mexican production because they weakened the state–civil society relations. Third, I have included those domestic policies which resulted from Mexico's earlier twentieth-century attempts to overcome prior globalization pressures by establishing autarkic development. This version of globalization is derived from a world-systems perspective, rather than the international relations perspective, and makes more transparent the consequences of Mexico's embeddedness in the global system.

NAFTA had the most notable effects on poultry production and its connection to migration because it provided the final blow to both Mexican domestic subsidies and trade protection. Davis describes the neoliberal trend as the "poisoned chalice of devaluation, privatization, removal of import controls and food subsidies, enforced cost recovery in health and education, and ruthless downsizing of the public sector" (2004, 18). These are the policies that rearranged relationships within the quartet of the Mexican government, Mexican commercial producers, Mexican farmers, and Mexico's trade partners.

Implications for the Immigration Debate

Unfortunately, the immigration debate is stuck on the moral plane, divided between groups pejoratively referred to as "racist" and "bleeding-heart liberals." There are numerous misspecified axioms in this debate; two have been challenged here. First, immigrant advocates treat the U.S. labor force as though it is still segmented, leaving the "jobs that nobody wants" to immigrants. The debate must look beyond the often cited lettuce worker. Second, what appears as segmented labor market vacancies are really the outcome of a split labor market conflict (Bonacich 1972). We must ask how those became the jobs that nobody wants. In the case described here, the causal ordering between native labor leaving jobs and immigrant labor taking does not follow the conventional wisdom. African Americans worked those jobs. And after the ethnic succession, they continued to live in poultry counties and experienced relatively high rates of unemployment and poverty. Scholars, particularly those using cross-sectional data sets to adjudicate the labor displacement theory, may erroneously conclude that "they take the jobs that nobody wants" because these analyses lack a longitudinal perspective. Case studies may capture the historical process, but they are susceptible to being idiosyncratic. By using data and reports from governments, industry, and academics as well as media reports and my own ethnography, I conclude that labor-management conflict contributed to ethnic succession.

In this book, I have not addressed the rise of anti-immigrant sentiments in the United States. To accomplish this, I believe, we need the understanding not just of psychology but also of the connection between racism and underdevelopment. Borrowing from Wallerstein (2001), racism is more than xenophobia, and underdevelopment is more than poverty. They are both part of the process by which our historical system has been organized. This global system is built on an unequal distribution of goods. The consequences include the dual labor displacements described in this book: migration and a growing native-born underclass. The current conflict over immigration can be better understood by placing it in the context of U.S. transformations, particularly the erosion of the social pacts created during the New Deal and expanded under the Great Society programs of the 1960s. Elsewhere I employ this template to analyze the conflict over birthright citizenship (Schwartzman 2011).

Public Policy for a New "American Dilemma"

The insularity of individual public policy debates (immigration reform, NAFTA, and domestic economic development) makes it difficult to understand the more general societal causes and consequences of immigration. We need to put the labor market effects of globalization back into the immigration debate.

The journey from analysis to public policy is complex. Short-term policy solutions on the U.S. side might include unionizing immigrant workers, a strategy recently embraced by some unions. Another solution would be to offer amnesty for undocumented workers. These would help create a single labor market and eliminate the threat of degrading working conditions and wages and immigrants undercutting labor organization. On the other hand, in times of recession, expanding the labor pool would exacerbate an already high unemployment rate.

Long-term solutions for the United States require a rethinking of the neoliberal principle of unfettered cross-border labor flows. Labor flexibility, both outsourcing and insourcing, is offered as the panacea for the economic difficulties of the United States, but it has been costly for U.S. labor. Beginning with case-by-case attacks on unions and aided by anti-union NLRB decisions such as the one on Harter Equipment Inc. (1986), workers have found it nearly impossible to defend their standard of living and economic security. Globalization and immigration have become part of a new American Dilemma. The United States is a nation that generates jobs that nobody wants, jobs that people do want that are shipped overseas, and other jobs that people want but for which they are unqualified. Globalization and the new American Dilemma are two aspects of the same phenomena.

Unfortunately, solutions for the United States will not address the global problem, which has half of the developing world packing suitcases for the journey north. International migration rates rise are on the rise. In 2009, it was estimated that worldwide there were 214 million immigrants (one human being out of every 33).

Theoretically, delinking global trade from global migration is a mistake. Advocates of NAFTA who were unequivocally certain that it would promote the well-being of all Mexicans need to reconsider the process of economic integration as it unfolded. In looking at the volume and persistence of illegal immigration, even in the face of heightened border control, Cornelius argues that the only policy alternative that will work is a "developmental approach" that creates a Mexican alternative to emigration (2004, 3). Many people who were forced to migrate for economic survival would remain in their country of birth if economic alternatives existed. NAFTA has not provided alternatives. In fact, Stiglitz thinks that the treaty has harmed Mexico's ability to build an "independently productive economy" (2004).

To the extent that NAFTA might have created some employment, its success is threatened by the growing competition for assembly work in

China, particularly since 2001, when China joined the WTO. Not only does China supply a larger portion of world exports, but its contribution to U.S. imports is also on the rise. In some areas it is in direct competition with Mexico (Iranzo and Ma 2006). Long-term (and seemingly utopian) policy solutions for global well-being would involve revising some of the practices of free trade and neoliberal restructuring. The challenge is to accomplish this without embracing, as Wise called it, "globophobia."

Solutions for Mexico seem limited. Mexico has recently expanded its foreign policy to include advocating for its immigrant-citizens in the United States. WTO and NAFTA weakened the economic solvency of many nations. What free trade and neoliberal restructuring took away, governments of emigrant nations seek to recoup for their emigrant citizens through international organizations such as UNESCO's International Convention on the Protection of the Rights of All Migrant Workers and Members of Their Families.[2] Unable to protect its economy in the face of WTO agreements, the Mexican government attempts to protect its emigrant citizens (and their remittances) through its foreign policies. The Mexican government, often in coalition with U.S. pro-immigrant groups, sends amicus letters for U.S. legal proceedings, lobbies U.S. congresspersons and presidents, and submits complaints to UNESCO.

Globalization is not a static process. Shifting global phases bring new benefits and new unintended consequences. However, as I mentioned earlier, the benefits for some nations become the social problems of other nations and the tragedies of individuals. Mutually beneficial global solutions depend on the involvement and compromises on the part of all stakeholders—those that benefit and those that suffer. The critics of WTO, trade agreements, and neoliberal reforms argue that we have not yet found the correct balance. The rise of societal conflict in impoverished countries and the impending global food crisis suggest that immigration will continue. Accompanying this are new conflicts between immigrants and the sometimes inhospitable citizens of developed nations. We must be hopeful that the analysis and discourse about these matters can rise above the passions of the moment. We must work for the future of the unemployed and displaced in the United States (and the rest of the developed world) *and* for the unemployed and evicted from Mexico (and the rest of the developing world).

We are in the throes of a new American Dilemma and of a new Global Dilemma.

Notes

Preface

1. U.S. government documents include the following terms: unauthorized noncitizens residing illegally, unauthorized immigrant population, unauthorized noncitizen workforce, undocumented, nonimmigrant overstays (in reference to visas), EWI (entry without inspection), illegal, and out-of-status unauthorized residents.

2. I subsequently found a three-part series published in the *Los Angeles Times* with the same title. Katz (1996) uses the term, but in a more literal fashion.

Chapter 1

1. There is a positive association (bivariate correlation of .385, significant at the .01 level [one-tail]) between the number of Hispanics in 2000 and the number of poultry firms in 1997. My calculations are based on data from the 483 counties in those five states from the U.S. Census and Economic Census.

Chapter 2

1. Parks, Alphonso. Conversations with author, 2004.
2. Marisala (pseud.). Conversation with author. Birmingham, AL, July 2004.
3. Nathan. Conversation with author. Birmingham, AL, July 2004.

4. Ethnic succession in poultry occurred later than in other meats. Stull and Broadway explored meatpacking workers in Garden City as it confronted the challenges accompanying an influx of new immigrants.

5. As one immigrant official unfavorably described the system, those who request asylum don't have to pay a smuggler (Briggs 2001, 181).

6. "The census in 1970 was the first to include a separate question specifically on Hispanic origin, although it was only asked of a 5-percent sample of households" (Guzmán 2001).

7. In the ranking of total population growth between 1990 and 2000 for all 3,141 U.S. counties, three of Georgia's counties ranked in the top ten: second with an increase of 123.2 percent, fourth with 103.2 percent, and seventh with a 96.3 percent. Author's calculation from U.S. Census files.

8. Not all Mexican migrants speak Spanish. In a Tennessee court case of child neglect, the judge ordered the immigrant mother to "learn English." The journalist noted that in Lebanon, twenty miles east of Nashville (population just over 20,000), it was once rare to hear a foreign language. "Now Lebanon has become home to more than 1,200 foreign born agricultural and manufacturing workers, including about 400 whose primary language is Mixteco" (Barry 2005).

9. When employers submit a Wage and Tax Statement (W-2) for a new employee, the SSA creates a new account and payroll funds go into the Master Earnings File (MEF), which connects earnings to earners (also called a "wage item"). If the W-2 contains erroneous information, the funds are placed into an Earnings Suspension File and a "no match" letter may be sent to the employer.

10. Author's calculations based data from the U.S. Social Security Administration (2003).

11. More recently, attempts to contact employers were halted in federal court due to concerns about errors in the SSA database that might lead to mistakenly firing or deporting legally authorized residents (Kandel 2008).

12. In 2008, the foreign-born share of workers in animal slaughtering and processing was 38 percent, divided equally between legal and unauthorized. Within the civilian labor force, 43 percent of butchers and other meat, poultry, and fish processing workers were foreign-born; of which more than half were unauthorized (Passel and Cohn 2009, 31–32).

13. The U.S. Census used different terms over the years. The 1970 census sampled households and included a question on "Spanish origin." The Current Population Survey (CPS) referred to "Hispanic" in 1999 and "Latino" in 2009.

14. When I substituted the category "foreign-born" instead of Hispanic/Latino, the correlations were essentially the same (.173 and .362, respectively). These are all statistically significant.

15. On the "long form" used to collect detailed information from approximately one-sixth of the total U.S. population in 2000, the U.S. Census asks questions of birth, citizenship, and year of immigration. They estimate a net census undercount for unauthorized residents of 10 percent (U.S. Census n.d.).

16. Also in 2006, ICE launched a nationwide operation called "Operation Return to Sender," which resulted in twenty-three thousand arrests at worksites and other locations.

Chapter 3

1. "Native" workers may be of any ethnic background (e.g., Anglo, African American, Hispanic).

2. Dickens and Lang (1988) describe characteristics of the dual (segmented) labor and conclude that workers are not able to choose their sector of employment.

3. This theme is developed in greater detail in Schwartzman (2008).

4. Some issues were resolved at a September 2003 Camp David summit between Presidents Bush and Putin.

5. This statistic from the USDA Poultry Yearbook is slightly higher than others reported in newspaper and magazines, possibly because the "ready-to-cook" data includes bones and water weight.

6. Author's calculations based on U.S. Economic Census data. In 1992, jobs were classified as SIC 2015 and in 1997 as NAICS 311615.

7. This conclusion holds for the total sample of 483 counties (not just poultry counties). The correlation between the percentage African American population in 1990 and the presence of poultry plants in 1992 was –.145** and for 2000–1997, it was –.141**. Controlling for the individual states did not change the finding.

8. As with all CPS unemployment rates (defined as those who had no employment during the reference week, were available for work except for temporary illness, and had made specific efforts to find employment at some time during the four-week period), they be may higher if one adds the marginally attached workers, including "discouraged workers," welfare recipients, and those who were "part time for some economic reason." For the United States as a whole, the CPS estimates that augmented rate in 2000 at 7.0 percent compared to the official unemployment rate of 4.0 percent.

9. Since whites and blacks comprise the bulk of the population in many counties, this would be expected statistically.

10. The Office of Federal Contract Compliance Programs, an agency of the U.S. Department of Labor's Employment Standards Administration, enforces Executive Order 11246 and other laws that prohibit employment discrimination by federal contractors.

Chapter 4

1. Tyson, in 2007, reported that it had contracts with 6,500 growers. Independent "growers" receive chicks (usually twenty days old), feed, and technical assistance until they are retrieved by Tyson. The grower provides the facility, utilities, and labor. The contract guarantees a consistent price regardless of price changes in feed or grocery markets.

2. The meat industry was undergoing a similar contraction. By 1979 the shakeout was peaking, as smaller firms were absorbed by agribusiness. Some agribusinesses like ConAgra were involved with both meat and poultry.

3. During the Carter administration, the allowable line speed had risen from 45 to 70 birds per minute.

4. The Treasury Department required virtually all nonfarm corporations with substantial inventory to use the accrual method because it believed it better reflected real income. In effect, it reduced current writeoffs on the total cost of inventory buildup (Rich 1977).

5. USAPEEC, a nonprofit dedicated to increasing exports of U.S. poultry and eggs worldwide, has worked closely with the Foreign Agricultural Service (FAS), an arm of the USDA, to help U.S. agriculture establish its presence in the global marketplace. This included administering export promotion funds allocated annually by the USDA.

6. The NLRB is the federal agency that administers the National Labor Relations Act (NLRA) by conducting elections to determine whether or not employees want union representation and investigating and remedying unfair labor practices (ULPs) by employers and unions.

7. Rates vary depending on the base: some are limited to private workers and others include public sector workers. Most exclude agriculture.

8. The number of certification elections is a useful benchmark despite several methodological deficiencies. First, rates do not include the public sector, airlines, or railways. Second, in recent times, unions have promoted "card check" recognition, which occurs when employers agree to recognize a union that proves (through an employee card check) that it has a majority of worker support. "Card check" avoids the delays associated with NLRB elections and minimizes

the opportunities for employers to engage in aggressive anti-union activities. Seen from the employers' perspective, it is "a somewhat dubious system where a union gets most of the workers at a firm to sign a pledge card and thus avoids NLRB-supervised secret-ballot elections" (*The Economist* 2005).

9. This NLRB decision "ratified" the 1981 actions of the Reagan administration. Following PATCO's illegal walkout and refusal to obey Reagan's back-to-work order, the 11,400 striking air traffic controllers were denied reemployment, their union was decertified (1982), strikers were barred from work in other branches of the federal government, and permanent replacement workers were hired.

10. A right-to-work law secures the right of employees to decide for themselves whether or not to join or financially support a union.

11. Naturally, state profiles are more volatile because they measure the activity of a smaller work force.

12. Here and in chapter 5, I present findings based on my analysis of the NLRB data set compiled by FAST. The data set is discussed in greater detail in chapter 5.

Chapter 5

1. The title refers to "poultry and smugglers." *Polleros* is the word used by many Mexicans for coyotes (alien smugglers). It is an analogy drawn from the activity of *polleros*—people who tend to small chicks.

2. This framework is adapted from Przeworski (1985, ch. 5).

3. The FAST/NLRB data set includes 62,691 elections and 537,798 unfair labor practices. From the original FAST files, I abstracted the information for the 3,053 elections in the five states from 1983 to 2000 and then the 91 elections that transpired in poultry industries (SIC 201/NAICS 311615). The data set does not provide industry code for ULPs, so I matched company names in the ULP file with those listed by USDA-FSIS to isolate the 718 cases.

4. An RD election also could result from a dispute between two unions.

5. These are ULPs that were filed and survived the initial investigation as being in violation of the NLRA.

6. An early version of this model for the Alabama case was presented in Schwartzman (2009).

7. The remainder are Decertification Elections (RDs).

8. Interview with author. Birmingham, AL, July 2004.

9. There are numerous qualitative and quantitative studies of the "displacement" argument that I have summarized in Schwartzman (2008).

Chapter 6

1. The global leader until 2004, when Brazil exported more.

2. In 2005, approximately 93 percent of the imports came from the United States; the rest came from Chile (UNA 2007, 8).

3. SISEMA reports both the number of birds and tons of meat. For the comparisons over time, I use the weight measure. "Total poultry imports" is a slight overestimation because it includes turkey and some other fowl. There are other minor concerns with data comparability. The first change in the codes used by the Mexican government to categorize commodities that were traded occurred in July of 1988. Since the data from January to June 1988 is not compatible with the rest of the year, I begin my calculations with 1989. The second change in the customs code took place in 1997, but data are comparable. In 2002, Mexico amended its customs categories to reflect the new World Customs Organization codes.

4. Article 2 of the WTO Agreement on Safeguards identifies a surge as occurring when "a product is imported into a country in such increased quantities, absolute or relative to domestic

production, and under such conditions as to cause or threaten to cause serious injury to the domestic industry that produces like or directly competitive products" (Sharma 2005).

5. Author's calculations and analysis based on price data from SAGARPA 2007a and the Consumer Price Index from Banco de Mexico.

6. Gonzales et al. converted current prices into 1994 prices (2003, 74).

7. By 2001, Tyson's total capacity in Mexico was approximately 2.2 million birds per week (PR Newswire 2001).

Chapter 7

1. The law created the National Foreign Investment Commission and established the National Foreign Investment Registry to track investments.

2. Ejidos are communally owned lands allocated on the basis of individual (or cooperative) usufruct and tenure.

3. Trust Funds for Rural Development initiated in 1954 (Fideicomisos Instituidos en Relación con la Agricultura, FIRA).

4. Funds came from Mexico's development bank Nacional Financiera (Nafin), in which the federal government holds 99.9 percent of the shares. They were administered through FAAEPPA, which was created to assist *ejidatarios* and small proprietors (Fondo de Apoyo a Agrupaciones Ejidales y Pequenos Propietarios Avicolas).

5. This program (Fondo de Garantía y Fomento para la Agricultura, Ganadería y Avicultura) was one of several administered by a second-tier bank—the Trust Funds for Rural Development (FIRA).

6. Although typically described in terms of support for small producers, CONASUPO (National Company of Popular Subsidies) included parastatals producing fertilizers, seeds and inputs, and credit and subsidies (King 2006, 6). Livestock producers also benefited from subsidized grain.

7. The 1941 Mexican Chambers Law, following the logic of corporatism, required all firms to join official business organizations, which subsequently would be regulated by the state. Shadlen offers an excellent discussion of Mexico's corporatist institutions and the state–civil society association (2000, 77).

8. This included contracting Burson and Marsteller, a Washington D.C. lobbying firm.

9. A TRQ establishes a two-tier tariff rate: a low (or free) rate on imports up to a certain quota level and a much higher rate on imports above that level.

10. According to Cameron and Aggarwal, maintaining an overvalued peso became more difficult by 1994 because the trade deficit required more and more of the foreign exchange reserves to close the balance of payments account (1996, 984). The authors argue that the overvalued peso may have resulted from policy errors, but those errors took place in the context of a nation held hostage by highly mobile investors looking for high returns.

11. Virgilio Arteaga Gonzalez. Interview with author, December 2007.

12. Direct employment includes everyone in the production process: workers, machine operators, administrators, managers, and owners of property. Tyson de Mexico in its vertically integrated operation includes associate "chicken growers" (Programa de Aparceria) and those who work in hatcheries and feed mills. Additional indirect employment is generated in the chain between production and consumption (Tyson Corporate).

Chapter 8

1. *Si Muero Lejos de Ti* ("If I die far from you"). This line from the famous song "México" Lindo (Beautiful Mexico) captures the nostalgia and loyalty that an immigrant felt about leaving his home land. The song continues "If I die far from you, may they say that I am asleep and may they bring me back to her (Mexico)."

2. Many have documented the connection between trade with rich countries and the fate of rural smallholders in Mexico (Avila 2008; Bacon 2007; Burstein 2007; Martinez 2007; Mekay 2003; Otero 2004; Oxfam 2003; Ros and Rodriguez 1987; Thompson 2002, and Wise 2003). Mexico joins other countries that experienced rising inequality and minimal poverty reduction following a high degree of trade openness.

3. These are also known as family farms (*huerto familiar, huerto casero*); poultry production, mostly chicken, is referred to as barnyard poultry (*aves de corral*).

4. This Project for the Production and Handling of Barnyard Poultry (Proyecto Tipo Producción y Manejo de Aves de Traspatio) was promoted under the umbrella of PESA, SAGARPA's Special Program for Nutritional Security (Programa Especial para la Seguridad Alimentaria).

5. Maria Jesus. Conversations with author. Sonora, Mexico, April, 2008.

6. In 2007, the per capita (measured) consumption of eggs in Mexico was 345. In that year, the per capita consumption was 349 in China and 250 in the United States (Poultry Site 2011).

7. Carmen Trujillo. Conversations with author. Sonora, Mexico, May, 2008

8. The percentages reported are not generalizable due to project sampling techniques (Massey, Douglas, and Zenteno 2000 or mmp.opr.princeton.edu).

9. On the eve of its 2008 expiration, President Felipe Calderón extended it until 2012.

10. Abundis reports that 80 percent of rural farmers were classified as poor and half as extremely poor (2003, 3), whereas the World Bank estimated that 42 of every 100 Mexicans live in poverty and nearly half of those in extreme poverty (Oxfam 2003, 15).

11. According to the balance sheet of a corn farmer in Puebla, he pays one third of his income to rent land on which he grows corn and has two temporary jobs because he needs money to buy insecticides and chemicals to improve the land (Oxfam 2003, 8).

12. The 1986 Immigration Reform and Control Act granted residency to undocumented immigrants who met certain requirements.

13. The 2008 drop in remittances could have resulted from (1) the same number of immigrants sending less because they became underemployed, unemployed, or experienced a rise in the cost of U.S. living; (2) a drop in number of immigrants as some return to Mexico or others are dissuaded from coming; (3) less need to send money as immigrants are joined by family members; or (4) a rise in the fees of formal sector intermediaries and banks that transfer funds.

14. Visas for immediate relatives (spouses, unmarried children under 21, and parents) of U.S. citizens are not subject to numerical limitation.

15. Individual Tax Identification Numbers (ITINs), created in 1996 by the IRS, are official U.S. tax numbers for the purpose of receiving taxes on dividends or income earned by nonresident aliens. They have been issued to illegal aliens, who sometimes use them to acquire work. From 1996 to 2002, over 5.5 million were issued.

16. She is part of the movement advocating for the "Dream Act," which would provide instate college tuition for Mexican-born undocumented high school graduates living in the United States.

Chapter 9

1. Eckholm (2006) surveys recent publications and summarizes crucial research findings. I have also included a summary of this research in Schwartzman (2008).

2. The Convention, ratified by members of the United Nations Educational, Scientific and Cultural Organization, went into force on July 1, 2003.

REFERENCES

Abundis, Monica Ramirez. 2003. "Con los pies en la tierra: Apertura agropecuaria; Universidade de Guadalajara." January 23. http://claves.udg.mx/pdf29-apertagro/ Apertura%20Agropecuaria.pdf.

Acuna, Rodolfo. 1981. *Occupied America: A History of Chicanos*. 2nd ed. New York: Harper and Row.

Alabama Development Office. 2007. "International Investment and Trade." *Alabama Profile*. http://web.archive.org/web/20070220093755/ and www.ado.state.al.us/ Alabama%20Profil.

Alonso, Maria de Lourdes Flores. 2002. *Los granos básicos en México ante la apertura comercial, 1980–2001*. Reportes de Investigación Económica, CIDE, México, Centro de Estudios Sociales y de Opinión Pública. Chamber of Deputies, September. www. diputados.gob.mx/cesop/boletines/n02/8.pdf.

Ammann, Melinda. 2002. "Breast Men: Mexican Immigrants Want to Fillet Our Chickens: The INS Is Determined to Stop Them." *Reason Magazine*, July. http:// reason.com/archives/2002/07/01/breast-men.

Aponte, Robert. 1996. "Urban Employment and the Mismatch Dilemma: Accounting for the Immigration Exception." *Social Problems* 43, no. 3 (August): 268–83.

Applebome, Peter. 1989. "Worker Injuries Rise in Poultry Industry as Business Booms." *New York Times,* November 6.

Arkansas Democrat-Gazette. 1997. "USDA May Allow Poultry Processed in Mexico into U.S." Bloomberg News Services. November 29.

Associated Press. 2005. "Mexican President's Racial Remark Criticized." May 15.

Atlas, Terry. 1996. "GOP Attacks Clinton Poultry Parley: Hyde, Others Wonder If President Aided Yeltsin Election Bid." *Chicago Tribune,* April 3.

Avila, Ricardo Monreal. 2008. "El campo mexicano y el TLC." *Diario Por Esto!*, January 17. http://fridaguerrera.blogspot.com/2008/01/el-campo-mexicano-y-el-tlc.html.

Bachoco. 2007. "Our History." Mexico: Bachoco. www.bachoco.com.mx.

Bacon, David. 2007. "What a Vote for Free Trade Means." *San Francisco Chronicle,* November 20.

Bagley, Carl, and Ricardo Castro-Salazar. 2009. *Undocumented Historias in the Desert of Dreams*. Video file, 25 minutes. http://villiers.dur.ac.uk/education/bagley//performancelong.wmv.

Barboza, David. 2001a. "Meatpackers' Profits Hinge on Pool of Immigrant Labor." *New York Times,* December 21.

———. 2001b. "Tyson Foods Indicted in Plan to Smuggle Illegal Workers." *New York Times,* December 20.

Barndt, Deborah, ed. 1999. *Women Working the NAFTA Food Chain: Women, Food and Globalization.* Toronto: Second Story Press.

Barry, Ellen. 2005. "Learn English, Judge Tells Moms." *Los Angeles Times,* February 14.

Bauer, Mary, and Mónica Ramírez. 2010. *Injustice on Our Plates: Immigrant Women in the U.S. Food Industry.* Montgomery, AL: Southern Poverty Law Center, November 20. www.splcenter.org/get-informed/publications/injustice-on-our-plates.

Bean, Frank D., and Gillian Stevens. 2003. *America's Newcomers and the Dynamics of Diversity.* New York: Russell Sage Foundation.

Becker, Edmund R., and John Thomas Delaney. 1983. "South/Non-South Differentials in National Labor Relations Board Certification Election Outcomes." *Journal of Labor Research* 4, no. 4 (December): 375–84.

Behar, Richard. 1992. "Arkansas Pecking Order." *Time Magazine* 140, no. 17 (October 26): 52. www.time.com/time/magazine/article/0,9171,976831,00.html.

Berg, Ivan, and Arne L. Kallenberg, ed. 2001. *Sourcebook of Labor Markets: Evolving Structures and Processes.* New York: Kluwer Academic.

Bobo, Kim. 2002. "Poultry Victory." *Labor Net*, May 10. www.labornet.org/news/0000/poultry.html.

Bonacich, Edna. 1972. "A Theory of Ethnic Antagonism: The Split Labor Market." *American Sociological Review* 37: 547–59.

Borjas, George J. 1999. *Heaven's Door*. Princeton, NJ: Princeton University Press.

Braverman, Harry. 1974. *Labor and Monopoly Capital*. New York: Monthly Review Press.

Breckenfeld, Gurney. 1977. "Business Loves the Sunbelt and Vice Versa." *Fortune* 95 (June): 132–46. UA microfilm 4932.

Brewer, Cynthia A., and Trudy A. Suchan. 2001. *Mapping Census 2000: The Geography of U.S. Diversity. Census 2000 Special Reports*. CENSR/01. U.S. Census Bureau. www.census.gov/population/www/cen2000/atlas.html.

Briggs, Vernon M. 2001. *Immigration and American Unionism*. Ithaca, NY: Cornell University Press.

Bronfenbrenner, Kate, and Tom Juravich. 1994. "The Impact of Employer Opposition on Union Certification Win Rates: A Private/Public Sector Comparison." Cornell University ILR School, Ithaca, New York. http://digitalcommons.ilr.cornell.edu/articles/19.

Brown, Robert H. 1994. "Broiler Companies Show Increasing Returns." *Feedstuffs* 66, no. 8 (February 21).

Brown, Warren. 1979. "Union Fighting Southern Traditions as Well as Mississippi Poultry Plant." *Washington Post,* December 2.

Bruce, Gene. 1990. "Dirty Chicken." *Atlantic Monthly* 266, no. 5 (November).

Brueggemann, John, and Cliff Brown. 2003. "The Decline of Industrial Unionism in the Meatpacking Industry: Event-Structured Analyses of Labor Unrest, 1946–1987." *Work and Occupations* 30, no. 3, 327–60.

Buckmaster. 2002. "Pilgrim's Pride 10-K Report." *Buckmaster Annual Stockholder Reports.* http://buck.com/10k?tenkyear=02&idx=P&co=PPC&nam=DEM02&pw=DEM02.

Buncombe, Andrew. 2005. "U.S. Poultry Giant under Fire after Segregation Scandal Is Revealed." *Independent,* September 17. http://news.independent.co.uk/world/americas/articles312981.ece.

Burke, Garance. 2008. "Union and States Try Recruiting Farm Workers from Mexico." Associated Press, April 29.

Burstein, John. 2007. *U.S.-Mexico Agricultural Trade and Rural Poverty in Mexico*. Washington, DC: Woodrow Wilson International Center for Scholars. www.wilsoncenter.org/topics/pubs/Mexico_Agriculture_rpt_English1.pdf.

Business Week. 1983. "The Slaughter of Meatpacking Wages." June 27.

——. 1984. "Hormel: Trying to Trim the Industry's Fattest Wages to Keep Making Money in Meat." September 10.

Cameron, Maxwell A., and Vinod K. Aggarwal. 1996. "Mexican Meltdown: States, Markets and Post-NAFTA Financial Turmoil." *Third World Quarterly* 57, no. 5, 975–87.

Canales, Alejandro I. 2000. "International Migration and Labour Flexibility in the Context of NAFTA." *International Social Science Journal* 165 (September): 409–19.

Castells, Manuel, and Roberto Laserna. 1989. "The New Dependency." *Sociological Forum* 4, no. 4 (December): 535–60.

Cave, Damien. 2011. "Better Lives for Mexicans Cut Allure of Going North." *New York Times,* July 6. www.nytimes.com/interactive/2011/07/06/world/americas/immigration.html?emc=eta.

Chavez, Leo. 1992. *Shadowed Lives*. Fort Worth, TX: Harcourt Brace Jovanovich College Publishers.

Cobb, Russell. 2004. "The Chicken Hangers." *In The Fray*, February 2. www.inthefray.org/content/v/208/39.

Constable, Pamela. 1995. "Poultry Plant Workers Face Deportation; 27 Latinos Arrested in Raid by Immigration Officials." *Washington Post,* July 23.

Cord, Louise and Quentin Wodon. 2001. "Do Mexico's Agricultural Programs Alleviate Poverty? Evidence from the Ejido Sector." World Bank. http://wbln0018.worldbank.org/LAC/LACInfoClient.nsf/49a0102c9b95cf028525664b006a17a4/60f53c9a666570b385256ae80057a73d/$FILE/MXAGPRO3.PDF.

Cornelius, Wayne. 2004. "Evaluating Enhanced U.S. Border Enforcement." Migration Information Source, May 15. www.migrationinformation.org/feature/display.cfm?ID=223.

Cornelius, Wayne, and Philip L. Martin. 1993. "The Uncertain Connection: Free Trade and Rural Mexican Migration to the United States." *International Migration Review* 27: 484–512.

Dale, Jack G., Susan Andreatta, and Elizabeth Freeman. 2001. "Language and the Migrant Worker Experience in Rural North Carolina Communities." In *Latino Workers in the Contemporary South*. Edited by Arthur D. Murphy, Colleen Blanchard, and Jennifer A. Hill, 93–125. Athens: University of Georgia Press.

Davis, Mike. 2004. "Planet of Slums: Urban Involution and the Informal Proletariat." *New Left Review* 26 (March–April): 5–34.

De Janvry, Alain. 1996. *NAFTA and Agriculture: An Early Assessment*. www.agrinet.tamu.edu/trade/papers/dejanvry.pdf.

Detzner, John A., and George R. Gonzalez. 1995. "Doing Business in Post-Devaluation Mexico." National Law Center for Inter-American Free Trade. *Inter-American Trade and Investment Law* 2, no. 12 (February 3): 244.

The Development Gap. 1998. "The Failure of the Mexico Bailout." Washington, DC: The Development Gap. www.developmentgap.org/americas/Mexico/The_Failure_of_the_Mexican_Bailout.htm.

DeWalt, Billie R., and Martha W. Rees. 1994. *The End of Agrarian Reform in Mexico: Past Lessons, Future Prospects*. San Diego: Center for U.S.-Mexican Studies, University of California.

Dickens, William T., and Kevin Lang. 1988. "The Reemergence of Segmented Labor Market Theory." *American Economic Review* 78, no. 2: 129–34.

Dickens, William T., and Jonathan S. Leonard. 1985. "Accounting for the Decline of Union Membership, 1950–1980." *Industrial and Labor Relations Review* 38, no. 3 (April): 323–34.

Diebel, Linda. 1993. "Unions Not Welcome." *Toronto Star,* June 6.

Dillon, Sam. 2001. "Profits Raise Pressure on U.S.-Owned Factories in Mexican Border Zone." *New York Times,* February 15.

Dine, Philip. 1990a. "Delta Dispute Divides Blacks, White Farmers." *St. Louis Post-Dispatch* (Missouri), October 11.

———. 1990b. " National to Switch Catfish Union Praises 'Uniform Support'; Here." *St. Louis Post-Dispatch* (Missouri), October 13.

Draper, Electa. 2008. "No Tidy Answer to Ag Labor Pinch." *Denver Post,* April 15.

Duchon, Deborah A., and Arthur D. Murphy. 2001. "Introduction: From Patrones and Caciques to Good Ole Boys." In *Latino Workers in the Contemporary South*. Edited by Arthur D. Murphy, Colleen Blanchard, and Jennifer A. Hill, 1–35.

Dugger, Celia. 2006. "Condoms Sent as Foreign Aid, Made in U.S.A." *New York Times,* October 29.

Dunne, Nancy. 1987. "U.S. Offers Subsidized Poultry to Middle East." *Financial Times,* November 6.

Durand, Jorge, Verónica Lozano, and Raúl Romo. 2005. *Proyecto de Migración Mexicana Proyecto de Migración Latino Americana: Interviewer's Manual*. Mexican Migration Project. http://mmp.opr.princeton.edu.

Durand, Jorge, Douglas S. Massey, and Rene Zenteno. 2001. "Mexican Immigration to the United States: Continuities and Changes." *Latin American Research Review* 36, no. 1: 107–27.

Eckholm, Erik. 2006. "Plight Deepens for Black Men, Studies Warn." *New York Times,* March 20.

Economist. 2003. "Buying Jobs Can Be Expensive." November 27. http://dr.economist.com/node/2245910.

———. 2005. "Card Check: A Somewhat Dubious System Where a Union Gets Most of the Workers at a Firm to Sign a Pledge Card and Thus Avoids NLRB-Supervised Secret-Ballot Elections." May 14.

Edwards, Richard C. 1973. "The Social Relations of Production in the Firm and Labor Market Structure." In *Labor Market Segmentation.* Edited by Richard C. Edwards, Michael Reich, and David Gordon, 3–26. Lexington, MA: D.C. Heath and Company.

Enchautegui, Maria E. 1998. "Low-Skilled Immigrants and the Changing American Labor Market." *Population and Development Review* 24, no. 4: 811–24.

Engormix. 2005. "International—Egg and Poultry Review." February 16. http://en.engormix.com/MA-poultry-industry/news/international-egg-poultry-review-t5121/p0.htm.

Engstrom, James D. 2001. "Industry and Immigration in Dalton, Georgia, 2001." In *Latino Workers in the Contemporary South.* Edited by Arthur D. Murphy, Colleen Blanchard, and Jennifer A. Hill, 44–56.

Erwin, Steve. 2005. "Toyota to Build 100,000 Vehicles per Year in Woodstock, Ont., Starting 2008." *Canadian Press,* July 14.

Espinosa, Guadalupe Hernandez. 2003. "Exigen regular la importación de cerdo." *El Universal,* October 28. www2.eluniversal.com.mx/pls/impreso/noticia.html?id_nota=36602&tabla=finanzas.

Espy, Mike. 1993. "Speech to National Grain and Feed Association." March 23. *Arizona-Mexico Journal* 2, no. 1 (June).

Evans, Peter. 1995. *Embedded Autonomy: States and Industrial Transformation.* Princeton, NJ: Princeton University Press.

Fantasia, Rick, and Kim Voss. 2004. *Hard Work: Remaking the American Labor Movement.* Berkeley and Los Angeles: University of California Press.

Fideicomisos Instituidos con Relación con la Agricultura (FIRA). 2007. "Acerca de Nosotros." Bank of Mexico. www.fira.gob.mx/AcercadeNosotrosXML/Acerca%20de%20Nosotros.jsp.

Fink, Leon. 2003. *The Maya of Morganton.* Chapel Hill: University of North Carolina Press.

Fleck, Susan, and Constance Sorrentino. 1994. "Employment and Unemployment in Mexico's Labor Force." *Monthly Labor Review* 117, no. 11 (November): 3–32.

Flessner, Dave. 2008. "Pilgrim's Pride Back in Business." *Chattanooga Times Free Press* (Tennessee), April 18.

Food and Agriculture Organization of the United Nations (FAO). 2006. "Import Surges: What Is Their Frequency and Which Are the Countries and Commodities Most Affected?" FAO Brief on Import Surges–Issues, no. 2. October. www.fao.org/es/esc/en/378/406/highlight_423.html.

Food and Allied Service Trades Department (FAST). AFL-CIO. "NLRB Elections, Unfair Labor Practices, and Petitions Withdrawn: 1980–2002." www.fastaflcio.org.

Fox, Jonathan, and Xochitl Bada. 2008. "Migrant Organization and Hometown Impacts in Rural Mexico." *Journal of Agrarian Change* 8, nos. 2 and 3: 435–61.

Frank, Andre Gunder. 1969. "Mechanisms of Imperialism." In *Latin America: Underdevelopment or Revolution,* 162–74. New York: Modern Reader.

Frontera NorteSur (FNS). 2008. "Carlos Salinas de Gortari and the Resurrection of the PRI." *Newspaper Tree*, August 3. http://newspapertree.com/features/2714.

FundingUniverse. n.d. "Pilgrim's Pride Corporation." *Company Histories and Profiles.* www.fundinguniverse.com/company-histories/Pilgrims-Pride-Corporation-Company-History.html.

Fussell, Elizabeth. 2004. "Sources of Mexico's Migration Stream: Rural, Urban, and Border Migrants to the United States." *Social Forces* 82, no. 3: 937–67.

Gallup Organization. 2008. "Immigration." Gallup Poll. www.gallup.com/poll/1660/immigration.aspx.

Galvin, Timothy J. 2000. "Statement before House Subcommittee on Agriculture, Rural Development, Food and Drug Administration, and Related Agencies." Washington, D.C., March 9. FASonline. www.fas.usda.gov/info/speeches/ct030900tg.html.

Garza, J. Trinidade Villarreal, Luis Lauro Flores Flores, and Pedro Castro Acevedo. 1998. "Programa de Aparceria Tyson de Mexico, S.A. de C.V." *Revista Mexicana de Agronegocios* 3 (July–December): 1–15.

Gates, Leslie. 2009. "Theorizing Business Power in the Semiperiphery: Mexico 1970–2000." *Theory and Society* 38: 57–95.

Gereffi, Gary, and Miguel Korzeniewicz. 1994. *Commodity Chains and Global Capitalism*. Westport, CT: Praeger.

Gilliam, Dorothy. 1986. "Unions and Minorities." *Washington Post,* October 20.

Gledhill, John. 1995. *Neoliberalism, Transnationalization, and Rural Poverty: A Case Study of Michoacan, Mexico.* Boulder, CO: Westview Press.

Goldfield, Michael. 1987. *The Decline of Organized Labor in the United States*. Chicago: University of Chicago Press.

Goodman, Peter S. 2007. "In Mexico, People Do Really Want to Stay." *Washington Post,* January 7.

Greenhouse, Steven. 1986. "Labor and Clergy Are Reuniting to Help the Underdogs of Society." *New York Times,* August 18.

——. 2005. "Union Organizers at Poultry Plants in South Find Newly Sympathetic Ears." *New York Times,* September 6.

Greer, Richard. 1992. "Labor in the South 58 Years after a Bitter Strike Sapped Their Power." *Atlanta Constitution,* September 7.

Griffith, David. 1990. "Consequences of Immigration Reform for Low-Wage Workers in the Southeastern U.S.: The Case of the Poultry Industry." *Urban Anthropology* 19, nos. 1–2: 155–84.

Guthey, Greig. 2001. "Mexican Places in Southern Spaces: Globalization, Work, and Daily Life in and around the North Georgia Poultry Industry." In *Latino Workers in the Contemporary South.* Edited by Arthur D. Murphy, Colleen Blanchard, and Jennifer A. Hill, 57–67.

Guzmán, Betsy. 2001. *The Hispanic Population: Census 2000 Brief.* May. C2KBR/01 3. U.S. Census Bureau. www.census.gov/prod/2001pubs/c2kbr01-3.pdf.

Hahn, William F., Mildred Haley, Dale Leuck, James J. Miller, Janet Perry, Fawzi Taha, and Steven Zahniser. 2005. "Market Integration of the North American Animal Products Complex." Electronic Outlook Report from the Economic Research Service/USDA, May. www.ers.usda.gov/publications/ldp/may05/ldpm13101/ldpm13101.pdf.

Halbfinger, David. 2002. "Factory Jobs, Then Workers, Leaving Poorest Southern Areas." *New York Times,* May 10.

Halpern, Rick, and Roger Horowitz. 1996. *An Oral History of Black Packinghouse Workers and Their Struggle for Racial and Economic Equality.* New York: Monthly Review Press.

Hamilton, Martha. 1980. "AFL-CIO Union Plans Boycott against Perdue." *Washington Post,* November 18.

Hanrahan, Charles E. 2008. *Agricultural Export and Food Aid Programs.* CRS Report for Congress, April 15. http://assets.opencrs.com/rpts/RL33553_20080415.pdf.

Hanrahan, Charles E., Beverly A. Banks, and Carol Canada. 2006. "U.S. Agricultural Trade: Trends, Composition, Direction, and Policy." CRS Report 98-253, National Council for Science and the Environment, September 25. www.au.af.mil/au/awc/awcgate/crs/98-253.pdf.

Hanson, Gordon H. 2006. "Illegal Migration from Mexico to the United States." *Journal of Economic Literature* 44: 869–924.

———. 2010. *Why Isn't Mexico Rich?* NBER Working Paper No. 16470. Issued in October NBER Program(s): ITI. National Bureau of Economic Research. www.nber.org/papers/w16470.

Hart, Ariel. 2004. "Anxiety for an American Family." *New York Times,* December 6.

Hernandez, Maria del Carmen Moreno. 2001. *Crisis avicola en Sonora: el fin de un paradigma, 1970–1999.* Mexico: Plaza y Valdes.

Hernandez, Maria del Carmen Moreno, and Carlos J. Maya. 2002. "Globalization and Pork Raising in Mexico." *International Journal of Sociology of Agriculture and Food* 10, no. 2: 25–31.

Hernandez, Maria del Carmen Moreno, Antonio Alberto Ulloa, and Ana I. Ochoa M. 1996. *Avicultura Sonorense Y T.L.C.* Ciad A.C.: Centro de Investigacion en Alimentacion y Desarrollo. http://agrinet.tamu.edu/trade/papers/mchdez⁻1.pdf.

Hernandez-Coss, Raul. 2005. *U.S.-Mexico Remittance Corridor: Lessons on Shifting from Informal to Formal Transfer.* Working Paper No. 47. Washington, DC: World Bank.

Hernandez-Leon, Ruben. 2004. "Restructuring at the Source: High-Skilled Industrial Migration from Mexico to the United States." *Work and Occupations* 31: 424–52.

Hetrick, Ron L. 1994. "Why Did Employment Expand in Poultry Processing Plants?" *Monthly Labor Review* 117, no. 6 (June): 31–35.

Hetzer, Michael. 1989. "Labor Lays an Egg." *Business North Carolina* 9, no. 3 (March).

Hirsch, Barry T., David A. Macpherson, and Wayne G. Vroman. 2001. "Estimates of Union Density by State." *Monthly Labor Review* 124, no. 7 (July): 51–55.

Hirschman, Albert O. 1970. *Exit, Voice, and Loyalty: Responses to Decline in Firms, Organizations, and States.* Cambridge, MA: Harvard University Press.

Hoodfires, John. 1992. "Overreaction to Hamlet Tragedy Will Only Create Additional Victims." *Atlanta Constitution,* September 3.

Hopkins, T. K., and Immanuel Wallerstein. 1986. "Commodity Chains in the World Economy prior to 1800." *Review* 10, no. 1: 157–70.

Horowitz, Roger. 1997. *Negro and White, Unite and Fight.* Urbana: University of Illinois.

Horwitz, Tony. 1994. "Nine to Nowhere." *Wall Street Journal,* December 1.

Huerta, Mario Miguel Carrillo. 2001. *El sector agropecuario Mexicano antecedentes recientes y perspectivas.* Mexico: Instituto Politecnico Nacional. www.libros.publicacio nes.ipn.mx/PDF/1242.pdf.

Hughes, Kathleen A. 1983. "Inspected Meat." *New York Times,* March 2.

Human Rights Watch. 2000. "'Deck Is Stacked' Against U.S. Workers." Human Rights Watch, August 30. www.hrw.org/en/news/2000/08/30/deck-stacked-against-us-workers.

Huntington, Samuel P. 2004. "The Hispanic Challenge." *Foreign Policy* (March/April). www.foreignpolicy.com/articles/2004/03/01/the_hispanic_challenge.

INEGI. 1996. *Indicadores Basicos Censales. VII Censos Agropecuarios 1991.* Mexico: INEGI.

———. 2002, 2003. *Sistema Anual del Comercio Exterior de Mexico (SACEM).* Mexico: INEGI.

Inter-American Development Bank (IDB). 2007. "IDB Survey of Remittances to Mexico and Central America: Findings and Analysis." IDB, August 8. http://idbdocs. iadb.org/wsdocs/getdocument.aspx?docnum=35057351.

Iranzo, Susana, and Alyson C. Ma. 2006. *The Effect of China on Mexico-U.S. Trade: Undoing NAFTA?* June 14. www.sandiego.edu/peacestudies/documents/tbi/iranzo_ma_tbi.pdf.

Ireland, Doug. 1998. "Birds of a Feather." *CityPages* (Minneapolis/St. Paul) 19, no. 892 (January 7). www.citypages.com/databank/19/892/article4074.asp.

Irvin, David. 2008. "Workers at Tyson to Pursue Wage Suit." *Arkansas Democratic Gazette,* February 16.

Isaac, Larry, and Lars Christiansen. 2002. "How the Civil Rights Movement Revitalized Labor Militancy." *ASR* 67 (October): 722–46.

Kallenberg, Arne. 2003. "Flexible Firms and Labor Market Segmentation." *Work and Occupations* 30, no. 2 (May): 154–75.

Kandel, William. 2008. "Hired Farmworkers a Major Input for Some U.S. Farm Sectors." USDA: Economic Research Service, April. www.ers.usda.gov/AmberWaves/April08/Features/HiredFarm.htm.

Katz, Jesse. 1996. "The Chicken Trail: How Migrant Latino Workers Put Food on America's Table." *Los Angeles Times,* November 10–12.

King, Amanda. 2006. "Ten Years with NAFTA: A Review of the Literature and an Analysis of Farmer Responses in Sonora and Veracruz, Mexico." CIMMYT Special Report 06-01. Mexico, DF: CIMMYT/Congressional Hunger Center. www.cimmyt. org/english/docs/special_publ/specialReport06-01.pdf.

Kirschenman, Joleen, and Kathryn M. Neckerman. 1991. "'We'd Love to Hire Them, But . . .': The Meaning of Race for Employers." In *The Urban Underclass.* Edited by Christopher Jencks and Paul E. Peterson, 203–32. Washington, DC: Brookings Institution Press.

Krau, Jon. 2002. "Capital, Power and Business Associations in the African Political Economy: A Tale of Two Countries, Ghana and Nigeria." *Journal of Modern African Studies* 40, no. 3: 395–436.

Kuwait News Agency (KUNA). 2008. "NGOs Defend Developing Countries Right to Special Safeguard Mechanism." July 28. www.kuna.net.kw/newsagenciespublicsite/ArticleDetails.aspx?Language=en&id=1927802.

Kwa, Aileen. 2008. "Why Food Import Surges Are an Issue at the WTO." IPS Inter Press Service Agency, March 17. http://ipsnews.net/news.asp?idnews=41502.

Labor Research Association (LRA). 2002. "Percentage of Representation Elections Won by Unions Rose in 2001; but Number of New Workers Organized Dropped." *Working Life,* June 25.

———. 2005. "Time for Card Check to Reverse the Course." *Working Life,* July 27. www.workinglife.org/index.php?content_id=6353&highlight.

Lee, Cheol-Sung. 2005. "International Migration, Deindustrialization and Union Decline in 16 Affluent OECD Countries, 1962–1997." *Social Forces* 84, no. 1: 71–88.

Lewis, Neil A. 1998. "Espy Is Acquitted on Gifts Received While in Cabinet." *New York Times,* December 3.

List, Friedrich. [1841] 2001. *The National System of Political Economy.* Kitchener, Ontario: Batoche Books.

Lugo, Bernardo Méndez. 2006. "Migración mexicana transnacional: Una nueva identidad mexicana, entre asimilación y resistencia cultural en Estados Unidos." *El Catoblepas* 58 (December). www.nodulo.org/ec/2006/n058p16.htm.

———. 2007a. "Migración mexicana transnacional (2): Una nueva identidad mexicana, entre asimilación y resistencia cultural en Estados Unidos." *El Catoblepas* 59 (January): 11. www.nodulo.org/ec/2007/n059p11.htm.

———. 2007b. "Migración mexicana transnacional (3) Una nueva identidad mexicana, entre asimilación y resistencia cultural en Estados Unidos." *El Catoblepas* 60 (February): 12. www.nodulo.org/ec/2007/n060p12.htm.

Lynch, David J. 2006. "Jobs Could Solve Some Mexico Woes." *USA Today,* May 30.

Malone, Nolan, Kaari F. Baluja, Joseph M. Costanzo, Cynthia J. Davis. 2003. *The Foreign-Born Population: 2000. Census 2000 Brief.* December. (C2KBR-34). U.S. Census Bureau. www.census.gov/prod/2003pubs/c2kbr-34.pdf.

Manger, William F. 1999. "The Hispanic Population of Rural Central Louisiana and Their Traditions: Agricultural Sector." Louisiana's Living Traditions. www.louisianafolklife.org/LT/Articles_Essays/TheHispanicPopulation.html.

Manning, L., R. N. Baines, and S. A. Chadd. 2007. "Trends in the Global Poultry Meat Supply Chain." *British Food Journal* 109, no. 5: 332–42. www.emeraldinsight.com/0007-070X.htm.

Marcelli, Enrico A., and Wayne A. Cornelius. 2001. "The Changing Profile of Mexican Migrants to the United States: New Evidence from California and Mexico." *Latin American Research Review* 36, no. 3: 105–31.

Martin, Philip. 1998–1999. "Economic Integration and Migration: The Case of NAFTA." *UCLA Journal of International Law and Foreign Affairs* 3 (Fall/Winter): 419–41.

Martinez, Jose. 2007. "Globalization and Its Impact on Migration in Agricultural Communities in Mexico." The Center for Comparative Immigration Studies. University of California, San Diego, February. www.ccis-ucsd.org/PUBLICATIONS/WP%20 161.pdf.

Marx, Karl, and Friedrich Engels. [1848] 1964. *The Communist Manifesto.* New York: Washington Square Press.

Mason, J., and P. Singer. 1980. *Animal Factories.* New York: Crown.

Massar, Keur. 2005. "Imports Threaten Senegal's Poultry Producers." STATpub, December 16. www.statpub.com/open/174415.html.

Massey, Douglas S. 1986. "The Settlement Process among Mexican Migrants to the United States." *American Sociological Review* 51, no. 5 (October): 670–84.

——. 1987. "Understanding Mexican Migration to the United States." *American Journal of Sociology* 92, no. 6 (May): 1372–1403.

Massey, D. S., J. Durand, and N. J. Malone. 2002. *Beyond Smoke and Mirrors: Mexican Immigration in an Era of Economic Integration.* New York: Russell Sage Foundation.

Massey, Douglas S., and Kristin Espinosa. 1997. "What's Driving Mexico-U.S. Migration? A Theoretical, Empirical, and Policy Analysis." *American Journal of Sociology* 102: 939–99.

Massey, Douglas S., Luin Goldring, and Jorge Durand. 1994. "Continuities in Transnational Migration: An Analysis of Nineteen Mexican Communities." *American Journal of Sociology* 99, no. 6: 1492–1533.

Massey, Douglas S., and René Zenteno. 2000. "A Validation of the Ethnosurvey: The Case of Mexico-U.S. Migration." *International Migration Review* 34, no. 3: 766–93. http://mmp.opr.princeton.edu/databases/studydesign-en.aspx.

Mauer, Marc, and Ryan S. King. 2007. *Uneven Justice: State Rates of Incarceration by Race and Ethnicity.* The Sentencing Project, July. www.sentencingproject.org/doc/ publications/rd_stateratesofincbyraceandethnicity.pdf.

Maviglia, Sandra F. 1986. "Mexico's Guidelines for Foreign Investment: The Selective Promotion of Necessary Industries." *American Journal of International Law* 80, no. 2 (April): 281–304.

Mayer, David. 2002. *Liberalization, Knowledge, and Technology: Lessons from Veterinary Pharmaceutics and Poultry in Mexico.* World Bank, May. http://wbln0018.worldbank. org/LAC/lacinfoclient.nsf/e9dd232c66d43b6b852567d2005ca3c5/a4b2846bcf2a4461 85256c3d007323bd/$FILE/LiberalizationKnowledgeTechnology.pdf.

McCarthy, Colman. 1980. "Striking a Blow for Unions in the South." *Washington Post,* May 18.

McGraw, Dan, and John Simons. 1994. "The Birdman of Arkansas: Don Tyson Revolutionized the Nation's Chicken Business; Now He's Hatching a Global Food Empire." *U.S. News and World Report* 117, no. 3 (July 18).

McLemore, David. 2008. "Refugees Fill Jobs in Cactus, Texas after Immigration Sweep." *Dallas Morning News,* April 22.

Mekay, Emad. 2003. "NAFTA No Model for Development." Global Policy Forum, November 18. www.globalpolicy.org/globaliz/econ/2003/1118naftanomodel.htm.

Milkman, Ruth. 2006. *L.A. Story.* New York: Russell Sage.

Miller, Eric. 2002. "The Outlier Sectors: Areas of Non-Free Trade in the North American Free Trade Agreement." Inter-American Development Bank. www.iadb.org/ intal/aplicaciones/uploads/publicaciones/i_intalitdsta_wp_10_2002_miller.pdf.

Miller, Lenore. 1992. "Revisiting the 'Jungle': The Case of the Hamlet Chicken Processing Plant Is Not Closed." *Washington Post,* October 20.

Miller, Tom. 1986. *The Panama Hat Trail.* New York: William Morrow.

Mitchell, Garry. 2004. "Poultry Industry Fears Loss of Trade with Cuba If Payment System Changes." Associated Press, December 2.

Moreno-Brid, Juan Carlos, Juan Ernesto Pardinas Carpizo, and Jaime Ros Bosch. 2009. "Economic Development and Social Policies in Mexico." *Economy and Society* 38, no. 1 (February): 154–76.

Moss, Philip, and Chris Tilly. 1996. "'Soft' Skills and Race: An Investigation of Black Men's Work and Occupations." *Work and Occupations* 23, no. 3: 252–76. doi: 10.1177/0730888496023003002.

Murjada, Tricia. 2002. "The 'Need' for Slave Labor: Tyson Corporation." *Free Republic.* www.freerepublic.com/focus/news/661357/posts.

Murphy, Arthur D., Colleen Blanchard, and Jennifer A. Hill, eds. 2001. *Latino Workers in the Contemporary South.* Athens: University of Georgia Press.

Nardi, Louis. 1999. "A Hearing on Immigrations Issues: Alien Smuggling and Visa Overstays Before the Subcommittee on Immigration and Claims." Committee on the Judiciary, U.S. House of Representatives, March 18. http://judiciary.house.gov/legacy/106-nard.htm.

National Labor Relations Board (NLRB). 1987. Lumbee Farms Cooperative, Inc. and Industrial Union Department, AFL-CIO. Cases 11-CA-11773 and 11-CA-11841. August 31. Decision and Order. By Chairman Dotson and Members Johansen and Babson. www.nlrb.gov/search/advanced/all/%28case%3A11-CA-011773%29%20AND %20%28name%3ALumbee%20Farms%20Cooperative%29.

——. 1992. "Choctaw Maid Farms, Ind. and Retail, Wholesale and Department Store Union, AFL-CIO." Cases 15-CA-11462 and 15-CA-11551. August 31, Decision and Order. By Members Devaney, Oviatt, and Raudabaughi.

——. 1993a. Marshall Durbin Poultry Company and United Food and Commercial Workers International Union, AFL-CIO and Billy Johnson. January 11. Decision and Order 310 NLRB no. 14, 71.

——. 1993b. Holly Farms Corporation and Its Successor, Tyson Foods, Inc. and Chauffeurs, Teamsters and Helpers Local Unions Nos. 29, 71, 355, 391, 592, 657, and 988, affiliated with International Brotherhood of Teamsters, AFL-CIO. Cases 11-CA-13184, 11-CA-13267, 11-CA-13487, 11-CA-13520, 11-CA-13619, and 11-RC-5583. Decisions of the National Labor Relations Board, 273–366.

——. 1993c. Tyson Foods, Inc. and United Food and Commercial Workers, Local 425, AFL-CIO. Cases 26-CA-14731 and 26-CA-14821. May 28. Decision and Order. By Chairman Stephens and Members Devaney and Oviatt. 311 NLRB no. 60.

New York Times. 1981. "ConAgra Positioning for Future." January 31.

——. 1984. "Faster Inspection of Turkey Favored." November 14.

——. 2003. "Mexican Farmers Renew NAFTA Protests." January 20.

——. 2005. "Cheap Border Politics." December 21.

NewsCenter. 1999. "Truth Squad Targets Vienna, Ga., Tyson Plant." Press release. NewsCenter Progressive Newswire, February 15. www.commondreams.org/press releases/feb99/021599a.htm.

O'Driscoll, Gerald P. 1999. *IMF Policies in Asia: A Critical Assessment; Backgrounder no. 1265.* Heritage Foundation, March 30. www.heritage.org/Research/Reports/1999/03/IMF-Policies-in-Asia.

Ollinger, Michael, James MacDonald, and Milton Madison. 2000. *Structural Change in U.S. Chicken and Turkey Slaughter.* Agricultural Economic Report No. AER787, November. www.ers.usda.gov/Publications/AER787/.

Orlandi, Lorraine. 2005. "Fox's Immigration Comments Backfire." *Seattle Times,* May 16.

Ortiz-Hernández, Luis. 2006. "Evolución de los precios de los alimentos y nutrimentos en México entre 1973 y 2004." *Archivos de Latin Americanos de Nutricion* 56, no. 3. www.alanrevista.org/ediciones/2006-3/evolucion_precios_alimentos_mexico.asp.

Ortiz, Petra Cruz. 2008. "Con un campo pobre, inseguro, descapitalizado y con severos rezagos tecnológicos, y con un coyotaje que tiende arraigarse cada vez más, entró México a competir con Estados Unidos y Canadá en el Tratado de Libre comercio." *Notiver,* January 7. www.notiver.com.mx/index.php?id=99974.

Otero, Gerardo. 2004. "Chapter 4. Transformaciones agrarias: crisis y diferenciación social." In *Adios al Campesindo? Democracia y formación política de las clases en México rural,* 89–112. Mexico: Miguel Angel Porrúa/Universidad de Zacatecas/Simon Fraser University. http://estudiosdeldesarrollo.net/coleccion_america_latina/adios_al_campesinado/Campesinado8.pdf.

Oxfam. 2003. *Dumping without Borders: How U.S. Agricultural Policies Are Destroying the Livelihoods of Mexican Corn Farmers.* Oxfam Briefing Paper 50, August. Oxfam GB. www.oxfam.org.uk/resources/policy/trade/downloads/bp50_corn.pdf.

Park, Robert E. 1936. "Succession, An Ecological Concept." *American Sociological Review* 1, no. 2: 171–79.

Parker, Suzi. 2006. "Finger-Lickin' Bad: How Poultry Producers Are Ravaging the Rural South." *Grist,* February 23. www.grist.org/article/parker1.

Passel, Jeffrey S., and D'Vera Cohn. 2009. *A Portrait of Unauthorized Immigrants in the United States.* Pew Hispanic Center. Pew Research Center, April 14. http://pewresearch.org/pubs/1190/portrait-unauthorized-immigrants-states and http://pewhispanic.org/files/reports/107.pdf.

———. 2011. *Unauthorized Immigrant Population: National and State Trends, 2010.* Pew Hispanic Center. Pew Research Center, February 1. http://pewhispanic.org/reports/report.php?ReportID=133.

Passel, Jeffrey S., and Roberto Suro. 2005. *Rise, Peak, and Decline: Trends in U.S. Immigration, 1992–2004.* Pew Hispanic Center. Pew Research Center, September 27. www.pewhispanic.org/files/reports/53.pdf.

Perez, Evan, and Corey Dade. 2007. "An Immigration Raid Aids Blacks for a Time." *Wall Street Journal,* January 17.

Perl, Peter. 1984. "AFL-CIO Calls for a Boycott of Marval Turkeys; Company Is Hit by Six-Week Strike." *Washington Post,* July 13.

Perry, M. J., and J. P. Schachter. 2003. *Migration of Natives and the Foreign Born: 1995 to 2000.* Census 2000 Special Reports (CENSR 11). August. www.census.gov/prod/2003pubs/censr_11.pdf.

Perry, Mark, and Paul J. Mackun. 2001. *Population Change and Distribution: 1990 to 2000. Census 2000 Brief* (C2KBR/01-2). April. www.census.gov/prod/2001pubs/c2kbr01-2.pdf.

Perusek, Glenn, and Kent Worcester, eds. 1995. *Trade Union Politics: American Unions and Economic Change, 1960s–1990s.* Atlantic Highlands, NJ: Humanities Press.

Pesado, Francisco Alonso. 1996. "Diagnostico de la Avicultura Nacional de 1972 a 1994." *Ciencia Veterinaria* 7: 147–86. www.fmvz.unam.mx/fmva/cienciavet/revistas/CVv017/CVv7c6.pdf.

———. 1997. "Descripción y análisis de la negociación definitiva de la avicultura nacional en el Tratado de Libre Comercio de América del Norte." October. www.fmvz.unam.mx/fmvz/pdfs/Conferencia%203.pdf.

Pickard, Miguel. 2005. "In the Crossfire: Mesoamerican Migrants Journey North." *Americas Program.* International Relations Center. March 18. www.cipamericas.org/archives/912.

St. James Press. Pilgrim's Pride Corporation. 1998. *International Directory of Company Histories.* Vol. 23. Reproduced in Business and Company Resource Center. Farmington Hills, MI: Gale Group. 2007. http://galenet.galegroup.com/servlet/BCRC. Document No. I2501304743.

Pingpoh, David Puewoh, and Jean Senahoun. 2007. "Extent and Impact of Food Import Surges in Developing Countries: The Case of Poultry Meat in Cameroon." AgEcon Search. http://purl.umn.edu/7931.

Poovey, Bill. 2006. "Ruling Helps Workers Claiming Tyson Hired Immigrants to Cut Wages." *Online Ledger,* October 12. http://mexicanoccupation.blogspot.com/2009/07/tyson-faces-lawsuit-for-giving-jobs-to.html.

Portes, Alejandro. 1979. "Illegal Immigration and the International System: Lessons from Recent Legal Immigrants from Mexico." *Social Problems* 26: 425–38.

Portes, Alejandro, and Ruben C. Rumbaut. 1990. *Immigrant America: A Portrait.* Berkeley and Los Angeles: University of California Press.

Portes, Alejandro, and Cynthia Truelove. 1987. "Making Sense of Diversity: Recent Research on Hispanic Minorities in the United States." *Annual Review of Sociology* 13: 359–85.

Poultry Site. 2011. "Prospects for Expanding Egg Consumption." ThePoultrySite.com, December 22. www.thepoultrysite.com/articles/1237/prospects-for-expanding-egg-consumption.

PR Newswire. 1987. "Pilgrim's Pride Announces Mexican Broiler Acquisitions." May 20.

———. 1995a. "LIUNA: National Poultry Workers' Alliance Proves Its Strength in North Carolina." June 29.

———. 1995b. "Pilgrim Acquires Additional Mexico Chicken Operation." July 5.

———. 1996. "Alliance Sends Thanksgiving Message to Reich: Labor Department Needs to Investigate Poultry Industry." November 26.

———. 1997. "Pilgrim's Pride Corporation Reports Record 1997 Net Income." November 5.

———. 2000. "United States Department of Labor: Tyson Foods Will Pay $230,000 to Settle Pay Discrimination Allegations at Mississippi Plant." February 29.

———. 2001. "Tyson Foods, Inc. Announces International Initiatives." June 8. www. just-food.com/news/tyson-foods-inc-announces-international-initiatives_id77977. aspx.

Przeworski, Adam. 1985. *Capitalism and Social Democracy*. Cambridge University Press.

———. 2007. "Is the Science of Comparative Politics Possible?" In *The Oxford Handbook of Comparative Politics*. Edited by Carles Boix and Susan Carol Stokes. Oxford: Oxford University Press.

Ramirez-Gonzales, Alejandro, Roberto Garcia Mata, Gustavo Garcia Delgado, and Jaime A. Matus Gardea. 2003. "Un modelo de ecuaciones simultaneas para el mercado de la carne de pollo en Mexico, 1970–1998." *Agrociencia* 37, no. 1 (January–February): 73–84.

Real, Gaspar Cabello. 1997. "Desarrollo agroindustrial y trabajadores agrícolas: el caso de San Rafael." In *El campo queretano en transición*. Edited by Gaspar Cabello Real, 33–48. Center for U.S.-Mexican Studies, U.C. San Diego. http://escholarship.org/uc/item/8nm6f6t7#page-38.

———. 2003. "The Mexican State and the Agribusiness Model of Development in the Globalisation Era." *Australian Journal of Social Issues* 38, no. 1: 129–39.

Reddington, John. 1997. "Diversity Is Key to Continued Success of U.S. Poultry Exports." FASonline. www.fas.usda.gov/info/agexporter/1997/January%201997/poul try.html.

Reddy, Anitha. 2002. "Ikea, Tyson Foods among U.S. Embargo Violators." *Washington Post,* July 3.

Reed, Deborah. 2001. "Immigration and Males' Earnings Inequality in the Regions of the United States." *Demography* 38, no. 3 (August): 366–73.

Rees, Martha W. 2001. "Mexican Females in Atlanta." In *Latino Workers in the Contemporary South*. Edited by Arthur D. Murphy, Colleen Blanchard, and Jennifer A. Hill, 36–43.

Rich, Spencer. 1977. "Two Hill Time Outs: Budget and Chickens; Senate Votes Poultry Processors Tax Relief; Senate Votes Tax Relief for Chicken Firms." *Washington Post,* April 29.

Robbins, John. 1987. *Diet for a New America*. Tiburon, CA: H. J. Cramer.

Roberts, Bryan R., Frank Bean, and Fernando Lozano-Ascencio. 1999. "Transnational Migrant Communities and Mexican Migration to the United States." *Ethnic and Racial Studies* 22, no. 2: 240–66.

Ros, Jaime, and Gonzalo Rodriguez. 1987. "Mexico: Study on the Financial Crisis, the Adjustment Policies and Agricultural Development." *CEPAL Review* 33.

Rosales, Rosa. 2006. "NAFTA Helped Spur Rise in Undocumented Immigrants." *Rio-GrandeGuardian.com*, April 6. http://list.afsc.org/pipermail/political_allies_ii/2006 q2/000091.html.

Rosenberg, Tina. 2003. "Why Mexico's Small Corn Farmers Go Hungry." *New York Times,* March 3.

Rosenbloom, Joseph. 2003. "Victims in the Heartland." *American Prospect* (July–August).

Rosenzweig, Andrés. 2005. *El debate sobre el sector agropecuario en el tratado de libre comercio de América del Norte*. United Nations. Economic Commission for Latin

America and the Caribbean, January 17. www.eclac.org/publicaciones/xml/4/20644/L650%20parte%201.pdf.

Rosenzweig Pichardo, Andrés. n.d. *Mexican Agricultural Trade under NAFTA: An Assessment after Five Years of Implementation*. 43–63. AgEcon Search. http://agecon search.umn.edu/bitstream/16844/1/ag010043.pdf.

Rudeclerk. 2007. "Farm Subsidies in Virginia." June 24. http://rudeclerk.blogspot.com/2007/06/farm-subsidies-in-virginia.html.

Ruiz, Miguel Angel J. Marquez. 2008. *Historia de la Union Nacional de Avicultores de Mexico (1958–2008)*. Mexico D. F., Mexico: UNA.

Rupert, Mark E. 1995. "(Re)Politicizing the Global Economy: Liberal Common Sense and Ideological Struggle in the US NAFTA Debate." *Review of International Political Economy* 2, no. 4 (Autumn): 658–92. www.jstor.org/stable/4177166.

Rural Migration News. 1998. "Midwest: Meat/Poultry Processing." *Rural Migration News* 4. no. 1 (January). http://migration.ucdavis.edu/rmn/comments.php?id=244_0_2_0.

SAGARPA. 2001. *Produccion avicola a pequena escala*. Undersecretary for Rural Development. Mexico: SAGARPA. www.sagarpa.gov.mx/desarrollorural/publicaciones/fichas/listfichas/p-12-01.pdf.

———. 2002. "Evaluación de la alianza para el campo 2001: Evaluación Fomento Avícola y Porcícola. Nuevo León 2001." Mexico: SAGARPA, October. www.nl.gob.mx/pics/pages/des_agropecuario_evaluaciones.base/AVICOLAYPORCICOLA2001.pdf.

———. 2003. "El Ingreso rural y la producción agropecuaria en México (1989–2002)." Mexico: SIAP. www.agronuevoleon.gob.mx/oeidrus/ESTUDIOS_E_INVESTIG ACIONES/SIAP/ingrural.pdf.

———. 2005. *Campaña contra influenza aviar en el estado de Michoacán*. Mexico: SAGARPA. www.sagarpa.gob.mx/dlg/michoacan/ganaderia/sanidad/campa%f1a%20de%20sal monelosis.html.

———. 2007a. "Estimación del Consumo Nacional Aparente 1990–2005." Mexico: SAGARPA, Special Project for Food Security (PESA). http://www.sagarpa.gob.mx.

———. 2007b. *Proyecto Tipo Producción y manejo de aves de traspatio*. Mexico: SAGARPA. www.sagarpa.gob.mx/DESARROLLORURAL/ASISTENCIACAPACITA CION/Paginas/manualespesa.aspx.

Salin, Delmy L., William F. Hahn, and David J. Harvey. 2002. *U.S.-Mexico Broiler Trade: A Bird's-Eye View*. USDA Economic Research Service, December. http://ers.usda.gov/publications/ldp/dec02/Ldpm10201/Ldpm102-01.pdf.

Schulman, Bruce J. 1991. *From Cottonbelt to Sunbelt*. New York: Oxford University Press. http://site.ebrary.com/lib/arizona/Top?id=10086800&layout=document.

Schultz, Eric. 2009. "The Pilgrim's Pride Plant in Athens Closes This Week, Putting 650 People Out of Work." Associated Press. October 5. http://blog.al.com/break ing/2009/10/pilgrims_pride_plant_closing_t.html.

Schwartz, Jeremy. 2007. "U.S. Immigration Laws Spark Anger in Mexico." *Atlanta Journal Constitution,* November 18.

Schwartzman, Kathleen C. 2006. "Globalization from a World System Perspective: A New Phase in the Core—A New Destiny for Brazil and the Semiperiphery?" *Journal of World-System Research* 12, no. 2: 265–307. http://jwsr.ucr.edu/archive/v0112/number2/pdf/jwsr v12n2_schwartzman.pdf.

———. 2008. "Lettuce, Segmented Labor Markets, and the Immigration Discourse." *Journal of Black Studies* 39, no. 1 (September): 129–56. Sage OnlineFirst, April 19, 2007. doi:10.1177/0021934706297009.

———. 2009. "The Role of Labor Struggle in the Shifting Ethnic Composition of Labor Markets." *Labor Studies Journal* 34, no. 2 (June): 189–218. http://lsj.sagepub.com/content/34/2/189.

———. 2011. "Anchor Baby." In *Anti-Immigration in the United States: A Historical Encyclopedia.* Edited by Kathleen R. Arnold, 15–20. Santa Barbara: ABC-CLIO, Inc.

Securities and Exchange Commission (SEC). 1994. FY 1994 Annual Report Pilgrim's Pride Corporation. Commission File number 1-9273 Washington, DC, 20549. www.getfilings.com/o0000802481-94-000021.html.

———. 1995. "Annual Report Fruit of the Loom Inc/DE · Form 10-K. For period ended 12/31/94 · EX-22. Filed on 3/29/95. SEC File 1-08941; Accession Number 771298-95-3." SEC Info. www.secinfo.com/dnH7d.ac.6.htm.

———. 1999. "An Excerpt from a 20-F SEC Filing, Filed by BACHOCO INDUSTRIES on 6/29/1999." SEC Info. http://sec.edgar-online.com/1999/06/29/17/0000903423-99-000248/Section2.asp.

———. 2004. "Industrias Bachoco SA De CV 20-F." SEC Info, December 31. www.secinfo.com/d16TCx.z29p.htm.

Seelye, Katharine Q. 1997. "T-Shirt Company Is Charged in Plot to Smuggle Mexicans." *New York Times,* December 23.

Seidman, Gay W. 1994. *Manufacturing Militance: Workers' Movements in Brazil and South Africa, 1970–1985.* Los Angeles and Berkeley: University of California.

Semple, Kirk. 2008. "A Somali Influx Unsettles Latino Meatpackers." *New York Times,* October 16.

Sengupta, Somini. 2006. "On India's Despairing Farms, a Plague of Suicide." *New York Times,* September 19.

Serrin, William. 1980. "200 Mississippi Women Carry on a Lonely, Bitter Strike." *New York Times,* February 27.

———. 1986. "Industries in Shift Aren't Letting Strikes Stop Them." *New York Times,* September 30.

Shadlen, Kenneth C. 2000. "Neoliberalism, Corporatism, and Small Business Political Activism in Contemporary Mexico." *Latin American Research Review* 35, no. 2: 73–106.

Sharma, Ramesh. 2005. *FAO Import Surge Project Working Paper No. 1. Overview of Reported Cases of Import Surges from the Standpoint of Analytical Content.* FAO. www.fao.org/es/esc/common/ecg/19/en/Surge1overview.pdf.

Silverside, D., and M. Jones. 1992. "Small-Scale Poultry Processing." FAO. www.fao.org/docrep/003/t0561e/T0561E01.htm#ch1.

Siobhán, McGrath. Compiled. 2005. *A Survey of Literature Estimating the Prevalence of Employment and Labor Law Violations in the U.S. April 15.* Brennan Center for Justice. http://nelp.3cdn.net/1ef1df52e6d5b7cf33_s8m6br9zf.pdf.

Smith, Rod. 2001. "Chicken Wrestle with New Reality of 'Commoditization.'" *Feedstuffs* 73, no. 46 (November 5): 15.

———. 2002. Demand Grows as Industry 'Follows Consumer Lifestyles." *Feedstuffs* 74, no. 5 (February 14): 11–12.

Smith, Sandra Susan. 2005. " 'Don't Put My Name on It': Social Capital Activation and Job-Finding Assistance among the Black Urban Poor." *AJS* 111, no. 1: 1–57.

Sparshott, Jeffrey. 2002. "Poultry Producers to Pay Tariffs to Mexico." *Washington Times,* December 31.

Starmer, Elanor, Aimee Witteman, and Timothy A. Wise. 2006. *Feeding the Factory Farm: Implicit Subsidies to the Broiler Chicken Industry.* Global Development and Environment Institute Working Paper No. 06-03. www.ase.tufts.edu/gdae/pubs/wp/06-03Broilergains.pdf.

Stein, Nicholas. 2002. "Tyson Son of a Chicken Man." *Fortune*, May 13. www.fortune.com/fortune/articles/0,15114,367405,00.html.

Stewart, D. R. 1996a. "Cost of Testing Poultry for Russia Will Be Minor: U.S. Firms Will Pay for Salmonella Inspections." *Arkansas Democrat-Gazette,* March 27.

———. 1996b. "Two More Arkansas-Based Poultry Producers Will Cut Chicken Production, Officials with the Firms Said Monday." *Arkansas Democrat-Gazette,* March 5.

Stiglitz, Joseph E. 2004. "The Broken Promise of NAFTA." *New York Times,* January 6.

Stone, Katherine Van Weizel. 1992. "The Legacy of Industrial Pluralism: The Tension between Individual Employment Rights and the New Deal Collective Bargaining System." *University of Chicago Law Review* 59: 575–644.

Striffler, Steve. 2002. "Inside a Poultry Processing Plant: An Ethnographic Portrait." *Labor History* 43, no. 3: 305–13.

———. 2005. *Chicken: The Dangerous Transformation of America's Favorite Food.* New Haven, CT: Yale University Press.

Studstill, John D., and Laura Nieto-Studstill. 2001. "Hospitality and Hostility: Latin Immigrants in Southern Georgia." In *Latino Workers in the Contemporary South.* Edited by Arthur D. Murphy, Colleen Blanchard, and Jennifer A. Hill, 68–81.

Stull, Donald D., and Michael J. Broadway. 2004. *Slaughterhouse Blues: The Meat and Poultry Industry in North America.* Belmont, CA: Thomson, Wadsworth.

Swarns, Rachel. 2006a. "Bridging a Racial Rift That Isn't Black and White." *New York Times,* October 6.

———. 2006b. "The Latino South in Georgia, Immigrants Unsettle Old Sense of Place." *New York Times,* August 4.

Swoboda, Frank. 1990. "Labor's Love Lost at Holly Farms; N.C. Chicken Producer Embroiled in Dispute with Teamsters." *Washington Post,* May 3.

Tabor, Mary B. 1991. "Poultry Plant Fire Churns Emotions over Job Both Hated and Appreciated." *New York Times,* September 6.

Tayler, Letta. 2003. "Squealing on NAFTA; Mexican Farmers Angry over Trade Pact." *Newsday,* January 26.

Thompson, Ginger. 2001. "Farm Unrest Roils Mexico, Challenging New Chief." *New York Times,* July 22.

———. 2002. "NAFTA to Open Floodgates, Engulfing Rural Mexico." *New York Times,* December 19.

Times Wire Services. 1999. "Fruit of the Loom Files for Chapter 11." *Los Angeles Times,* December 30. http://articles.latimes.com/1999/dec/30/business/fi-48844.

Tobar, Hector. 2008. "Mexican Farmers Protest NAFTA." *Los Angeles Times,* January 3. www.spokesman.com/stories/2008/jan/03/mexican-farmers-protest-as-last-nafta-barriers/.

Tobler, Christopher. 1995. "Tyson Foods Splurges with Two Poultry Acquisitions." *Arkansas Business* 12, no. 32 (August 7).

Tomaskovic-Devy, Donald, and Vincent J. Roscigno. 1997. "Uneven Development and Local Inequality in the U.S. South: The Role of Outside Investment, Landed Elites, and Racial Dynamics." *Sociological Forum* 12, no. 4: 565–97.

U.S. Census. 1997. "Manufacturing by Major Group (2-digit SIC)." Economic Census 1997. www.census.gov/epcd/ec97sic/E97SUSD.HTM#D.

———. 1999. *Poultry Processing: 1997.* Manufacturing Industry Series. 1997 Economic Census. www.census.gov/prod/ec97/97m3116d.pdf.

———. 2004. *Poultry Processing: 2002.* Manufacturing Industry Series. 2002 Economic Census. www.census.gov/prod/ec02/ec0231i311615.pdf.

———. 2005. *Alabama: 2002. Manufacturing.* Geographic Area Series. 2002 Economic Census. www.census.gov/prod/ec02/ec0231aal.pdf.

———. 2010. "*NAICS 311615; Poultry Processing.*" Industry Statistics Sampler. 2007 Economic Census. www.census.gov/econ/industry/current/c311615.htm.

U.S. Census Bureau. 2001. *Two or More Races.* Census Special Reports. www.census.gov/population/cen2000/atlas/censr01-110.pdf.

———. 1981, 1991, 2001. *Statistical Abstract of the United States.* Washington, DC.

———. 2002. *Foreign-Born Population: 2000.* Table FBP-1. Census 2000 Brief. Profile of Selected Demographic and Social Characteristics: 2000. www.census.gov/population/cen2000/stp-159/foreignborn.pdf.

———. 2008. "Question and Answer Center: Question 306; Why Collect Hispanic Origin Information?" http://ask.census.gov.

U.S. Department of Agriculture (USDA). 1996. "Poultry Outlook 1996." Economic Research Service. November 18. http://usda01.library.cornell.edu/usda/ers/LDP-P/1996/ldpp1196.txt.

———. 1997. *U.S. Broiler Meat Exports Sluggish.* Foreign Agricultural Service. www.fas.usda.gov/dlp2/circular/1997/97-10LP/poult_cmpt.htm.

———. 1998. *Livestock and Poultry World Markets and Trade March 1998.* www.fas.usda.gov/dlp2/circular/1998/98-03LP/poultry1.html.

———. 2000. *Mexico Poultry and Products Annual 2000.* GAIN Report No. MX0127. September 27. www.fas.usda.gov/gainfiles/200009/30678259.pdf.

———. 2002. "U.S. Broiler Industry Structure." National Agricultural Statistics Service. November 27. Agricultural Statistics Board, Washington, D.C. http://usda.mannlib.cornell.edu/usda/nass/industry-structure/specpo02.txt.

———. 2003. *Mexico Poultry and Products: Creation of Tariff Lines for Chicken Leg Quarters.* GAIN Report No. MX3003. www.fas.usda.gov/gainfiles/200301/145785029.pdf.

———. 2007. *Dairy and Poultry Statistics.* 1–42. www.nass.usda.gov/Publications/Ag_Statistics/2007/CHAP08.PDF.

———. 2009. "Global Food Markets: Foreign Direct Investment." July 29. Economic Research Service. www.ers.usda.gov/Briefing/GlobalFoodMarkets/Investment.htm.

———. 2012. "Chickens, Turkeys, and Eggs: Annual and Cumulative Year-to-Date U.S. Trade." Economic Research Service. *www.ers.usda.gov/Data/MeatTrade/Data/BroilerTurkey_Yearly-Full.xls*

———. n.d. Meat, Poultry and Egg Product Inspection Directory. Food Safety and Inspection Service. www.fsis.usda.gov/regulations_&_policies/Meat_Poultry_Egg_Inspection_Directory/index.asp.

U.S. Department of Homeland Security (DHS). 2001. *The President's Second Triennial Comprehensive Report on Immigration.* Citizen and Immigration Services. www.uscis.gov/USCIS/Resources/Reports%20and%20Studies/tri3fullreport.pdf.

U.S. Department of Labor (DOL). 2002. "Labor Department Files Suit Against Tyson Foods." News release, May 9. www.dol.gov/opa/media/press/opa/OPA2002287.htm.

———. 2005. "Employment Status of the Civilian Noninstitutional Population." Bureau of Labor Statistics. www.bls.gov/lau/table14ful105.pdf.

———. 2006a. "Tyson Foods Inc. Agrees to Pay $1.5 Million in Back Pay for Hiring Discrimination: More than 2500 Minorities and Women Benefit from U.S. Labor Department Action." Employment Standards Administration (ESA). News release No. 06-1658-NAT, September 27.

———. 2006b. "Wage and Hour Collects $172 Million in Back Wages for over 246,000 Employees in Fiscal Year 2006." Employment Standards Administration (ESA). www.dol.gov/esa/whd/statistics/200631.htm.

———. Various years. "Local Area Unemployment Area Statistics Map." Bureau of Labor Statistics. http://data.bls.gov/map/MapToolServlet?survey=la.

U.S. Federal Register. 2007. "Federal Register Notices" 72, no. 61 (March 30). www.fas.usda.gov/info/fr/2007/033007MAPapps.asp.

U.S. Government Accountability Office (GAO). 1990. *U.S.-Mexico Trade: Trends and Impediments in Agricultural Trade.* http://archive.gao.gov/d27t7/140595.pdf.

———. 1991. *U.S.-Mexico Trade: Impact of Liberalization in the Agricultural Sector.* March 29. http://archive.gao.gov/d20t9/143693.pdf.

———. 2000. *Worker Protection: OSHA Inspections at Establishments Experiencing Labor Unrest.* www.gao.gov/archive.2000/he00144.pdf.

———. 2005a. *Report to Congressional Committees: Social Security: Better Coordination among Federal Agencies Could Reduce Unidentified Earnings Reports.* GAO-05-154. Washington, D.C., February 2005. www.gao.gov/new.items/d05154.pdf.

———. 2005b. *Workplace Safety and Health. Safety in the Meat and Poultry Industry, While Improving, Could Be Further Strengthened.* Washington, D.C., January. www.gao.gov/new.items/d0596.pdf.

U.S. Grains Council. 2010. "Sorghum." www.grains.org/sorghum.

U.S. Immigration and Naturalization Service (INS). 2003. *Estimates of Unauthorized Immigrant Population Living in the United States: 1990–2000.* Report 1211. Office of Policy and Planning. www.dhs.gov/files/statistics/publications/archive.shtm

U.S. News and World Report. 1986. "Frank Perdue; Chatting Up a Mob Boss." March 17.

——. 2002. "Playing Chicken." April 29.

U.S. Occupational Safety and Health Administration (OSHA). 1997. "Hudson Foods, Missouri Poultry Processor, Faces $332,500 Fine for Safety Violations." News release, July 22. www.osha.gov/pls/oshaweb/owadisp.show_document?p_table=NEWS_RELEASES&p_id=466.

U.S. Social Security Administration (SSA). 1999. *Patterns of Reporting Errors and Irregularities by 100 Employers with the Most Suspended Wage Items.* Report A-03-98-31009. September 29. Office of the Inspector General. http://oig.ssa.gov/sites/default/files/audit/full/pdf/98-31009.pdf.

——. 2001a. *Management Advisory Report: Review of Service Industry Employer with Wage Reporting Problems.* Report A-03-00-10022. September 27. http://oig.ssa.gov/sites/default/files/audit/full/pdf/A-03-00-10022.pdf.

——. 2001b. *Misuse in the Agriculture Industry.* Report A-08-99-41004. January 22. http://oig.ssa.gov/sites/default/files/audit/full/pdf/A-08-99-41004.pdf.

——. 2002. *Recent Efforts to Reduce the Size and Growth of the Social Security Administration's Earnings Suspense File.* Report A-03-01-30035. May. http://oig.ssa.gov/sites/default/files/audit/full/pdf/A-03-01-30035.pdf.

——. 2003. *Follow-Up Review of Employers with the Most Suspended Wage Items.* October.

Uehling, Mark D., with Rich Thomas. 1986. "Tax Reform: Congress Hatches Some Loopholes." *Newsweek,* September 29.

Union Nacional de Avicultores (UNA). 2003. *Salvaguarda definitiva para pierna y muslo de pollo de EU.* UNA, July 28. www.UNA.org.mx.

——. 2003, 2005, 2007, 2008. *Compendio de Indicadores Económicos del Sector Avícola.* UNA. www.una.org.mx.

United Food and Commercial Workers International Union (UFCW). 2001. "History of Tyson Greed." http://knowmore.org/wiki/index.php?title=Tyson_Foods.

——. 2005. "Injury and Injustice—America's Poultry Industry." Reprinted at Southern Poverty Law Center, November 2010. www.splcenter.org/get-informed/publications/injustice-on-our-plates.

United States–Mexico Chamber of Commerce. 1999a. *NAFTA: Five Years Linking U.S. and Mexican Markets.* Proceedings from a May conference examining sector-by-sector successes, strategies and challenges under the trade agreement. June. www.usmcoc.org/b-nafta6.php.

——. 1999b. "U.S.-Mexico Agriculture: A Trade Success Story." www.usmcoc.org/b-nafta8.html.

University of California, Los Angeles (UCLA). 2002. *Statistical Abstract of Latin America* 38: 676, 770.

Vasquez, Ian. 2003. "A Retrospective on the Mexican Bailout." *Cato Journal* 21, no. 3 (Winter): 545–51.

Vaughan, Jessica. 1997. "Immigrant Visa Waiting List at 3.6 Million." *Immigration Review* no. 28 (April): 5–6.

Vicini, Jim. 2001. "U.S. Charges Tyson Foods with Immigrant Smuggling." Organic Consumers Association, December 19. www.organicconsumers.org/Corp/Tyson Busted.cfm.

Villamar Angulo, Luis, Herminio V. Guzman, and Nadia Ruiz Sanchez. 2004. "Situación actual y perspectiva de la producción de carne de pollo en Mexico 2004." *Claridades Agropecuarias.* June. www.infoaserca.gob.mx/claridades/marcos.asp?numero=130.

———. 2004. *Situación actual y perspectiva de la producción de carne de pollo en Mexico 2004.* Mexico: SAGARPA. http://www.sagarpa.gob.mx/ganaderia/estudio/sitpoll004.pdf.

Villamar Angulo, Luis, Miguel A. Castillo Mangas, and Herminio Guzman V. 2003. "Situación actual y perspectiva de la producción de carne de pollo en Mexico 2003." Mexico: SAGARPA. www.sagarpa.gob.mx/ganaderia/estudio/sitpoll003.pdf.

Villamar Angulo, Luis, Cesar Segura M., Marco A. Barrera, W. Herminio Guzman V., Ramon Dominguez I. 2001. *A produccion de Carnes en Mexico y sus perspectivas 1990–2000.* Mexico: SAGARPA. www.sagarpa.gob.mx/ganaderia/estudio/carne.pdf.

Villamar Angulo, Luis, Nadia Ruiz Sanchez, Miguel A. Castillo Mangas, Herminio Guzman Valenzuela, and Alfredo Garcia Bustamante. 2003. "Situation and Outlook of Poultry Meat Production in Mexico 2003." Mexico: SAGARPA. www.sagarpa.gob.mx/Dgg/estudio/sitpoll003i.pdf.

Waldinger, Roger. 1997. "Black/Immigrant Competition Re-Assessed: New Evidence from Los Angeles." *Sociological Perspectives* 40, no. 3: 365–86.

Walker, Herman. 1964. "Dispute Settlement: The Chicken War." *American Journal of International Law* 58. no. 3 (July): 671–85.

Wall Street Journal. 1987. "Pilgrim's Pride Announces Mexican Broiler Acquisitions." May 21.

Wallerstein, Immanuel. 1974. *The Modern World System.* New York: Academic Press.

———. 2001. "The Myrdal Legacy: Racism and Underdevelopment as Dilemmas." In *Unthinking Social Science: The Limits of XIX Century Paradigms,* 80–103. Philadelphia: Temple University Press.

Warren, Robert Penn. 1965. *Who Speaks for the Negro?* New York: Vintage Books.

Washington, Booker T. [1895] 1974. "Atlanta Compromise Speech to the Atlanta Exposition." In *The Booker T. Washington Papers,* vol. 3. Edited by Louis R. Harlan, 583–87. Urbana: University of Illinois Press, 1974.

Washington Post. 2005. "Washington in Brief." April 20.

Weiler, Paul. 1993. "One Strike and You're Out? Creating an Efficient Permanent Replacement Doctrine." *Harvard Law Review* 106, no. 3: 669–86.

White, Gregory L., Scott Kilman, and Sprin Thurow. 2004. "The Farms Race; Chicken Fight." *Wall Street Journal,* December 15.

Whittaker, William G. 2005. *Labor Practices in the Meat Packing and Poultry Processing Industry: An Overview.* CRS Report for Congress. July 20. www.nationalaglawcenter.org/assets/crs/RL33002.pdf.

Williams, Winston. 1986. "Business Brings Back the Lockout." *New York Times,* October 5.

Wilson, William J. 1980. *The Declining Significance of Race.* Chicago: University of Chicago Press.

Wise, Timothy A. 2003. "NAFTA's Untold Stories: Mexico's Grassroots Responses to North American Integration." *Americas Program Policy Report,* June 10. www.americaspolicy.org/reports/2003/0306globalization.html.

Yost, Hunter, 2007. "Do You Wonder Why Salads Cost More than a Big Mac?" *Lovin' Life after 50,* December. Tucson, Arizona.

Young, Ben. 2009. "Jackson County: Getting Ready for Round Two." *Georgia Trend,* February 27. www.georgiatrend.com/February-2009/Jackson-County-Getting-Ready-For-Round-Two/.

Yunez-Naude, Antonio. 2001. "How Changes in Mexican Agriculture Affect Mexico-U.S. Migration." Presented at workshop in Imperial Valley, California, January 16–18. www.iga.ucdavis.edu/reapwp/changes.pdf.

Zamora, Luis. 2005. "A Mexican Leader Revealed Reality of Labor." *Tampa Tribute,* May 29.

Zarate, Angel Juarez. 2003. *Produccion de pollo para carne en Mexico (1980–2002): (Estudio descriptivo y análisis de la cadena productiva).* http://orton.catie.ac.cr/cgi-bin/wxis.exe/?IsisScript=CIESTAAM.xis&method=post&formato=2&cantidad=1&expresion=mfn=003161.

Zavodny, Madeline. 1999. "Determinants of Recent Immigrants' Locational Choices." *International Migration Review* 33, no. 4 (Winter): 1014–1030.

Zengerle, Jason. 2003. "Not a Prayer." *New Republic* (September 22): 13–15.

Zepeda, Guillermo. 2000. *Transformación agrarian: los derechos de propiedad en el campo mexicano bajo el nuevo marco institucional.* Mexico City: Miguel Angel Porrúa and Centro de Investigación para el Desarrollo.

Zuniga, V., and Ruben Hernandez-Leon. 2001. "A New Destination for an Old Migration: Origins, Trajectories, and Labor Market Incorporation of Latinos in Dalton, Georgia." In *Latino Workers in the Contemporary South.* Edited by Arthur D. Murphy, Colleen Blanchard, and Jennifer A. Hill, 126–35.

Index